INTERNATIONAL DEVELOPMENT IN FOCUS

Adaptive Social Protection

Building Resilience to Shocks

THOMAS BOWEN, CARLO DEL NINNO, COLIN ANDREWS,
SARAH COLL-BLACK, UGO GENTILINI, KELLY JOHNSON,
YASUHIRO KAWASOE, ADEA KRYEZIU, BARRY MAHER,
AND ASHA WILLIAMS

WORLD BANK GROUP

Contents

Figures

Maps

Tables

Foreword

At the time of finalizing this publication on Adaptive Social Protection (ASP), the world entered the midst of the COVID-19 pandemic, which has left no country unaffected by its sweeping impacts. Although the long-term trajectory of these widespread health, economic, and social impacts is uncertain, its immediate consequences have already resulted in significant losses in terms of lives and livelihoods. A period of prolonged, often extreme, hardship is being endured by many who are undergoing social distancing and experiencing reduced income and diminished consumption. This is especially true for the poorest among us, with the lowest capacity to cope.

As the crisis has taken hold, policy makers have been reminded of the value of having strong social protection systems in place that are capable of reaching affected households with immediate assistance. Toward the end of April 2020, as many as 133 countries had planned, introduced, or adjusted social protection programs in response to COVID-19. At the same time, the crisis is shining a light on both the enabling and constraining factors that affect governments' ability to leverage social protection systems to address large, covariate shocks of this sort.

At the World Bank Group, we consider ASP to be a dedicated area of focus within the wider field of social protection, examining and identifying the ways in which social protection systems can be prepared and enhanced ahead of large covariate shocks like COVID-19 to build the resilience of poor and vulnerable households—before, during, and after such shocks occur.

The report begins by highlighting how, when designed appropriately, social protection programs that are delivered to the poorest and most vulnerable households can have a transformative impact on their resilience to these kinds of shocks. Through the provision of transfers and services to the poorest and most vulnerable households, adaptive social protection directly supports their capacity to prepare for, cope with, and adapt to the shocks they face. Over the long term, by supporting these three capacities, ASP can provide a pathway to a more resilient state for households that may otherwise lack the resources to move out of chronically vulnerable situations.

Further, the organizing framework for ASP that is articulated in this report provides insights into the ways in which social protection systems can be made more capable of building household resilience. Through its four building blocks—programs, information, finance and institutional arrangements, and partnerships—the framework highlights both the elements of existing social protection systems that are the cornerstones for building household resilience to shocks, as well as the additional priorities and core investments that will be instrumental in enhancing these outcomes and making the social protection system more prepared in advance of the next crisis.

By way of some key examples, the report highlights the need to modify traditional targeting methods to factor in household vulnerability to shocks; integrate and layer programming among poor and vulnerable households in "hot-spot" areas of recurrent shocks; invest in delivery systems and contingency planning to enable the increased responsiveness of programs after a shock hits; expand coverage of social registries, with a focus on the inclusion of high-risk households; preposition risk financing to ensure funding is readily available to fund response programs in a timely manner; invest in fostering collaboration and coordination with nontraditional but essential partners across government—including those involved disaster risk management and climate change adaptation—as well as nongovernment, humanitarian actors. These are only a few of the priorities within the four building blocks that are outlined in the report.

As the COVID-19 pandemic eventually begins to recede, other shocks and crises will remain on the horizon, many of which will become increasingly severe under the influence of climate change. The framework in this report can provide directions along the path toward the development of ASP in advance of those shocks materializing in the future. Indeed, the World Bank Group is increasingly working with governments to develop ASP in some of the poorest and highest-risk countries around the world. The report provides the basis for a structured approach to implementing these engagements, each of which will, in turn, continue to inform our collective learning on this evolving and important agenda.

Michal Rutkowski
Global Director
Social Protection and Jobs Global Practice
The World Bank Group

Acknowledgments

This report is the product of a sustained conversation among colleagues within the World Bank Group's Social Protection and Jobs Global Practice over the past several years. In particular, many of the concepts, as well as the framework outlined here, were developed for the South-South Learning Forum 2018, "Building Resilience through Adaptive Social Protection." The work conducted as part of the Sahel Adaptive Social Protection Program has also been key in driving many of the ideas outlined in this report. As such, the report has benefited enormously from the myriad views, insights, and experiences related to the evolving concept of adaptive social protection that have been shared by these many direct or indirect contributors, not all of whom can be captured in this acknowledgments section.

The report was prepared by a team that was led by Thomas Bowen (social protection specialist) and included coauthors Carlo del Ninno (lead economist), Colin Andrews (program manager), Sarah Coll-Black (senior economist), Ugo Gentilini (senior economist), Kelly Johnson (senior social protection specialist), Yasuhiro Kawasoe (junior professional officer), Adea Kryeziu (social protection specialist), Barry Maher (senior financial sector specialist), and Asha Williams (social protection specialist).

In addition to the research completed by the authors, in several places this report draws heavily on unpublished background papers prepared by Oxford Policy Management (OPM). The OPM background paper team was led by Valentina Barca and included coauthors Sarah Bailey, Rodolfo Beazley, Andrew Kardan, Gabrielle Smith, and Ana Solórzano. Catherine Fitzgibbon, an independent consultant, also contributed to the background paper related to finance. All background paper references are cited throughout the text and are noted in the chapter reference lists.

Overall guidance and quality control for this report were provided by Michal Rutkowski (global director), Margaret Grosh (senior adviser), Anush Bezhanyan (practice manager), and Jehan Arulpragasam (practice manager) of the Social Protection and Jobs Global Practice. Comments received during the peer review process from John Blomquist (lead economist), Yashodhan Ghorpade (economist), Aylin Isik-Dikmelik (senior economist), and Laura Rawlings (lead economist) helped to sharpen and enrich this report throughout. Cathy Ansell (financial sector specialist), Evie Calcutt (financial sector specialist),

Kenichi Chavez (senior social protection specialist), Aline Coudouel (lead economist), Jesse Doyle (young professional), Matthew Hobson (senior social protection specialist), Phillippe Leite (senior social protection economist), Olivier Mahul (practice manager), and Ruslan Yemtsov (lead economist) were also key contributors to the development of many of the concepts outlined in this report.

The team would also like to thank members of the Sahel Adaptive Social Protection Program's Partnership Council, who provided important insights and guidance related to the adaptive social protection building blocks and the concept of resilience that proved instrumental in helping to develop this report, namely: Laura Garn, Heidi Gilert, and Harriet McDonald (Department for International Development—DFID); Daniel Longhurst, Ralf Radermacher, and Anne-Sophie Vollmecke (Deutsche Gesellschaft für Internationale Zusammenarbeit—GIZ); and Thibault Van Langenhove (Agence française de développement—AFD). The messages contained within this report do not necessarily reflect the opinions of these Partnership Council members or the positions of their respective organizations.

Lastly, the authors would like to sincerely thank Darcy Gallucio for her thorough, patient, and precise editorial assistance; Nita Congress and Andres de la Roche, who provided graphic design support to finalize the publication; as well as Janice Tuten who led the finalization of the publication as part of the World Bank's International Development in Focus series.

This report was commissioned and financed by the World Bank's Global Facility for Disaster Reduction and Recovery (GFDRR).

About the Authors

Colin Andrews is a program manager in the Social Protection and Jobs Global Practice at the World Bank. He has more than 15 years of experience working in social protection across Africa and South Asia and at the global policy level. He leads the Partnership for Economic Inclusion, a multipartner initiative to support the scale-up of national economic inclusion programs, linking several sectors. Colin has managed several lending operations on safety nets and service delivery in the Africa region. He has published widely on safety net impacts, crisis response, and financing. Before joining the World Bank, he worked at the Food and Agriculture Organization of the United Nations, at the European Commission, and within international nongovernmental organizations. He holds an MA in economics from Trinity College, Dublin.

Thomas Bowen is a social protection specialist in the Social Protection and Jobs Global Practice. He has worked extensively on issues related to adaptive social protection (ASP), focusing on the design and implementation of safety net programs as a means for building household resilience to disasters and climate change. Thomas has supported the development of ASP programs in the East Asia and Pacific Region, including in the Philippines, Vietnam, and the Pacific Island Countries. More recently, he has been supporting ASP engagements in West Africa, including in The Gambia, Sierra Leone, and the six Sahelian countries within the Sahel Adaptive Social Protection Program. He holds an MA in economics and international relations from the School of Advanced International Studies at The Johns Hopkins University in Washington, DC.

Sarah Coll-Black is a senior economist in the Social Protection and Jobs Global Practice at the World Bank, with a focus on the social assistance and jobs in Eastern Europe and Central Asia. Previously, she worked extensively on social protection in East and West Africa, managing the design and delivery of national safety net programs, including links to disaster risk management and humanitarian response, and youth employment and productive inclusion programs. Before joining the World Bank, she worked in the Philippines with the World Health Organization Regional Office for the Western Pacific, the Canadian International

Development Agency, and nongovernmental organizations. She holds an MPhil from the Institute of Development Studies at the University of Sussex and a BS in economics from the University of King's College.

Carlo del Ninno is a lead economist in the Social Protection and Jobs Global Practice for the Middle East and North Africa Region. Over the past 18 years, he has worked on analytical and operational issues on safety net programs covering several countries in South Asia and Sub-Saharan Africa. In the Africa Region, he worked on safety net policies and programs and managed the Sahel Adaptive Social Protection Program. Before joining the World Bank, he worked on food security policy for the International Food Policy Research Institute in Bangladesh, and on poverty analysis in several countries for the Policy Research Division of the World Bank and for Cornell University. He has published on safety nets, food policy, and food security and holds a PhD in agriculture and applied economics from the University of Minnesota.

Ugo Gentilini is a global lead for social safety nets in the Social Protection and Jobs Global Practice at the World Bank. With more than 20 years of experience, he has worked across the analytics and practice of social assistance as it relates to disaster risk management, labor markets, urbanization, subsidy reforms, displacement, humanitarian assistance, and food security in high-, middle-, and low-income countries. His latest book, *Exploring Universal Basic Income: A Guide to Navigating Concepts, Evidence, and Practices* (World Bank, 2020) provides a comprehensive analysis of universal basic income. Ugo produces a newsletter that reaches more than 10,000 practitioners weekly (ugogentilini.net). He holds a PhD in economics.

Kelly Johnson is a senior social protection specialist in the Office of the Managing Director at the World Bank. Previously, she worked in the Social Protection and Jobs Global Practice in the Africa Region on Eswatini, Ethiopia, and Lesotho and in the South Asia Region on Afghanistan, Pakistan, and Sri Lanka. She joined the World Bank in 2010 in the Fragile and Conflict-Affected Countries Group. She specializes in emergency response, cash transfers, safety nets, and institutional reform. Kelly holds an MSc from the London School of Economics and a BA with distinction from Queen's University in Canada.

Yasuhiro Kawasoe is a junior professional officer in the Social Protection and Jobs Global Practice at the World Bank. His interests encompass the analytics and practice of social protection and disaster risk management, with a focus on the role of cash transfer programs in building household resilience to disasters. Yasuhiro holds an MA in architecture from the Graduate School of Creative Science and Engineering at Waseda University in Japan.

Adea Kryeziu is a social protection specialist in the Social Protection and Jobs Global Practice at the World Bank. She has published extensively on social protection matters, including on linkages with climate change, disaster risk management, and energy subsidy reform. Her analytical background has been complemented by operational experience in East Asia, the Middle East and North Africa, and West Africa. She serves as co-chair and task team leader of the Intra-Agency Social Protection Assessments Partnership, playing a key role in managing relationships with donors and partner organizations. Before joining the World Bank, Adea served as a sustainable development fellow at the Aspen Institute and a researcher in the Ministry of Economic Development in her native Kosovo. Adea holds an MA in international economics and energy, resources, and environmental policy from The Johns Hopkins University and a BA in economics from John Cabot University in Rome.

Barry Maher works in the Finance, Competitiveness, and Innovation Global Practice at the World Bank, based in Pretoria, South Africa. He leads the financial resilience policy dialogue in several African countries and coordinates the work on crisis and disaster risk financing in the Africa Region. Barry is a qualified actuary with experience in the non-life insurance sector, the carbon and renewable energy markets, financial inclusion, social protection, and disaster risk financing. He has worked for a Lloyds of London reinsurance syndicate, as a chief actuary in an insurance agency, and with the United Nations to help drive financial inclusion in the Pacific. At the World Bank, Barry has led the work on developing public-private partnerships to support agriculture insurance in Bangladesh, India, Kenya, Rwanda, South Africa, and Uganda; he spearheaded the work on developing financing strategies to support shock-responsive safety nets. Barry has also been working closely on the joint workplan between the African Risk Capacity and the World Bank. He holds a BA with distinction in actuarial and financial studies from the University College of Dublin and a Masters in statistics with distinction from the University of Oxford.

Asha Williams is a social protection specialist in the Social Protection and Jobs Global Practice at the World Bank. Her analytic and operational work on social protection spans more than a decade and covers a range of topics, including adaptive social protection, social protection systems, social safety nets, labor market programs, youth, and people with disabilities. Before joining the World Bank, she worked at the Organization of American States, where she managed a multicountry skills training program for at-risk youth; in her home country of Trinidad and Tobago, she was a researcher with the Ministry of Social Development. Asha has authored several journal articles and reports. She is a Fulbright scholar and holds an MA in international development and graduate certificate in Latin American studies from the University of Pittsburgh, and a BS in government from University of the West Indies.

Abbreviations

ASP	adaptive social protection
BRACED	Building Resilience and Adaptation to Climate Extremes and Disasters
DRM	disaster risk management
HSNP	Hunger Safety Net Program
IVACC	Vulnerability to Climate Hazards Index (Índice de Vulnerabilidad ante Choques Climáticos)
NGO	nongovernmental organization
PSNP	Productive Safety Net Programme
SASPP	Sahel Adaptive Social Protection Program
SP	social protection
UNICEF	United Nations Children's Fund

All dollar amounts are US dollars unless otherwise indicated.

Overview

A FRAMEWORK FOR ADAPTIVE SOCIAL PROTECTION

INTRODUCTION

Today's global landscape is fraught with interconnected and often devastating covariate shocks such as natural disasters, economic crises, pandemics, conflicts, and forced displacement.[1] In the last 50 years, natural disasters have followed an increasing trend in terms of occurrence and human devastation (figure O.1).[2] Climate change is expected to exacerbate these trends and, without climate-informed development, to push an additional 100 million people into extreme poverty by 2030 (Hallegatte et al. 2016). Forced displacement also has hit record highs in recent years, with an estimated 20 persons fleeing their homes every 60 seconds and more than 64 million people being displaced worldwide in 2016 (UNHCR 2016). In addition, the COVID-19 pandemic is providing a vivid reminder of the devastating potential impact of pandemics on the lives and livelihoods of those who are directly and indirectly affected.

Adaptive social protection (ASP) is a response to widespread demand for the use of social protection as a tool to build the resilience of poor and vulnerable households to these kinds of covariate shocks. ASP is outlined in this report as a specific focus area within the wider field of social protection that is dedicated to identifying the ways in which social protection can be leveraged and enhanced to build household resilience to these kinds of shocks. In doing so, this report draws inspiration and insight from the concept of ASP promulgated by researchers at the Institute of Development Studies (for example, Arnall et al. 2010; Davies et al. 2009, 2012). These authors first highlighted the value of integrating the often disconnected social protection, disaster risk management (DRM), and climate change adaptation sectors for a mutually reinforcing approach to reduce household vulnerability and build household resilience. In equal measure, the report draws on the proliferating literature on and operational experiences related to shock-responsive social protection, especially the Oxford Policy Management shock-responsive social protection series, 2015–18. Finally, the report draws on and adapts the Building Resilience and Adaptation to Climate Extremes and Disasters (BRACED) framework developed by Bahadur et al. (2015), as the primary basis for its definition of household resilience.

FIGURE O.1

Natural disasters: Increasingly frequent and devastating impacts, 1967–2017

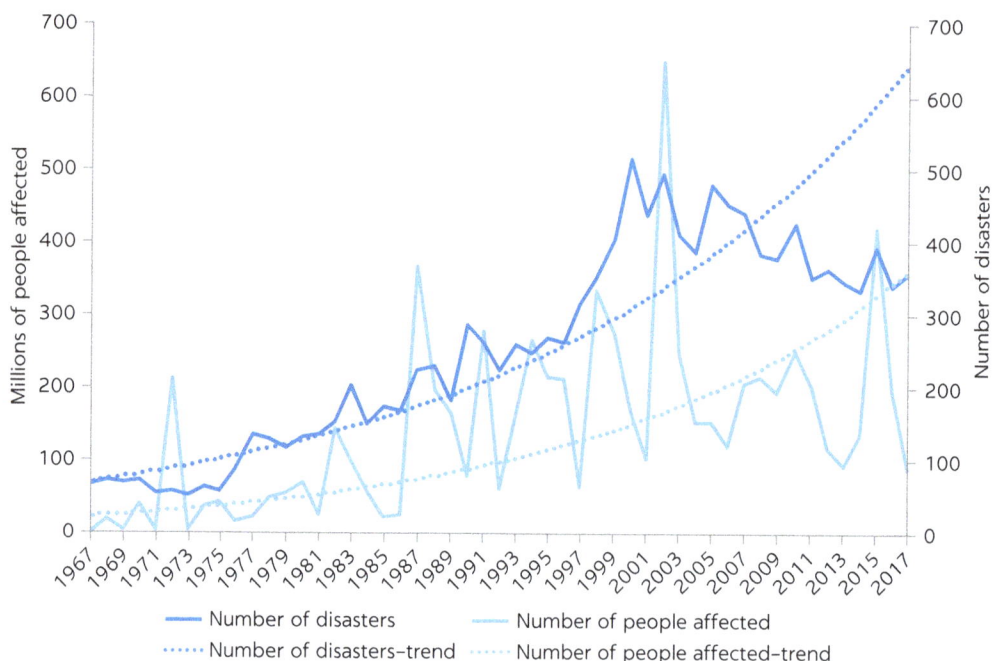

Source: EM-DAT: The Emergency Events Database, Université catholique de Louvain (UCL)—CRED, www.emdat .be, accessed May 2019.

In response to this growing demand for ASP, this report outlines and elaborates on a concise framework to help inform its design and implementation. To do so the report first outlines a working definition of ASP that is anchored to a definition of household resilience. Building from these foundational definitions, the main contribution of the report is an organizing framework for ASP that is composed of four building blocks—programs, data and information systems, finance, and institutional arrangements and partnerships. In developing this framework, the report highlights the specific priorities and core investments aligned to each building block that support the design and implementation of ASP. In this way, the report identifies several priorities and investments that are above and beyond those that are business as usual for regular social protection, generated by the unique demands of building household resilience to covariate shocks.

This report focuses primarily on elaborating this framework in relation to natural disasters and climate change. Each type of covariate shock transmits its impacts to households in a different way: primarily, if not exclusively, through the labor market for economic shocks, through food insecurity for drought, and through asset loss for destructive shocks such as earthquakes. This implies different policy and programmatic prescriptions to mitigate the impacts, including, for example, the timing of an intervention and the most appropriate type of assistance. Natural disasters lay at the intersection of those covariate shocks where more is known on the role of social protection—such as economic and financial crises—and those where lessons are only beginning to emerge— including pandemics such as COVID-19 and forced displacement. The building blocks and the priorities that are outlined in this report offer a foundation for a structured approach to advance ASP globally, across each type of shock.

RESILIENCE TO SHOCKS: THE CAPACITY TO PREPARE, COPE, AND ADAPT

To understand how ASP can build household resilience to shocks, it is important to first define resilience. The concept of resilience has enjoyed widespread adoption across (as well as outside of) international development organizations and sectors, from finance to health to infrastructure, to name but a few. The concept has gained traction, significance, and influence in part because it highlights a positive capacity for a unit of analysis to manage adversity (that is, a system, a society, a community, a household, or a person; for detailed synopses, see Béné et al. 2012; de Weijer 2013; and appendix A). Definitions for resilience abound and any given two definitions are rarely the same across or even within institutions. For conceptual clarity, in this report resilience is defined as:

> The ability for a household to prepare for, cope with, and adapt to shocks in a manner that protects their well-being: ensuring that they do not fall into poverty or become trapped in poverty as a result of the impacts.

A household's resilience to a shock can be thought of as the product of its capacity to prepare for, cope with, and adapt to it. Drawing inspiration from the BRACED framework (Bahadur et al. 2015), conceptually, a more resilient household will possess three interlinked capacities that help to minimize and resist a shock's negative impacts. The higher the household's capacity to prepare, cope, and adapt, the lesser the implied impact of the shock on well-being and the increased likelihood that the household will "bounce back faster" (Schipper and Langston 2015), recovering to pre-shock levels of well-being. By extension, vulnerability and resilience can be simplistically seen as "two sides of the same coin" (Jorgensen and Siegel 2019), where a household is vulnerable to a shock because of a limited capacity to prepare, cope, and adapt, translating into an inability to minimize and resist the negative impacts, bouncing back slowly, if at all.

For greater precision, taking each interlinked capacity in turn, a more resilient household can do the following.

- **Prepare for a shock:** *mitigating the impacts, informing and enabling coping and adaptation.*[3] First, the capacity to prepare is, to a large extent, determined by a household's access to information on the risks it faces, enabling a better understanding of the factors that drive its own exposure and vulnerability to those risks (Bahadur et al. 2015). Adequate information on risk is essential for informing the actions needed to minimize exposure and vulnerability, including through preparing to cope with the immediate impact of a shock, as well as strategies for long-term adaptation. At the same time, a more resilient household tends to have access to savings in the form of cash and assets to create a buffer that it can draw upon after a shock. Similarly, a more resilient household is typically more prepared as a result of having access to a range of private (insurance) and public (social protection) instruments to draw upon when savings are depleted and/or a shock is especially severe.
- **Cope with a shock:** *minimizing the immediate impact of a shock on well-being in the short term.*[4] The capacity to cope with a shock is highly correlated to the capacity to prepare. A more resilient household possesses a higher capacity to cope with the impact because it can draw upon its savings

and leverage private (insurance) and public (social protection) resources as appropriate to smooth consumption and lost income. Together, these strategies and instruments help to resist the negative impact on their well-being and enable households to bounce back to their pre-shock state as quickly as possible.

- **Adapt to a shock:** *reducing exposure and vulnerability over the long term, enabling a movement toward a more resilient state.* With sufficient adaptive capacity, a more resilient household can make investments that reduce both its exposure and vulnerability to shocks over the longer term. This includes diversifying or adjusting livelihood portfolios away from sources of income that are especially vulnerable to the impacts of a shock; building a larger and more diversified asset base, including productive, financial, and human capital-related assets to enable these adjustments in livelihood portfolios; and/or leveraging such assets to relocate away from an area of spatially concentrated risk. Indeed, the ultimate expression of adaptive capacity may be the household's ability to reduce its exposure to a shock altogether through relocation and planned migration when in situ adjustments to livelihood and assets portfolios fail and where remaining in place would lead to chronic vulnerability and even maladaptation.[5]

POVERTY AND VULNERABILITY: CONSTRAINTS TO THE CAPACITY TO PREPARE, COPE, AND ADAPT

Shocks disproportionately impact poorer households, who tend to be particularly exposed to shocks and more vulnerable to their impacts (Hallegatte et al. 2016). The generalized vulnerability of poorer households to shocks can be ascribed to a deficit in terms of the capacity to prepare, cope, and adapt. For example, it is widely documented that poorer households resort to "negative coping mechanisms" to smooth consumption, including by cutting consumption, selling productive assets, and removing children from school (Hill, Skoufias, and Maher 2019). Poverty also can prevent the adoption of livelihood strategies and higher-risk investments in support of greater preparedness and longer-term adaptation, leading to a state of chronic vulnerability to shocks (Bahadur et al. 2015). For many poorer households, the ability to bounce back to a pre-shock state of well-being is acutely limited, creating poverty traps and, at a societal level, undermining poverty reduction (UNISDR 2015).

Shocks routinely impoverish nonpoor households when their capacity to prepare, cope, and adapt is overwhelmed. The data and research are replete with examples of how local and national poverty rates increase substantially after severe and less severe shocks (see appendix A). Many households live close to the poverty line, meaning they are especially vulnerable to poverty as a consequence of even small variances in income and consumption (figure O.2). In this way, households that are vulnerable to poverty due to shocks often possess similar constraints as poor households to prepare, cope, and adapt to shocks. Particularly severe shocks—especially those that are rapid-onset, destructive shocks such as earthquakes and severe typhoons—can erase assets and livelihoods and impoverish even wealthier households. Further, within a

FIGURE O.2

Africa: Chronic and transient poverty

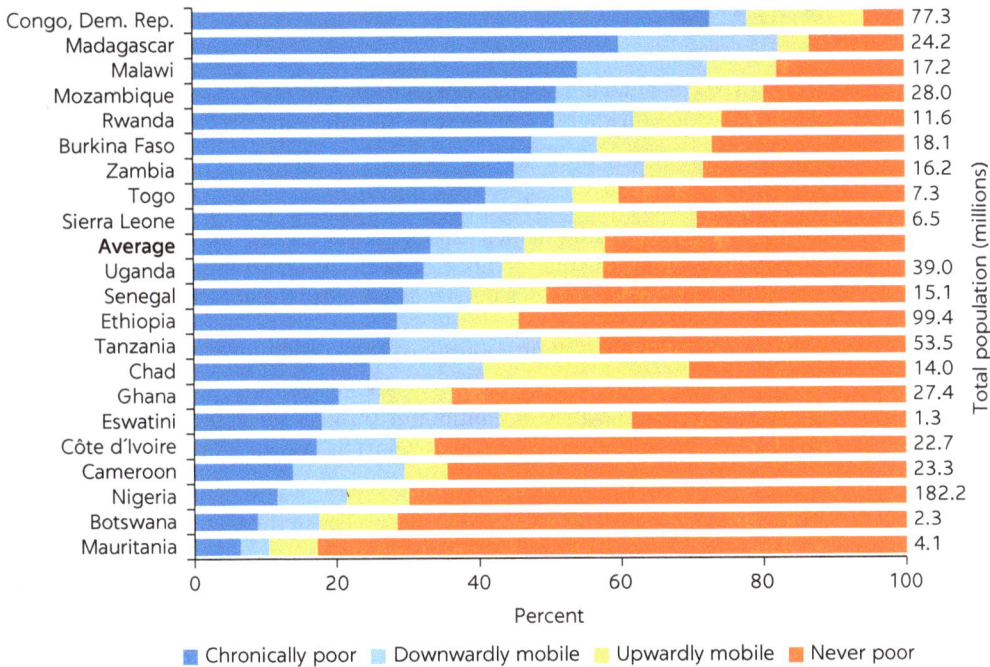

Source: Dang and Dabalen 2017, as cited in Beegle, Coudouel, and Monsalve 2018.
Note: Poverty statistics are from the latest household survey year for each country. "Chronically poor" are households that were poor in both periods of the analysis; "downwardly mobile" are households that fell into poverty in the second period; "upwardly mobile" are those that were poor in the first period but not in the second; and "never poor" are households that were nonpoor in both periods.

household, women, children, the disabled, and the elderly are often found to be especially vulnerable to the impacts from shocks (see, for example, Holmes 2019; UNICEF 2018).

Adapting to shocks and "bouncing back better" after they hit is critical for poor and vulnerable households. Priority 4 of the Sendai Framework for Disaster Risk Reduction emphasizes that reconstruction after a disaster offers an opportunity to build more resilient societies (Hallegatte, Rentschler, and Walsh 2018). The concept of "building back better," aligned to Priority 4, highlights the necessity of not re-creating the same vulnerabilities that exacerbated the impacts of the previous disaster. Applying the same principle in relation to household resilience, it is critical to ensure that poor and vulnerable households can "bounce back better" to a more resilient state of lower exposure and vulnerability (Frankenberger et al. 2012; Manyena et al. 2011). Further, under the influence of climate change, and alongside societal adaptation initiatives, a household's ability to adapt over the long term to increased uncertainty and worsening climatic conditions will become increasingly critical. The limited capacity of poorer households to adapt to climate change means they are likely to be among the hardest hit by the worsening impacts (Hallegatte et al. 2016).

ADAPTIVE SOCIAL PROTECTION: BUILDING RESILIENCE BY SUPPORTING THE CAPACITY TO PREPARE, COPE, AND ADAPT

ASP can help to build the resilience of poor and vulnerable households to shocks by directly investing in their capacity to prepare, cope, and adapt. As such, the report defines ASP in the following way:

> Adaptive social protection helps to build the resilience of poor and vulnerable households by investing in their capacity to prepare for, cope with, and adapt to shocks: protecting their wellbeing and ensuring that they do not fall into poverty or become trapped in poverty as a result of the impacts.

This definition of ASP promotes government-led investment in the three resilience capacities of households who are particularly vulnerable to shocks along the pre- and post-shock continuum, through social protection programs (table O.1). Together, social safety nets, social insurance, and labor market programs constitute the social protection "system" along with the policies that guide them and the delivery systems that underpin them (ILO 2017; Robalino, Rawlings, and Walker 2012; World Bank 2012).

The pronounced ability of safety net programs in particular to build the resilience of poor and vulnerable households can be harnessed and enhanced in relation to covariate shocks. Unemployment insurance and social insurance programs are widely understood to be instruments that can help households to cope with the impacts of a shock, if they have access to these programs. That said, in many countries, the share of the formal labor force is limited, and access to unemployment insurance is highly constrained, especially among the poorest households. Safety nets, on the other hand, routinely reach among the

TABLE O.1 The social protection system: Objectives and types of social protection and labor programs

SOCIAL PROTECTION AND LABOR PROGRAM	OBJECTIVES	TYPES OF PROGRAMS
Social safety nets/ social assistance Noncontributory	Reduce poverty and inequality	• Unconditional cash transfers • Conditional cash transfers • Social pensions • Food and in-kind support • School feeding programs • Public works projects • Fee waivers and targeted subsidies • Other interventions
Social insurance Contributory	Ensure adequate standards in the face of shocks and life changes	• Contributory old-age, survivor, and disability pensions • Sick leave • Maternity/paternity benefits • Health insurance coverage • Other types of insurance
Labor market programs Contributory and noncontributory	Improve chances of employment and earnings; smooth income support during unemployment	• Active labor market programs: training, employment intermediation services, and wage subsidies • Passive labor market programs: unemployment insurance and early retirement incentives

Source: World Bank 2018.

poorest households with various forms of noncontributory assistance—most typically unconditional or conditional cash transfers, in-kind support such as food and nonfood items, and public works programs. For these reasons, while there is ample room to explore the role of all types of social protection programs in building resilience, the focus of this report is squarely on safety net programs.

The impact of assistance delivered to a poor or vulnerable household through a safety net can be transformative across its resilience capacities. A cash transfer, for example, provides a supplementary source of income that can enable the beneficiary household to undertake preparedness measures (such as saving) and to invest in higher-risk, higher-return livelihoods, supporting adaptation. If a shock hits, the beneficiary household is better able to smooth consumption and to avoid negative coping strategies. Moreover, after a shock, if preparedness measures are overwhelmed (for example, depleted savings), the continued provision of transfers can directly support the beneficiary household's capacity to cope. More specifically, table O.2 summarizes the impact of safety net programs across the three resilience capacities—prepare, cope, and adapt—highlighting the ways ASP can build the resilience of poor and vulnerable households.

TABLE O.2 Adaptive social protection: Supporting the capacity to prepare, cope, and adapt

	PREPAREDNESS	COPING	ADAPTATION
A more resilient household	• More savings (cash, assets) to draw upon if a shock occurs • Access to public (social protection) and private (insurance) instruments if needed after a shock • Access to information on their own exposure and vulnerability to shocks (including early warning information) to inform action	• Activates coping mechanisms: acting on information (including early warning information), leverages savings, assets, public and private instruments to smooth consumption and to supplement lost income	• Capable of making long-term investments to reduce exposure and vulnerability over time • Adjustment of asset and livelihood portfolios away from sources of risk and vulnerability • Planned movement and migration away from areas of spatially concentrated, chronic risk
Poor and vulnerable households	• Limited savings and assets to draw on if a shock occurs • Limited or no access to public (social protection) and private (insurance) instruments if needed should a shock occur • Limited access to information on their exposure and vulnerability (including early warning information) to inform action	• In the absence of adequate savings and access to social protection and/or private insurance, resort to negative coping strategies— cutting consumption, removing children from school, distress sale of assets, among others	• Fewer resources with which to make long-term investments in adaptation through adjustments in livelihood and asset portfolios that can lead to • Maladaptation and chronic vulnerability • Forced displacement and unplanned migration
Role of safety net programs in supporting preparedness, coping, and adaptation among the poor and vulnerable households	• Increased access to safety nets among the poor and vulnerable, especially those identified as at-risk from shocks • Transfers to at-risk households before shocks occur to support savings and asset accumulation • Safety nets leveraged to transmit information on exposure and vulnerability, enabling the increased anticipation of shocks, and informing actions in support of preparedness, coping, and adaptation	• Support to post-shock coping through continued delivery during and after a shock to existing beneficiaries • Shock-responsive programs capable of adjusting benefit package and temporarily increasing the number of beneficiaries as needed based on post-shock needs	• Support to long-term adjustment of asset and livelihood portfolios, including through cash, cash plus, and productive inclusion interventions • Community asset-building projects through public works programs that address key drivers of community-level vulnerability • Support to human capital accumulation for intergenerational adaptation through increased opportunity

Source: World Bank.

An overriding priority for ASP is the continued extension of access to safety net programs, especially for the households that are identified as being most vulnerable to shocks. Recently, safety net coverage has increased dramatically, globally (see, for example, Beegle, Coudouel, and Monsalve 2018; World Bank 2018), providing a strong platform for their use in building resilience to covariate shocks. However, while the rise of safety nets has been impressive and is at the heart of several increasingly ambitious social protection–related agendas (including ASP), the undercoverage of and limited access to safety net programs, particularly among the poorest households, remain widespread (ILO 2017; World Bank 2018). Low social protection coverage of those most vulnerable to covariate shocks inevitably limits the role of social protection in building resilience (Bastagli and Holmes 2014). Indeed, many countries at high risk of natural disasters have especially low coverage, as highlighted in figure O.3. In that sense, the development of ASP is consistent with and integral to the advancement of the universal social protection agenda: access to social protection for all in need, when they need it, including in relation to shocks.[6]

The remainder of this report highlights how specific priorities and core investments can enhance the ability of safety net programs to build household resilience to covariate shocks. In order to highlight these priorities and core investments, the report outlines a framework that delineates four key building blocks for the development of ASP: (1) programs, (2) data and information systems, (3) finance, and (4) institutional arrangements and partnerships (figure O.4). This report is structured around these building blocks, with each chapter dedicated to expanding on the key priorities and core investments aligned to each. In that way, chapter 1, "Programs: Design Considerations for Building Resilience," focuses on some of the design features that can enhance the ability of safety net programs to build resilience by supporting preparedness, coping, and adaptation. Chapter 2, "Data and Information: Understanding

FIGURE O.3

Social safety nets: Global coverage compared to World Risk Index ranking

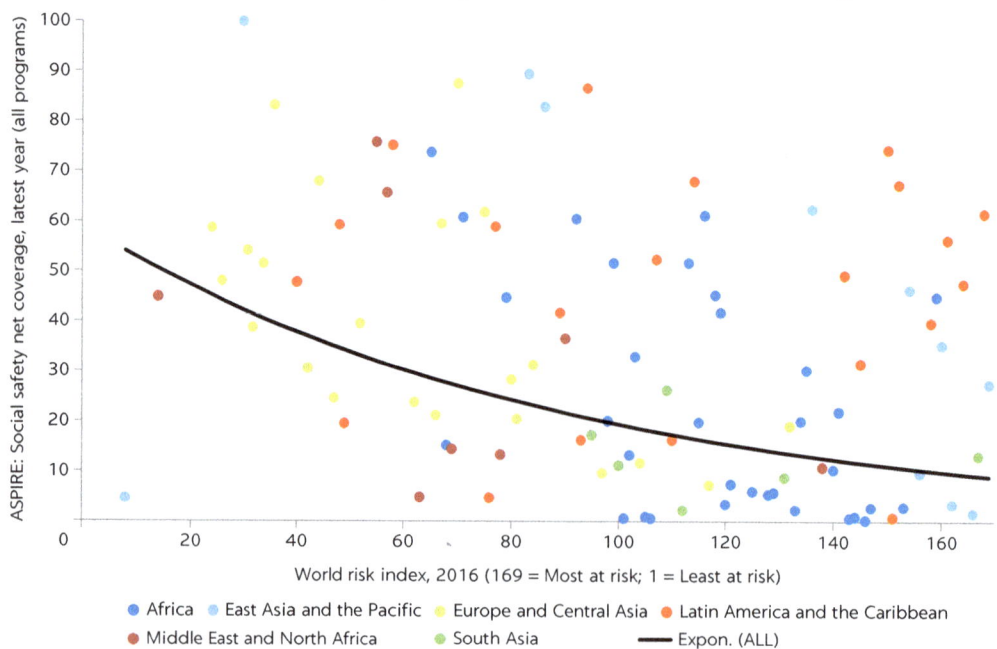

Sources: Atlas of Social Protection (ASPIRE), http://datatopics.worldbank.org/aspire/; UNU-EHS 2016.

FIGURE O.4
Framework for adaptive social protection: Four building blocks

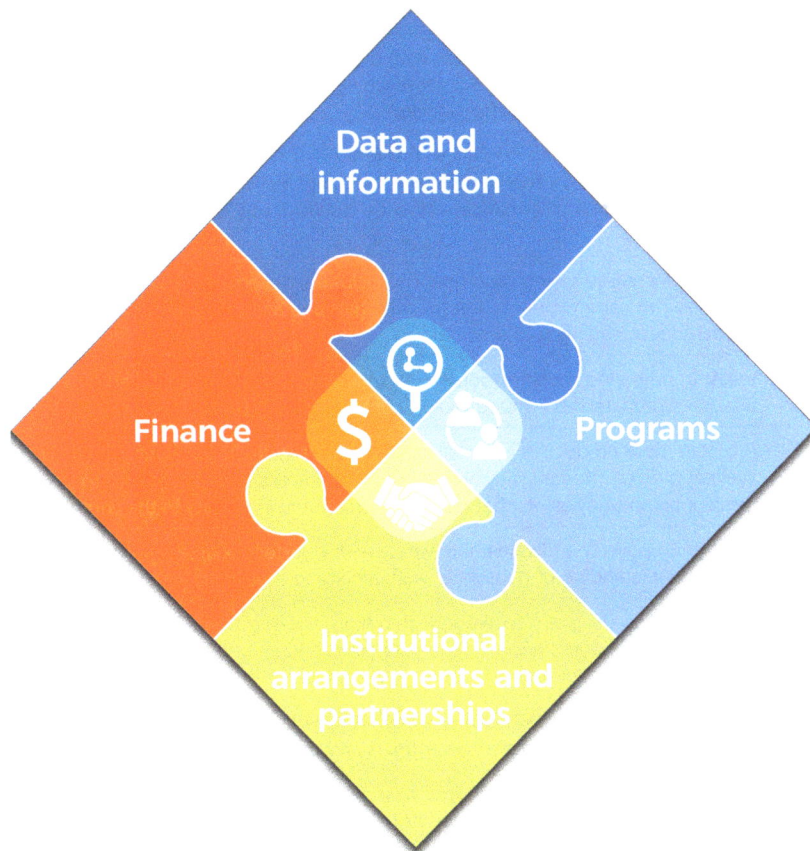

Source: World Bank.

Risk and Household Vulnerability," identifies some of the data and information requirements that underpin the design and implementation of these programs. Chapter 3, "Finance: Applying a Disaster Risk Financing Approach," then focuses on outlining the role of risk financing in enabling timely response to shocks with ASP. Lastly, chapter 4, "Institutional Arrangements and Partnerships: Multisectoral Coordination and Humanitarian Linkages," unbundles some of the multisectoral institutional arrangements and partnerships that are critical for ASP both across government line ministries as well as with nongovernment partners. These key priorities and core investments are summarized in table O.3 and the remainder of this overview section.

ASP building block 1: Programs

As noted, investing in a stronger, more comprehensive social protection system composed of multiple programs with high coverage provides the foundation for building household resilience. Moreover, beyond the traditional social protection system itself, ASP highlights the need for strong coordination with the disparate programs working on building the resilience of households to shocks from other sectors. Take for example the many agriculture, human development (health and education), and disaster risk reduction programs that explicitly or

TABLE O.3 Summary of the key priorities and investments, by building block

BUILDING BLOCK	PRIORITY/INVESTMENT	DESCRIPTION
Programs	Strengthen the overall social protection system and expand coverage	A stronger social protection system with higher coverage across several programs provides more avenues for reaching poor and vulnerable households with assistance before and after shocks
	Appraise and adjust the design parameters of existing programs within the system	Adjusting targeting approaches to integrate risk and household vulnerability into eligibility criteria and beneficiary selection, as well as fine-tuning benefit parameters to enhance resilience-building outcomes among those households
	Design features to support preparedness	Promote increased savings and financial inclusion; disseminate risk information within at-risk communities to inform strategies and actions for household preparedness, coping, and adaptation
	Design features to support coping	Invest in preparing shock-responsive, flexible programs that are backed by adequate preparedness measures and contingency plans
	Design features to support adaptation	Promote more productive and resilient livelihoods including through asset and livelihood diversification; support to human capital accumulation; building resilient community assets that address sources of vulnerability in the community
Data and information	Household risk and vulnerability assessments	Integrating poverty and vulnerability data with disaster risk assessments for a spatial understanding of household vulnerability to shocks
	Social registries	Expanding social registry coverage within high-risk areas, enabling more frequent updating and ensuring the data contained in registries are useful in the assessment of household vulnerability to shocks
	Early warning systems	Linking to early warning systems as a basis for predicting needs and promoting timely action based on predefined triggers and thresholds for action
	Post-shock needs assessment	Investing in the capacity to conduct post-shock assessments, or linking to assessment from other sectors, to ensure an up-to-date understanding of household needs—especially after less predictable, destructive shocks
	Data sharing platforms and protocols	Facilitating exchange of data between social protection and relevant line ministries, including DRM, as well as nongovernment partners
Finance	Cost estimation of shock response	Use historical shock data to analyze the predicted cost of future responses with social protection
	Preplanned risk financing and risk layering for shock response	Preposition financial instruments to cover those costs, layering different instruments for different risks and ensuring timelier responses
	Linking to disbursement mechanisms	Ensure that programs and their payment platforms are prepared to efficiently disburse available funds to beneficiaries once released
	Secure long-term financing in support of resilience building	Financing for the expansion of long-term programs, supporting household resilience, including through preparedness and adaptation
Institutional arrangements and partnerships	Government leadership	Internalizing responsibility to build the resilience of poor and vulnerable households to shocks, owning the ASP agenda and setting government objectives and strategy accordingly
	Policy coherence and cross-sector collaboration	Especially among the core sectors of social protection, DRM, and those involved in climate change adaptation
	Institutional capacity	Beyond policy coherence and coordination mechanisms: investing in the additional human, financial, and physical capacity required for ASP delivery
	Strategic partnerships with nongovernment actors	Pursuing a collaborative, coordinated approach with nongovernment partners engaged in building resilience
	National and nongovernment actor specificity in roles and responsibilities	Beyond simple dichotomies, identifying specific comparative advantages in design and delivery of ASP programs across humanitarian/government divide

Source: World Bank.
Note: ASP = adaptive social protection; DRM = disaster risk management.

implicitly seek to build household resilience to covariate shocks. Similarly, after a shock hits, many emergency response and recovery programs deliver from a multitude of ministries, departments, and agencies as well as from nongovernmental and humanitarian organizations to help people cope with the impacts. Where such coordination, coherence, and integration of programming is achieved in practice, household gains in resilience building could be more significant and sustainable; see, for example, the integrated and layered programmatic approaches to building resilience undertaken by the World Food Programme (WFP 2015, 2018).

More specifically, traditional approaches to safety net beneficiary selection need to be re-evaluated to ensure coverage of the households that are most vulnerable to shocks. Geographic targeting that is based on a spatial understanding of risks and that prioritizes extending and/or deepening coverage within high-risk areas will enhance the ability of safety net programs to support resilience building. Within program eligibility criteria, measures of vulnerability to covariate shocks can further enhance the ability to identify and reach households most vulnerable to shocks in support of preparedness, coping, and adaptation (del Ninno and Mills 2015). For example, climate-smart targeting incorporates area and household data to help identify the households vulnerable to natural hazards and climate-change risks (ADB 2018; Bastagli and Holmes 2014; World Bank 2013).

Appraising and adjusting existing program benefit package parameters can enhance their resilience-building impact. Building on risk and vulnerability–informed beneficiary selection, an assessment of existing safety net program benefit packages can inform specific adjustments to maximize their impact on resilience building. For example, it is worthwhile considering how the benefit package design parameters—type (cash, vouchers, food), timing, frequency, duration, and amount—mediate their impact on preparedness, coping, and adaptation. Concretely, smaller, more frequent cash transfers in support of consumption smoothing are associated with support to coping, especially when they are timed with predictable shocks such as lean seasons. Larger, lump-sum, infrequent transfers are more likely to spur investments in support of adaptation and preparedness. More generally, where transfers are not predictable and reliable, they will undermine resilience-building impacts, with beneficiaries more likely to continue to resort to negative coping strategies and not factor the transfers into longer-term investment decisions, hampering preparedness and adaptation.

Safety net support to the capacity to prepare for shocks

Savings and financial inclusion can directly increase the preparedness of poor and vulnerable households, enhancing their ability to cope with and adapt to a shock. Financial inclusion can be explicitly supported where safety net beneficiaries are given access to a store-of-value transaction account (increasingly common practice for cash transfers) and encouraged to save and/or are given access to savings groups in their community. Even where social protection does not explicitly support financial inclusion and saving, beneficiaries often use the transfer for this purpose, especially in contexts of recurrent crises. Recent evaluations of safety net programs indicate significant impacts on increased savings, improved creditworthiness, and reduced debt (Andrews, Hsiao, and Ralston 2018; Bastagli et al. 2016; Hidrobo et al. 2018; Ulrichs and Slater 2016). In Mexico, beneficiaries of the former national conditional cash transfer program (Prospera) who lived in communities highly exposed to droughts and hurricanes largely used the transfer "to save for the bad times" (Solórzano 2016). In Africa, safety net beneficiary households are 4–20 percentage points more likely to save relative to comparable nonbeneficiary households (figure O.5); given the initial low savings rate among such households, this implies an expansion by a factor of almost two in the incidence of savings (Beegle, Coudouel, and Monsalve 2018). Financial inclusion provides the additional benefit of making beneficiaries more easily reachable with swift electronic cash transfer assistance after a shock.

Safety net programs can also provide channels for communicating early warning information, disaster preparedness training, and guidance on adaptation to recipient households. Access to early warning systems is low and biased against poor households in developing countries (Hallegatte et al. 2017).

FIGURE O.5

Africa: Safety net beneficiaries tend to use the transfers to save

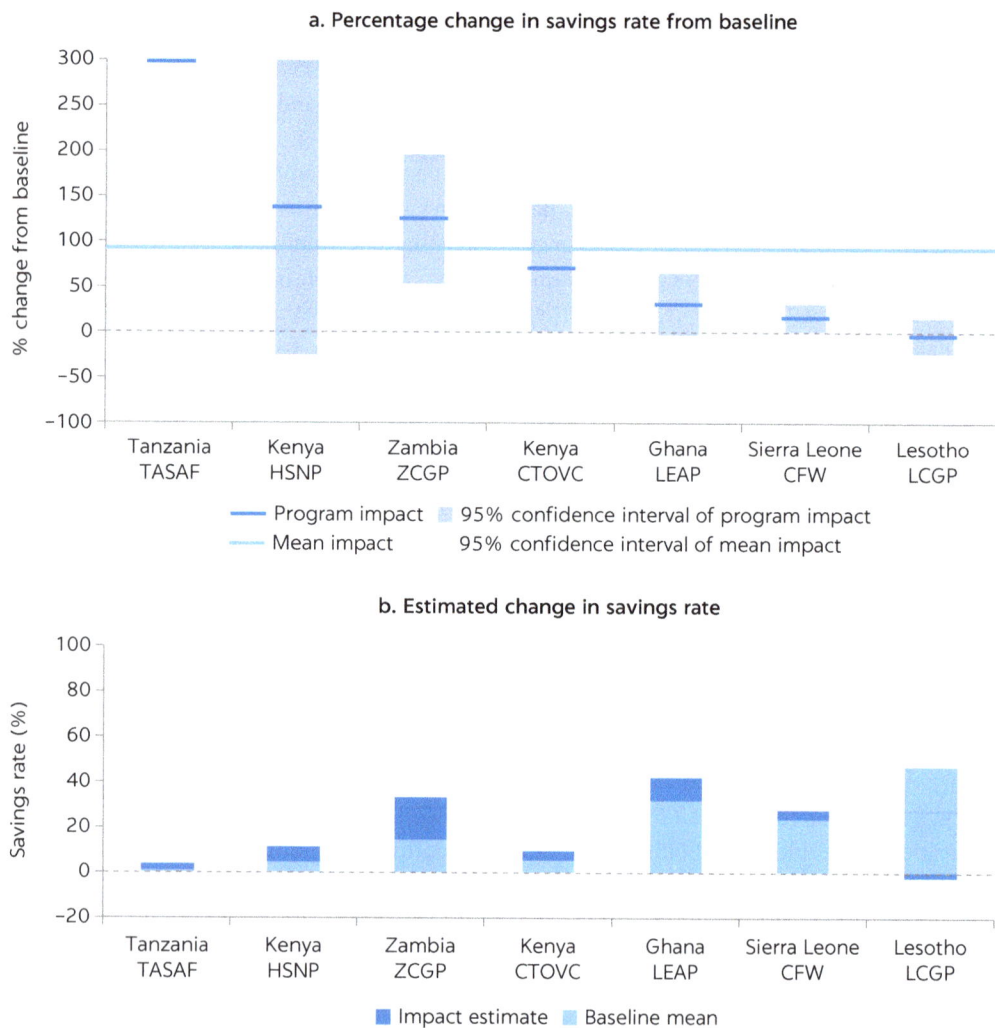

a. Percentage change in savings rate from baseline

b. Estimated change in savings rate

Source: Beegle, Coudouel, and Monsalve 2018.
Note: The mean value of the household transfer (in 2011 US$ purchasing power parity) is Tanzania Social Action Fund $48; Kenya's Hunger Safety Net Program $47; Zambia's Child Grant Program $27; Kenya Cash Transfer for Orphan and Vulnerable Children $71; Ghana's Livelihood Empowerment against Poverty $24; Sierra Leone Cash for Work $83; and Lesotho Child Grants Program $34.

This deficit is notable insofar as households can only be so prepared without access to early warning information to anticipate the coming shocks. Safety net programs rely on a network of implementers who often reach into the poorest communities, including social workers and village/community leaders. Leveraging these networks and the behavioral change sessions that increasingly accompany program delivery within communities can provide the means and venues for communicating this information. These venues can also be utilized to disseminate information on household and community disaster risk, risk reduction, and adaptation measures to beneficiary households and the wider community that are otherwise hard to reach (ADB 2018). For example, in the Philippines, Family Development Sessions, an integral component of the national conditional cash transfer program (Pantawid Pamilya Pilipino Program), are used as a vehicle and venue for delivering disaster preparedness information to all beneficiaries (Bowen 2015).

Safety net support to the capacity to cope with shocks

Safety net programs have well-documented, positive impacts on a poor household's capacity to cope with shocks, supporting food security and lessening the need to resort to negative coping alternatives (Ulrichs and Slater 2016). Of the resilience capacities, safety nets tend to demonstrate the strongest impact on supporting a household's capacity to cope. Evaluations of safety net programs across six African countries describe "unambiguous" increases in the food security of beneficiary households (Asfaw and Davis 2018).[7] The receipt of transfers through Ethiopia's Productive Safety Net Programme reduced the initial impact of a drought on beneficiaries by 57 percent, eliminating the adverse impact on food security within 2 years (Hidrobo et al. 2018).

In the context of covariate shocks, safety net programs can provide extraordinary support to help households cope with often devastating impacts. In their shock-responsive social protection framework, O'Brien et al. (2018) outline five potential ways that social protection programs can be leveraged to respond to large-scale shocks:

- **Design tweaks** are small adjustments to a routine social protection program. They can introduce flexibility to maintain the regular service for existing beneficiaries in a shock (for example, by waiving conditionalities). Alternatively, they can address vulnerabilities that are likely to increase in a crisis, through adjustments to program coverage, timeliness or predictability (for example, by altering the payment schedule), without requiring a flex at the moment of the shock.
- **Vertical expansion** is the temporary increase of the value or duration of a social protection intervention to meet the additional needs of existing beneficiaries. For such vertical expansions to be relevant, the program or programs must have good coverage of the disaster-affected area and also of the neediest households.
- **Horizontal expansion** is the temporary inclusion of new beneficiaries from disaster-affected communities into a social protection program, by extending geographic coverage, enrolling more eligible households in existing areas, or altering the enrollment criteria.
- **Piggybacking** occurs when an emergency response uses part of an established system or program while delivering something new. Exactly which and how many elements of the system or program are borrowed will vary; it could

be, for example, a specific program's beneficiary list, its staff, a national database, or a particular payment mechanism.

- **Alignment** describes designing an intervention with elements resembling others that already exist or are planned, but without integrating the two. For example, this could be an alignment of objectives, targeting method, transfer value, or delivery mechanism. Governments may align their systems with those of humanitarian agencies or vice versa, either because an existing intervention is not operational as needed in a crisis or because it may not yet exist (O'Brien et al. 2018).

Where a safety net exists and has a good degree of coverage among affected households, vertical expansion offers a relatively simple method of providing more assistance to existing beneficiaries that have been affected by a shock (figure O.6). Recent examples include the vertical expansion of the social protection system in Fiji following Tropical Cyclone Winston in 2016 and of the national conditional cash transfer program in the Philippines, through additional grants from humanitarian actors (the World Food Programme and UNICEF) following Typhoon Haiyan (Yolanda) and Typhoon Ruby. In the case of Fiji, an impact assessment, conducted 3 months after the disaster, found that households that received the vertical expansion were more likely to report having recovered from the shock more quickly; for instance, they were 8–10 percent more likely to have recovered from housing damage than nonbeneficiaries (Mansur et al. 2017). However, vertical expansions generally do not reach shock-affected, nonbeneficiary households that may be in equal or greater need of assistance (Barca and O'Brien 2017). As such, the ability to at least temporarily reach additional households that may be equally or more in need of support to their coping capacity but that may not be regular beneficiaries of social protection programs is critical for shock-responsive social

FIGURE O.6

Social protection programs: Vertical and horizontal expansion

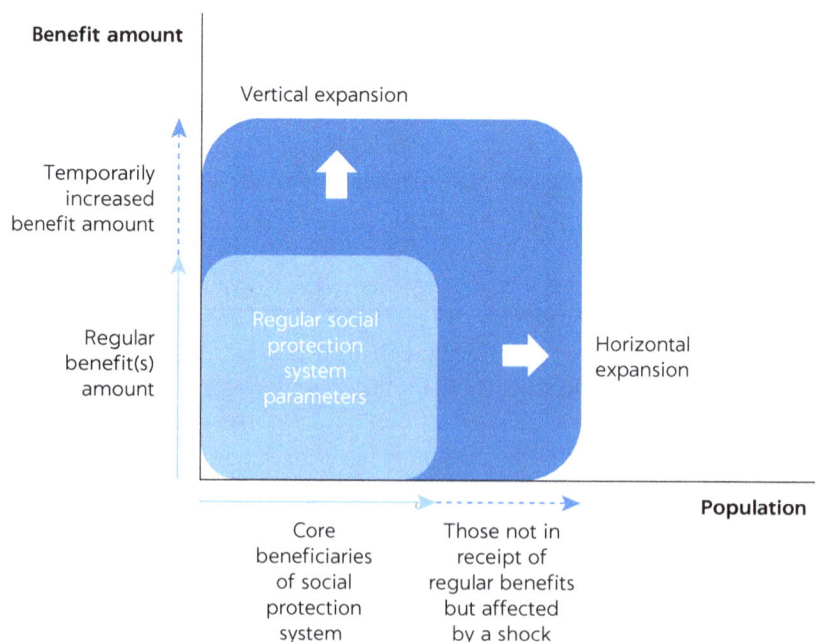

Source: World Bank.

protection. This can be achieved through horizontal expansion, or dedicated emergency programs that may piggyback on social protection delivery systems.

Horizontal expansion enables a safety net program to temporarily expand its caseload after a shock to include new households based on eligibility from a shock's impacts (figure O.6). Introducing the ability to horizontally expand in this manner is far more complex than undertaking vertical expansion to existing beneficiaries. Horizontal expansion benefits from significant ex ante investment in the processes and procedures for delivering the program, often in challenging postdisaster settings. Several countries have invested in the capacity to horizontally expand a safety net program, including most prominently Ethiopia with the Productive Safety Net Programme and Kenya with the Hunger Safety Net Program; each is prepared to undertake horizontal expansions based on household needs generated by drought and related food insecurity in drought-prone parts of the country.

Some countries use a dedicated emergency program with characteristics similar to a safety net (cash, in-kind, and public works), which may piggyback on core safety net delivery systems and capacity. Emergency programs have dedicated response objectives and operate alongside an existing safety net program. Such programs can be located within or outside of the social protection ministries, departments, and agencies and can leverage underlying safety net delivery systems such as social registries, payment systems, and front-line social protection staff. In Pakistan, one such emergency program, the Citizen's Damage Compensation Program, responded to widespread flooding in 2010 (World Bank 2013). The Citizen's Damage Compensation Program model has since been adopted as a permanent approach to reaching those affected by shocks in Pakistan. In the Sahel, Mauritania has developed a dedicated response program ("Elmaouna") that piggybacks on existing social protection social registries and payment platforms for its delivery.

Whichever approach is taken, the timeliness of shock-responsive social protection is critical for the protection of household well-being and is a function of adequate preparedness measures. Specifically, contingency planning is a critical preparedness measure that enhances the timeliness of response. Indeed, operational processes for shock response need to be clearly defined in advance—who does what, when—in relevant operational manuals, standard operating procedures, and the wider government shock response plans. Ultimately, such planning can better ensure faster, more effective, and more coordinated implementation. To a large extent, social protection programs across countries rely on common phases of delivery to ensure that programs provide the right amount/composition of benefits and services, to the right persons at the right time. This "delivery chain" is centered on four implementation phases: assess, enroll, provide, and manage (figure O.7). The delivery chain provides a useful schematic for considering the preparedness measures and contingency plans that are required at each phase of delivery to enable the operationalization of shock responsive social protection. These considerations for shock response along the social protection delivery chain are explored further in appendix B.

Safety net support to the capacity to adapt to shocks

Alongside supporting short-term coping after a shock, governments can use safety nets to invest in the capacity for poor and vulnerable households to adapt to shocks over the long term. There has been an increasing and

FIGURE O.7
Social protection delivery chain

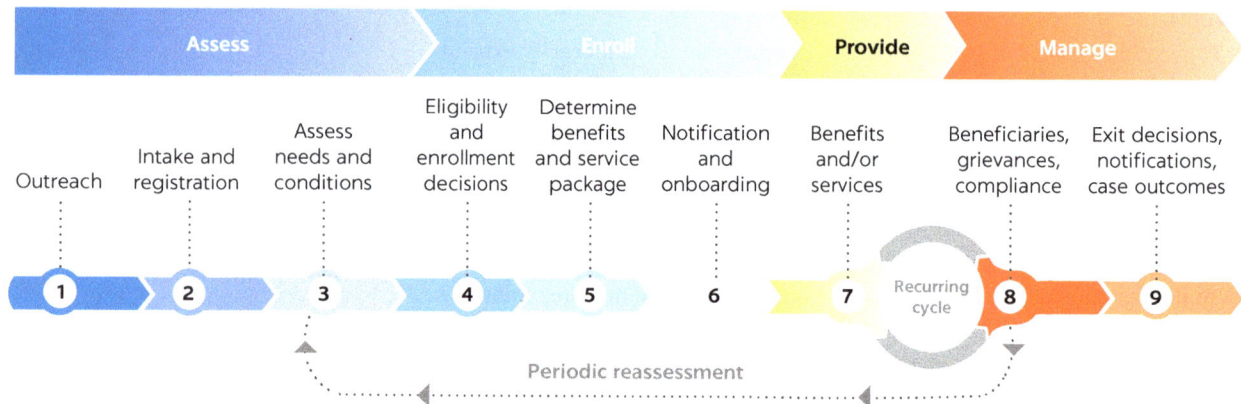

Source: Lindert et al., forthcoming.

justifiable focus on the role of shock-responsive social protection in supporting post-shock coping. That said, ASP and the wider definition of resilience used here highlight the central importance of supporting a vulnerable household's longer-term adaptation in order to reduce its vulnerability to a shock over time. By broadening the focus in this way, safety net programs can provide pathways toward a more resilient state for poor and vulnerable households (see also Tenzing 2019). By extension, where successful, these investments may serve to reduce future post-shock needs over time.

Concretely, safety nets can support adaptive capacity when designed to help the poor and vulnerable households accumulate and diversify assets and livelihoods (Bahadur et al. 2015; FSIN 2015; Jorgensen and Siegel 2019). The promotion of more productive and resilient livelihoods among poor and vulnerable households is one of the primary ways in which safety net programs can support adaptive capacity. Interventions that promote more productive and resilient livelihoods have the potential for empowering beneficiaries to diversify their asset and livelihood portfolios and to reduce their exposure and vulnerability to shocks. For example, a study by Macours, Premand, and Vakis (2012) found that the provision of vocational training or a productive investment grant in addition to a cash transfer to beneficiaries vulnerable to drought in Nicaragua provided full protection against drought shocks 2 years after the end of the intervention (relative to a control group that only received a cash transfer). Similarly, safety nets can contribute to livelihood promotion through specific programs that link cash transfer recipients to complementary interventions in other sectors (for example, agricultural inputs, training, and microfinance), leading to positive—yet varied—impacts on production and diversification into on-farm and off-farm opportunities (FAO 2016; Mariotti, Ulrichs, and Harman 2016).

As such, productive inclusion programs are emerging as powerful instruments for supporting the adaptive capacity of the poorest by supporting transitions into more productive and resilient livelihoods. Productive inclusion complements and links the provision of routine transfers with other interventions. These other interventions include skills and micro-entrepreneurship training tailored to livelihood opportunities; promotion of and support for saving groups; provision of seed capital and productive grants; linkage to existing value chains and markets; and mentoring, behavior, and life skills to build confidence and reinforce existing skillsets, among others (Bossuroy and Premand 2016; PEI 2016; Roelen et al. 2017).

Additionally, climate-sensitive public works programs enable beneficiaries to build assets that address structural vulnerabilities within their community. When designed to do so, public works programs can engage communities in climate-smart agriculture and integrated natural resource management, including a focus on waste management, reforestation, rainwater harvesting, soil/water conservation, and drought-resistant horticulture, among others.[8] A series of case studies of India's Mahatma Gandhi National Rural Employment Guarantee Scheme (MGNREGS) found that it can help to build resilience to various climate shocks. The MGNREGS was found to do so by providing integrated natural resource management and soil conservation infrastructure, agriculture-based investments, and other local infrastructures (Esteves et al. 2013; Kaur et al. 2017).

Lastly, safety net programs that contribute to building human capital can equip future generations with the tools to adapt to shocks. Promoting the accumulation of human capital among poorer households is critical in terms of connecting those households with the skills to adapt over the long term. Indeed, human capital can empower the next generation with the means to move out of at-risk areas toward employment opportunities in lower-risk livelihoods or lower-risk areas. To encourage the accumulation of human capital among beneficiaries, safety net benefits often come with conditions such as, most prominently, those aligned to conditional cash transfer (CCT) programs. CCT programs typically provide cash transfers to households when a household meets conditions related to investing in the education and health of its children. In cases where the capacity to monitor compliance with "hard" conditions in CCT programs may be lower, "soft" conditions are increasingly being used. For example, behavioral change sessions are increasingly accompanying cash transfer programs in Africa, delivered in the community to transmit information on health, nutrition, and education to beneficiaries.

ASP building block 2: Data and information

Information on household vulnerability to shocks and their relative capacity to cope and recover is crucial for the design and implementation of ASP programs. Critical questions for ASP include: What kinds of hazards does the country face? How frequently? Where? Which assets and population groups are exposed, and among them, which are the most vulnerable? The analysis of disaster risk is a core pillar of work conducted by the DRM sector. As highlighted above, ASP will need to draw on these analyses and assessments of disaster risk, integrating them with assessments of household poverty and vulnerability to poverty to provide an informed, needs-based foundation for policy dialogue and program design.

Beyond foundational analyses of risk and vulnerability, the global expansion of social registries is framing much of the current discussion around the ASP information agenda (Barca 2017; Bastagli 2014; Bastagli et al. 2016; IEG 2011; Kuriakose et al. 2012). Social registries are information systems that support outreach, intake, registration, and determination of potential eligibility for inclusion in one or more social programs. While many technical considerations are involved in designing and implementing social registries, their role in social policy is simple: provide a "gateway" for potential inclusion of intended populations into social programs (Leite et al. 2017). Social registries have been noted as especially useful tools for estimating the effects of a disaster on a household and for providing information on social protection beneficiaries and nonbeneficiaries that can enable shock-responsive social protection.

However, the business-as-usual expansion of social registries alone may not meet the information requirements for ASP. Many countries operate registries with "fixed lists" of registrants and program beneficiaries, and they generally update the lists every 4–5 years. Thus, social registries often comprise dated information and partial population coverage. For example, in Ecuador, only 15 percent of households in the database of affected households collected after the 2016 earthquake, Registro de Damnificados, were linked to the country's flagship social assistance program, Bono de Desarrollo Humano (Beazley 2017). Figure O.8 compares the coverage of social registries in four countries to demonstrate the varying population shares that are more or less easily identified and reached with post-shock assistance. Even with a complete social registry, existing information may not be fully up to date or

Lesotho, Mozambique, Pakistan, and the Philippines: Social registry coverage and utility for shock response

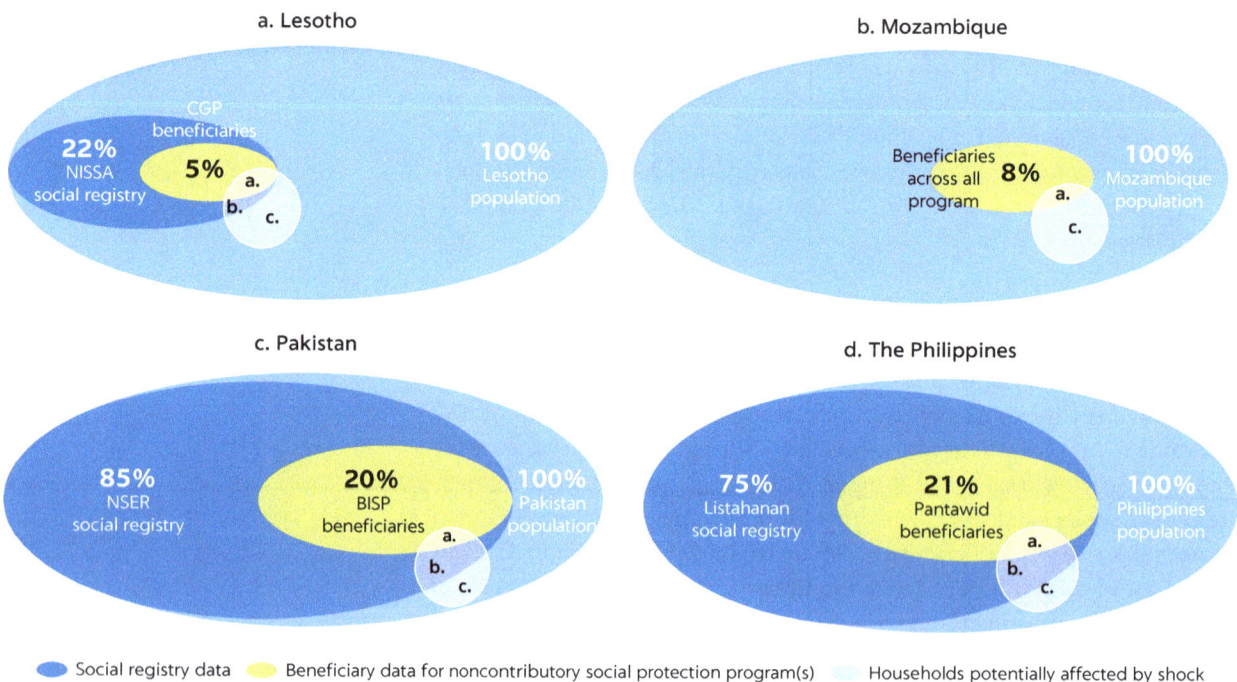

Source: Barca and O'Brien 2017.
Note: BISP = Benazir Income Support Program; CGP = Child Grants Programme; NISSA = National Information System for Social Assistance; NSER = National Socioeconomic Registry. Figures do not represent the totality of social protection databases in each country. The original source material also referred to Listahanan's coverage in the Philippines as 60 percent, which has since expanded to the 75 percent pictured here.
a = households that can be reached through vertical expansion or piggybacking (on the beneficiary databases); b = households that can be easily reached through horizontal expansion or piggybacking (on the social registry); c = households less easily reached through horizontal expansion or piggybacking (not covered by existing social protection databases).

accessible or may not be fully complete to reflect the multidimensional data requirements to inform a response after a shock (Barca and O'Brien 2017).

With that said, social registries can enhance their relevance for ASP by expanding into and within high-risk areas, updating information in those areas more frequently, and including variables related to household vulnerability. The prioritization of identified hotspot areas, in tandem with the expansion of programming to those areas, can help to increase the relevance of the social registry for ASP. In Mauritania, the government developed a methodology to determine the ideal number of households in the social registry in each commune to ensure it was more capable of informing response to drought. The analysis recommended including an additional 50,000 households that were expected to be food insecure. Additionally, the social registry data collected on households in those high-risk areas can be adapted to include key indicators related to their livelihoods and vulnerability to the hazards they face. In the Dominican Republic, the Vulnerability to Climate Hazards Index (Índice de Vulnerabilidad ante Choques Climáticos; IVACC) quantifies the likelihood of a household being vulnerable to hurricanes, storms, and floods. The index uses data from the country's national social registry, Sistema Unico de Beneficiarios, which covered approximately 85.5 percent of the population in 2015 (UNDP-UNEP PEI 2018) (map O.1).

ASP also highlights a significant need to link to information systems that are typically disconnected from the social protection sector. Early warning systems continue to play a critical role in providing and monitoring information for response and in triggering early action, especially in a context of growing climate-related risks.[9] Drought–food security hybrid systems typically use a range of information on food production, access, and livelihood outcomes from national agencies and international assessments (such as the Famine Early Warning Systems Network and the Integrated Food Security Phase Classification) and merge the information into an assessment of the food-security status and likely risk (Wilkinson et al. 2018). More recently, forecasts have started using a growing range of climate information. Systems using probabilistic forecast information typically draw on products from international, regional, and national forecasting centers. Products from international and regional forecasting centers are most common, as these are freely available and considered reliable. Where appropriate, these are complemented with products from national hydrological and meteorological services. Indeed, countries are already linking social protection responses to early warning information and developing index-based triggers for response, particularly for slow-onset shocks. In Uganda, satellite data and the Normalized Difference Vegetation Anomaly Index provide the basis for triggering earlier response to drought through the Northern Uganda Social Action Fund's (NUSAF) cash-for-work program.

In addition to early warning systems, post-shock data collection can play a key role in reflecting socioeconomic conditions and household needs, especially after fast-onset, less predictable, and destructive disasters. A postdisaster household assessment helps to gather real-time information and data for better understanding a disaster's impact on household well-being and livelihoods, thereby informing the choice of response programs and the appropriate benefit package. Social registry information on households can help inform and can be informed by the postdisaster household assessment process. In Chile, for example, the electronic Basic Emergency Sheet (Ficha Básica de

MAP O.1

Dominican Republic: The Vulnerability to Climate Hazards Index (IVACC)

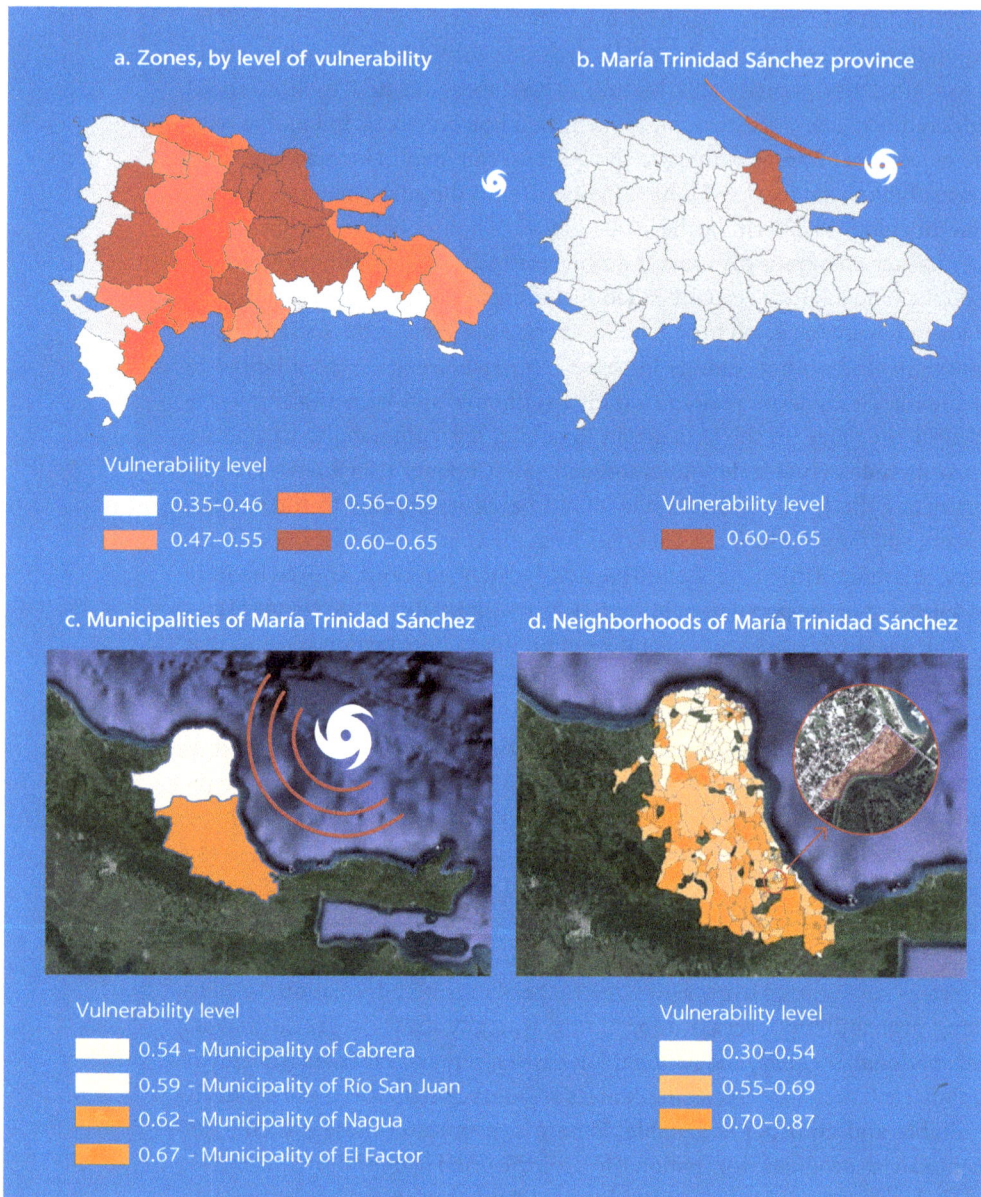

a. Zones, by level of vulnerability

b. María Trinidad Sánchez province

Vulnerability level

0.35–0.46	0.56–0.59
0.47–0.55	0.60–0.65

Vulnerability level

0.60–0.65

c. Municipalities of María Trinidad Sánchez

d. Neighborhoods of María Trinidad Sánchez

Vulnerability level

0.54 - Municipality of Cabrera
0.59 - Municipality of Río San Juan
0.62 - Municipality of Nagua
0.67 - Municipality of El Factor

Vulnerability level

0.30–0.54
0.55–0.69
0.70–0.87

Source: UNDP-UNEP 2018.
Note: The Vulnerability to Climate Hazards Index has a scale of 0–1, where provinces, municipalities, neighborhoods, and households with values close to 0 are the least vulnerable, and those with values close to 1 are the most vulnerable.

Emergencia—FIBE) collects and links postdisaster household assessment data to the social registry, providing a model for merging existing social registry data with up-to-date, post-shock needs assessments and for facilitating virtual, two-way data flows.

That said, when balancing the trade-off between a timely versus an accurate shock response, speed is more important. The literature on the topic is unequivocal: overall timeliness is more important than full targeting accuracy, especially in the first phase of assistance (Beazley, Solórzano, and Sossouvi 2016;

O'Brien et al. 2018; Pelham, Clay, and Braunholz 2011). Specifically, inclusion errors can and should be tolerated in the short term, especially as they can contribute to controlling tensions within recipient communities. As shock responses evolve and refocus on longer-term recovery, more precise targeting of losses and needs will become increasingly important to identify the households most in need of longer-term support.

ASP building block 3: Finance

Disaster risk financing is part of a global shift in thinking from seeing disasters as unpredictable humanitarian crises to predictable events that can be planned for and managed to minimize their impact. This involves moving from a reactive approach that addresses the impact of shocks once they happen to a more proactive approach, putting in place the required systems and financing to respond to shocks before they take place. This approach highlights the need for governments to develop risk financing strategies that enable funding to flow in the event of a shock and thus enable a faster response to disasters.

The application of these principles and related risk financing instruments to ASP can transform the ability to mobilize a faster response through a social protection system. Indeed, this highlights a strong synergy: when disaster risk financing strategies are established, a shock-responsive safety net program represents a preprepared mechanism through which financial instruments can disburse directly to affected households. Conversely, the availability of the kinds of risk financing instruments outlined in this building block and the extent of their linkage to safety net programs will to a large extent determine the speed of the response to affected households.

As a first step, financial modeling can better forecast the costs of responding to shocks through safety net programs. Leveraging a long time series of historic shock data, models can assess the retrospective incidence and scale of shocks to extrapolate future cost scenarios. In Kenya, the Hunger Safety Net Program is capable of horizontally expanding to drought; using a 15-year time series, financial models were able to avail policy makers of the program's cost implications to be planned for accordingly (figure O.9).

Based on such analyses, a disaster risk financing strategy can be developed for shock-responsive social protection. No single financial instrument can or should cover all risk financing requirements. Risk-layering considers how to meet the financial cost of response using a menu of financial instruments (figure O.10). Each instrument has its own terms and conditions and, therefore, advantages and disadvantages (table O.4). When assessing how to finance contingent liabilities from adaptive social protection, assessing which instruments are the most appropriate, adequate, and cost-effective is critical. In most cases, multiple financial instruments will be required to meet the financial cost of the anticipated response(s).

Establishing effective disbursement mechanisms (that is, how funding reaches beneficiaries) and linking disaster risk financing instruments to them is as important as securing funds in the first place. Having funds available in-country is of limited benefit if they cannot be transferred in a timely manner to the relevant institutions and, in turn, to the shock-affected households. A key factor affecting the disbursement of funds to affected households is the

FIGURE O.9

Kenya: Modeling the cost of responding to drought

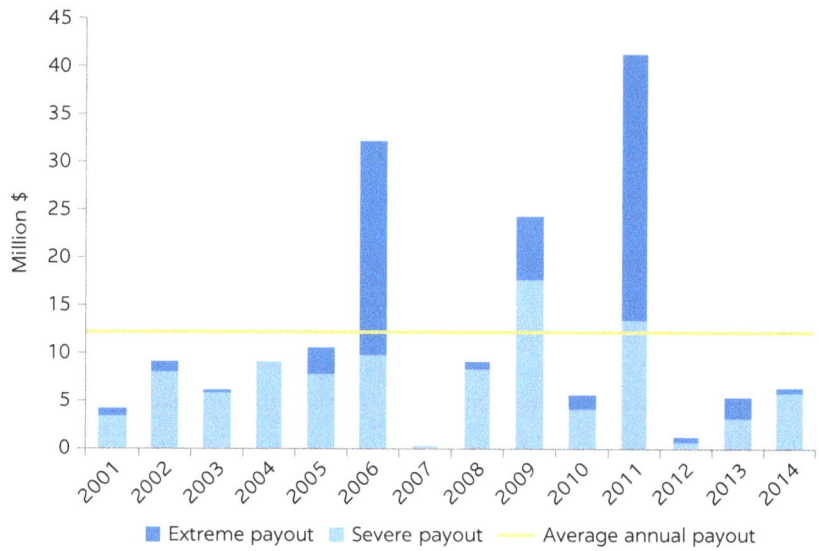

■ Extreme payout ■ Severe payout — Average annual payout

Source: Maher, Fitzgibbon, and Solórzano 2018.
Note: Annual scalability costs are totaled across the four Hunger Safety Net Program counties.

FIGURE O.10

Risk layering: Financial instruments, by frequency and severity of a shock

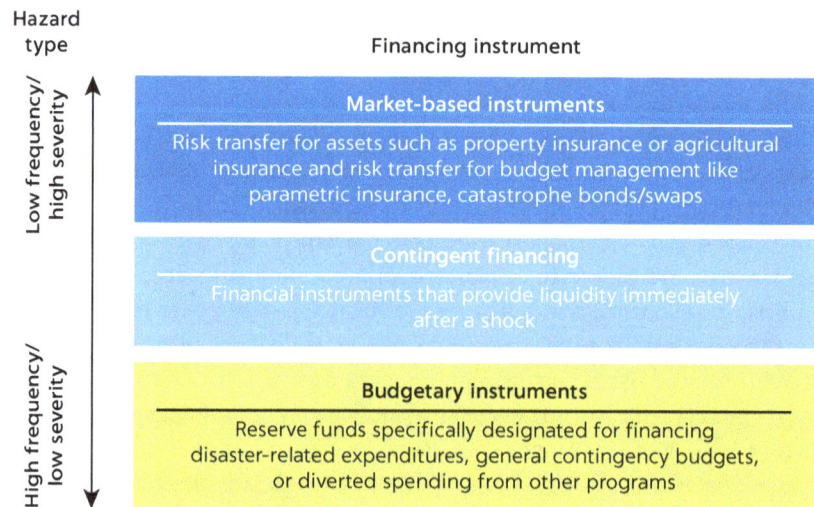

Hazard type — Financing instrument

Low frequency/high severity

Market-based instruments
Risk transfer for assets such as property insurance or agricultural insurance and risk transfer for budget management like parametric insurance, catastrophe bonds/swaps

Contingent financing
Financial instruments that provide liquidity immediately after a shock

High frequency/low severity

Budgetary instruments
Reserve funds specifically designated for financing disaster-related expenditures, general contingency budgets, or diverted spending from other programs

Source: Financial Protection Forum 2018.

existence of effective safety net payment systems. Countries use different approaches for the delivery of cash-based emergency responses including manual systems ("over-the-counter"), electronic transfers to bank accounts, or via mobile phone payments. Indeed, e-payment systems are emerging as a preferred option to deliver postdisaster assistance as they have the advantages of speed and flexibility, even in challenging environments (Maher, Fitzgibbon, and Solórzano 2018).

TABLE O.4 **Risk layering: Advantages and disadvantages of individual financial instruments**

TYPE	ADVANTAGES	DISADVANTAGES	BEST SUITED
Ex ante			
Contingency/ reserve funds	• Can be cheap, particularly for frequent shocks • Fast • Allows implementers to plan • Approach has been used in many contexts; thus, experience is available for countries to build upon	• Requires fiscal discipline • High opportunity cost of funds, given high rates of return on other government investments • Can be hard to defend given the opportunity cost	Low risk layer such as frequent low-level events (annual flooding, localized drought, conflict)
Contingent credit	• Can be cheap, particularly for midfrequency shocks • Fast, when conditions for disbursement are met • Allows implementers to plan • Can incentivize proactive actions to reduce risk (for example, policy actions in disaster risk reduction and DRM)	• Has conditionality • Opportunity cost of loan • Adds to country's debt burden, must be repaid • Current low (but growing) uptake of Cat DDOs as some countries prefer investment projects guaranteed resources over contingent instruments	Mid-risk layer such as higher-magnitude, less frequent events whose damages exhaust the resources of national contingencies (widespread flooding, hurricanes)
Market-based risk transfer instruments	• Can be cheap, particularly for extreme shocks • Can be fast • Allows implementers to plan • Supports fiscal discipline • Risk diversification	• Can be expensive for frequent shocks • Can be vulnerable to criticism and "regret" • Can miss need • Need a level playing field to negotiate • Trade-off between the cost of premiums and the frequency or scale of the pay-out	High-risk layer such as extreme, less frequent events, less than every 5–10 years (severe droughts, hurricanes, earthquakes)
Ex post			
Humanitarian assistance	• Flexible—can respond to need • Doesn't have to be repaid	• Can be slow to be mobilized • Can be unreliable • Undermines preplanning	Only as a last resort
Other ex post instruments	• Approach has been used in many contexts; thus, experience is available for countries to build upon	• Can be slow • Can have negative impact on long-term development/investment programs • Can be expensive	Only as a last resort

Source: Maher, Fitzgibbon, and Solórzano 2018.
Note: Cat DDO = Catastrophe Deferred Drawdown Option.

Lastly, where finance for ASP is concerned, interventions that support people's longer-term adaptation could reduce future household needs, and by extension, response costs—but more evidence is needed. Programs that support household adaptation over the longer term can be costly at scale (for example, in contexts of widespread chronic and severe poverty in high-risk areas). Yet, initial evidence indicates that more expensive investment scenarios are broadly offset by the avoided cost of humanitarian response (Cabot Venton 2018; Wilkinson et al. 2018). In Bangladesh, the Chars Livelihoods Program focused on building an annual contingency budget into its project design for disaster response, but the need for this contingency fund decreased over time because of the program's specific focus on reducing vulnerabilities and supporting the adaptation of poor households living in the chars to regular flooding (ADB 2018). Where resources are limited, more evidence is needed on the cost-effectiveness of and trade-offs between ex ante resilience-building interventions in support of adaptation and risk reduction at the household level over the long term versus the cost of ex post shock response to support short-term coping.

ASP building block 4: Institutional arrangements and partnerships

A defining feature of ASP is the many actors within government that may be involved in its implementation. The inherent multidisciplinary and interagency nature of resilience building across the three capacities of preparedness, coping, and adaptation requires diversified expertise and coordination among actors. Indeed, the number of potential actors and complementary programs aligned to ASP objectives calls for institutional arrangements that anchor the planning, management, and delivery of this assistance. In practice, the development of ASP in many countries has shifted attention from a singular focus on national social protection systems, the policies that guide them, and the organizations that deliver social protection programs to a wider focus inclusive of the policies, organizations, and programs involved in DRM and climate change adaptation.

Strong government leadership is necessary to ensure coordination of the often disconnected actors, based on a clear articulation of respective roles and responsibilities. Concretely, governments are required to lead the ASP agenda by setting resilience-related objectives in policies and strategies, including social protection, DRM, and climate change adaptation. Policy commitments can instill the necessary budgetary allocations for national ministerial structures to translate objectives into outcomes among poor and vulnerable households. In practice, government leadership also includes establishing the standards and procedures to guide the integration of nongovernmental organizations and humanitarian actors into ASP implementation.

National social protection policies and strategies should provide the foundation for ASP. Most countries have social protection policies and strategies that set out the government's vision for the sector. The extent to which these policies and strategies are rooted in legislation varies (see, for example, Beegle, Coudouel, and Monsalve 2018). The functions of social protection often are equity, which provides protection against deprivation; resilience, which is insurance against shocks; and, opportunity, which seeks to promote human capital and access to income earning opportunities (World Bank 2012).[10] Articulated in this manner, these policies and strategies provide a foundation for the aims of further elaboration of and commitment to ASP objectives.

At the same time, the strategies of other sectors such as—prominently—DRM also can support the advancement of ASP. This is particularly true given the ongoing shift from disaster response to disaster preparedness within the DRM community, as encapsulated in the Sendai Framework for Disaster Risk Reduction.[11] In Kenya, ASP emanated out of the government's resolve to address poverty and vulnerability as a cause of and outcome from drought emergencies; a framework developed by the government (Ending Drought Emergencies) laid the policy foundation for the Hunger Safety Net Program, which expands vertically and horizontally for drought emergencies. Where the political appetite for social protection is low, national DRM policies, and the DRM sector more broadly, can provide additional impetus for introducing ASP as part of a comprehensive disaster risk management strategy. This suggests a government's commitment to ASP can come from sectors other than social protection itself.

Policy commitment for ASP, to be credible, needs to be backed with appropriate implementation capacity, financing, and accountability. To be effective, these policies require enough capacity within the parts of government charged with delivery as well as clear roles and responsibilities, such as those set out in contingency plans and the decision-making in response to early warning data (chapters 1 and 2). In addition, they also need to be backed by the levels of financing required to achieve the stated objectives (chapter 3). The source of this financing may be from national governments or development partners, depending on the prevailing context in the country. Accountability mechanisms and feedback loops are central to help ensure that citizens are aware of available programs, inform governments when services are failing, and ultimately, hold governments accountable to their commitments and objectives.

Additionally, in many contexts of limited national government capacity and/or especially severe shocks, the development and coordination of ASP with humanitarian actors is essential. However, humanitarian assistance tends to be provided in parallel to national structures. Only 1.0–2.5 percent of global humanitarian flows channel through host governments (Gentilini, Laughton, and O'Brien 2018). Factors for this often include a risky operating environment; the need for timely assistance in life-threatening situations; possible lack of government sovereignty over a territory in full or in part; legislation preventing domestic assistance to particular groups; concerns about the impartiality of governments, especially in relation to conflicts; low government capacity; and ensuring transparency and accountability of resources.

The humanitarian Grand Bargain and the increasing shift to cash-based assistance are strengthening linkages with national social protection systems and providing impetus for closer integration. The 2016 World Humanitarian Summit, and the resulting Grand Bargain, created high-level policy support to strengthen humanitarian linkages with social protection. The Grand Bargain is a series of 10 commitments to improve assistance to crisis-affected populations and included a commitment to "increase social protection programmes and strengthen national and local systems and coping mechanisms in order to build resilience in fragile contexts" (Grand Bargain 2016, 14). Cash transfers are simultaneously on the rise in national social protection systems and humanitarian programming. Cash now claims about 10 percent of global humanitarian assistance, highlighting a strong synergy with national cash transfer programs (CaLP 2018; World Bank 2016, 2018). Table O.5 summarizes these and other features of the humanitarian system, along with their implication for ASP.

Identifying the precise roles and responsibilities of government and humanitarian actors can help establish actionable, operational partnerships for the delivery of ASP. Conceptually, government and humanitarian actors are often viewed simplistically in "either-or" terms. A framework laid out by Seyfert et al. (2019) attempts to facilitate the identification of workable pathways for progress among national and humanitarian actors (figure O.11). Instead of falling back on the "either–or" choice, the framework lays out four strategic options (parallel systems, alignment, piggybacking, and national-led systems). It also discusses how collaborations may emerge around select programmatic "functions" and the "degrees" of possible connection between national and humanitarian actors within a given function. While a work-in-progress, such a granular analytical approach holds the potential to move beyond strategic dialogue and strategies in support of coordination; that is, coordination toward an operationally relevant delineation of roles and responsibilities based on relative comparative advantages in differing country contexts.

TABLE O.5 International humanitarian system: Features and implications for adaptive social protection

FEATURE	CHARACTERISTICS	IMPLICATIONS
Policy commitments and the Grand Bargain	High-level policy support for building resilience and increasing the role of social protection	Opportunities to advance aims of ASP but need to be translated into more concrete and strategic actions
Bifurcation of humanitarian/ development and rise of resilience building	Humanitarian and development assistance often underpinned by different financing channels, coordination structures, mandates, and principles	Divide between humanitarian and development systems may remain an obstacle; need for specificity on "resilience building"
Humanitarian financing	Very little direct funding goes to national governments; significant flows to fragile and conflict settings, and year-on-year to the same places	Limited potential for humanitarian financing to be channeled to governments for national safety nets; scope to fund nongovernmental organizations operating within national frameworks for ASP in some countries
	Shares of humanitarian financing go to some areas and populations supported by national safety nets	
Humanitarian principles	Humanitarian assistance is guided mainly by the four principles of humanity, impartiality, independence, and neutrality	Humanitarian principles should inform the response function of ASP to shocks; can be referenced to advocate for a principled engagement around ASP with governments by humanitarian agencies
	Differing views on flexibility of principles exist, but they are not incompatible with working with governments	
Coordination	Established mechanisms for coordination (see the cluster system, chapter 4) but varying coordination approaches because of differing levels of national involvement in those mechanisms	Need for engagement of ASP at various levels of humanitarian operational and strategic coordination and for bilateral engagement with major donors and aid agencies
Increasing shift to cash transfers	Cash transfers increasingly accepted as mainstream tool of humanitarian response, but programs often fragmented and still represent only a small share of total assistance	Offers an entry point for engagement of national ASP programs with humanitarian system

Source: Bailey 2018.

FIGURE O.11

ASP delivery approaches: A mix across national and humanitarian actors

	Parallel systems	Alignment	Piggy-backing	National-led systems
Financing	●			
Legal and policy framework		●		
Setting eligibility criteria and qualifying conditions		●		
Setting transfer type, level, frequency, duration			●	
Governance and coordination				●
Outreach	●			
Registration		●		
Enrollment	●			
Payment			●	
Case management				●
Complaints and appeals				●
Protection			●	
VAM/M&E		●		
Information management	●			

Source: Seyfert et al. 2019.
Note: VAM/M&E = Vulnerability analysis and mapping/monitoring and evaluation.

NOTES

1. Shocks may be either idiosyncratic or covariate in nature. An idiosyncratic shock is felt by an individual or household, with the negative impacts to their well-being typically not shared more widely by others outside of the immediate household. Idiosyncratic shocks include things such as ill health, injury, disease, disability, a death in the family, and job loss. Covariate shocks are larger in scale, affecting multiple individuals and households at once, with the negative impacts to well-being spread across a (typically large) number of persons.

2. An undetermined share of this increase is undoubtedly due to better recording of events and their impact during that time period.

3. This capacity also is referred to as "anticipatory" capacity in the BRACED 3As framework (Bahadur et al. 2015). The term "preparedness" is used here to more explicitly reflect the meaning of the capacity as used in this report. The capacity to anticipate a shock based on appropriate information is recognized as a critical component of the capacity to prepare, informing appropriate action.

4. This capacity also is referred to as "absorptive" capacity in the BRACED 3As framework (Bahadur et al. 2015; similar in Béné et al. 2012). The term "coping" is chosen here because of its widespread use in the social protection community and its interchangeability with the term "absorptive."

5. Defined as a failure to adjust adequately or appropriately to a shock.

6. Led by the "International Labour Organization (ILO) and the World Bank Group (WBG), in partnership with the African Union, the Food and Agriculture Organization (FAO), the European Commission, the Inter-American Development Bank (IDB), Organization of Economic Cooperation and Development (OECD), the United Nations Development Programme (UNDP) and its International Poverty Centre for Inclusive Growth (IPC-IG), the United Nations Children's Fund (UNICEF), and others, along with Belgian, Finnish, French, and German development cooperation, and international civil society organizations such as HelpAge, the International Council of Social Welfare (ICSW), Save the Children, among others" (World Bank and ILO 2018, 1).

7. The six African countries are Ethiopia, Ghana, Kenya, Lesotho, Malawi, and Zambia.

8. These are sometimes classified as "soft resilience measures" typically low cost and adaptable to deliver benefits in changing conditions (Cabot Venton et al. 2012).

9. The United Nations International Strategy for Disaster Reduction defines early warning systems as "an integrated system of hazard monitoring, forecasting and prediction, disaster risk assessment, communication and preparedness activities systems and processes that enables individuals, communities, governments, businesses and others to take timely action to reduce disaster risks in advance of hazardous events" (www.unisdr.org/we/inform/terminology).

10. See also Devereux and Sabates-Wheeler (2004), who set a similar framework of protection, prevention, promotion, and transformation.

11. Sendai Framework, https://www.unisdr.org/we/coordinate/sendai-framework.

REFERENCES

ADB (Asian Development Bank). 2018. "Strengthening Resilience through Social Protection Programs." Guidance Note. ADB, Manila.

Andrews, C., A. Hsiao, and L. Ralston. 2018. "Social Safety Nets Promote Poverty Reduction, Increase Resilience, and Expand Opportunities. In *Realizing the Full Potential of Social Safety Nets in Africa,* edited by K. Beegle, A. Coudouel, and E. Monsalve, 87–137. Washington, DC: World Bank.

Arnall, A., K. Oswald, M. Davies, T. Mitchell, and C. Coirolo. 2010. "Adaptive Social Protection: Mapping the Evidence and Policy Context in the Agriculture Sector in South Asia." IDS Working Paper, Institute of Development Studies, Brighton, UK.

Asfaw, S., and B. Davis. 2018. "Can Cash Transfer Programmes Promote Household Resilience? Evidence from Sub-Saharan Africa." In *Climate Smart Agriculture*, edited by L. Lipper, N. McCarthy, D. Zilberman, S. Asfaw, and G. Braca, 227–50. Rome: Food and Agriculture Organization of the United Nations. http://www.fao.org/3/a-i7931e.pdf.

Bahadur, A., K. Peters, E. Wilkinson, F. Pichon, K. Gray, and T. Tanner. 2015. "The 3As: Tracking Resilience across BRACED." Working Paper, Building Resilience and Adaptation to Climate Extremes and Disasters (BRACED), London.

Bailey, S. 2018. "Institutions for Adaptive Social Protection: External Linkages and the Humanitarian Sector." Background Paper. Oxford Policy Management, Oxford, UK.

Barca, V. 2017. *Integrating Data and Information Management for Social Protection: Social Registries and Integrated Beneficiary Registries.* Canberra: Commonwealth of Australia, Department of Foreign Affairs and Trade. https://dfat.gov.au/about-us/publications /Documents/integrating-data-information-management-social-protection-full.pdf.

Barca, V., and C. O'Brien. 2017. "Factors Affecting the Usefulness of Existing Social Protection Databases in Disaster Preparedness and Response." Policy Brief. Oxford Policy Management, Oxford, UK. https://assets.publishing.service.gov.uk/media/5a942c50ed915d57d4d0ef98 /Policy-Brief-Factors-affecting-usefulness-existing-social-protection-databases.pdf.

Bastagli, F. 2014. "Responding to a Crisis: The Design and Delivery of Social Protection." ODI Working Paper, Overseas Development Institute, London.

Bastagli, F., J. Hagen-Zanker, L. Harman, V. Barca, G. Sturge, and T. Schmidt. 2016. "Cash Transfers: What Does the Evidence Say? A Rigorous Review of Programme Impact and of the Role of Design and Implementation Features." Overseas Development Institute, London.

Bastagli, F., and R. Holmes. 2014. "Delivering Social Protection in the Aftermath of a Shock: Lessons from Bangladesh, Kenya, Pakistan, and Viet Nam." Overseas Development Institute, London.

Beazley, R. 2017. "Study on Shock-Responsive Social Protection in Latin America and the Caribbean: Ecuador Case Study." Oxford Policy Management, Oxford, UK.

Beazley, R., A. Solórzano, and K. Sossouvi. 2016. "Study on Shock-Responsive Social Protection in Latin America and the Caribbean: Theoretical Framework and Literature Review." Oxford Policy Management, Oxford, UK.

Beegle, K., A. Coudouel, and E. Monsalve. 2018. *Realizing the Full Potential of Social Safety Nets in Africa.* Washington, DC: World Bank. http://documents.worldbank.org/curated /en/657581531930611436/pdf/128594-PUB-PUBLIC.pdf.

Béné, C., S. Devereux, and R. Sabates-Wheeler. 2012a. "Shocks and Social Protection in the Horn of Africa: Analysis from the Productive Safety Net Programme in Ethiopia." IDS Working Paper 395, Institute of Development Studies, Brighton, UK.

Béné, C., R. Wood, A. Newsham, and M. Davies. 2012b. "Resilience: New Utopia or New Tyranny? Reflection about the Potentials and Limits of the Concept of Resilience in Relation to Vulnerability Reduction Programmes." IDS Working Paper 405, Institute of Development Studies, Brighton, UK.

Bossuroy, T., and P. Premand. 2016. "Boosting Productive Inclusion and Resilience of the Poor: Perspectives from the Sahel Adaptive Social Protection Program." Presentation, World Bank, Washington DC.

Bowen, T. 2015. "Social Protection and Disaster Risk Management in the Philippines: The Case of Typhoon Yolanda (Haiyan)." Policy Research Working Paper 7482, World Bank, Washington, DC. http://documents.worldbank.org/curated/en/681881468181128752/pdf /WPS7482.pdf.

Cabot Venton, C. 2018. "Economics of Resilience to Drought in Ethiopia, Kenya and Somalia: Executive Summary." Center for Resilience, U.S. Agency for International Development, Washington, DC.

Cabot Venton, C., C. Fitzgibbon, T. Shitarek, L. Coulter, and O. Dooley. 2012. "The Economics of Early Response and Disaster Resilience: Lessons from Kenya and Ethiopia: Economics of Resilience Final Report." Department for International Development, London.

CaLP 2018. The State of the World's Cash Report: Cash Transfer Programming in Humanitarian Aid. Oxford, UK. http://www.cashlearning.org/downloads/calp-sowc-report-web.pdf.

Dang, H.-A., and A. Dabalen. 2017. "Is Poverty in Africa Mostly Chronic or Transient? Evidence from Synthetic Panel Data." Policy Research Working Paper 8033, World Bank,

Washington, DC. http://documents.worldbank.org/curated/en/172891492703250779 /pdf/WPS8033.pdf.

Davies, M., C. Béné, A. Arnall, T. Tanner, A. Newsham, and C. Coirolo. 2012. "Promoting Resilient Livelihoods through Adaptive Social Protection: Lessons from 124 Programmes in South Asia." *Development Policy Review* 31 (1): 27–58.

Davies, M., B. Guenther, J. Leavy, T. Mitchell, and T. Tanner. 2009. "Adaptive Social Protection: Synergies for Poverty Reduction." *IDS Bulletin* 39 (4): 105–12.

de Weijer, F. 2013. "Resilience: A Trojan Horse for a New Way of Thinking?" ECDPM Discussion Paper 139, European Centre for Development Policy Management, Maastricht.

del Ninno, C., and B. Mills, eds. 2015. *Safety Nets in Africa: Effective Mechanisms to Reach the Poor and Most Vulnerable.* Washington, DC: World Bank. http://documents.worldbank.org /curated/en/869311468009642720/pdf/Safety-nets-in-Africa-effective-mechanisms-to -reach-the-poor-and-most-vulnerable.pdf.

Devereux, S., and R. Sabates-Wheeler. 2004. "Transformative Social Protection." IDS Working Paper 232, Institute of Development Studies, Brighton, UK.

Esteves T., K. V. Rao, B. Sinha, S. S. Roy, B. B. Rai, I. B. Rao, N. Sharma, S. Rao, V. Patil, I. K. Murthy, J. Srinivasan, R. K. Chaturvedi, J. Sharma, S. K. Jha, S. Mishra, A. B. Singh, H. S. Rakhroy, S. Rai, R. Sharma, S. Schwan, K. Basu, N. Guerten, I. Porsché, N. Ranjan, K. K. Tripathy, and N. H. Ravindranath. 2013. "Environmental Benefits and Vulnerability Reduction through Mahatma Gandhi Rural Employment Guarantee Scheme (NREGS): Synthesis Report." Ministry of Rural Development, Government of India and Deutsche Gesellschaft für Internationale Zusammenarbeit (GIZ), New Delhi.

FAO (Food and Agriculture Organization of the United Nations). 2016. *Adapting Agriculture to Climate Change. FAO's Work on Climate Change Adaptation.* Rome: FAO. http://www.fao .org/3/a-i6273e.pdf.

Financial Protection Forum. 2018. "Disaster Risk Finance: A Primer, Core Principles, and Operational Framework." World Bank, Washington, DC. https://financialprotectionforum .org/publication/disaster-risk-finance-a-primercore-principles-and-operational -framework.

Frankenberger, T., T. Spangler, S. Nelson, M. Langworthy. 2012. "Enhancing Resilience to Food Insecurity amid Protracted Crisis." United Nations High-Level Expert Forum, Rome. http:// www.fao.org/fileadmin/templates/cfs_high_level_forum/documents/Enhancing _Resilience_FoodInsecurity-TANGO.pdf.

FSIN (Food Security Information Network). 2015. "Measuring Shocks and Stressors as Part of Resilience Measurement." Technical Series 5. Resilience Measurement Technical Working Group, FSIN Secretariat, World Food Programme. http://www.fsincop.net/fileadmin/user _upload/fsin/docs/resources/1_FSIN_TechnicalSeries_5.pdf.

Gentilini, U., S. Laughton, and C. O'Brien. 2018. "Lessons on Better Connecting Humanitarian Assistance and Social Protection." Social Protection and Labor Discussion Paper 1802. World Bank, Washington, DC. http://documents.worldbank.org/curated/en/94640154 2689917993/pdf/Human-itarian-Capital-Lessons-on-Better-Connecting-Humanitarian -Assistance-and-Social-Protection.pdf.

Grand Bargain. 2016. "The Grand Bargain: A Shared Commitment to Better Serve People in Need." World Humanitarian Summit, Istanbul. https://reliefweb.int/sites/reliefweb.int /files/resources/Grand_Bargain_final_22_May_FINAL-2.pdf.

Hallegatte, S., M. Bangalore, L. Bonzanigo, M. Fay, T. Kane, U. Narloch, J. Rozenberg, D. Treguer, and A. Vogt-Schlib. 2016. *Shock Waves: Managing the Impacts of Climate Change on Poverty.* Washington, DC: World Bank.

Hallegatte, S., J. Rentschler, and B. Walsh. 2018. "Building Back Better: Achieving Resilience through Stronger, Faster, and More Inclusive Post-Disaster Reconstruction." World Bank, Washington, DC. http://documents.worldbank.org/curated/en/420321528985115831 /pdf/127215-REVISED-BuildingBackBetter-Web-July18Update.pdf.

Hallegatte, S., A. Vogt-Schilb, M. Bangalore, and J. Rozenberg. 2017. *Unbreakable: Building the Resilience of the Poor in the Face of Natural Disasters.* Washington, DC: World Bank. https:// www.gfdrr.org/sites/default/files/publication/Unbreakable_FullBook_Web-3.pdf.

Hidrobo, M., J. Hoddinott, J. Kumar, and M. Oliver. 2018. "Social Protection, Food Security, and Asset Formation." *World Development* 101: 88–103.

Hill, R., E. Skoufias, and B. P. Maher. 2019. *The Chronology of Disaster: A Review and Assessment of the Value of Acting Early on Household Welfare*. Washington, DC: World Bank. http://documents.worldbank.org/curated/en/796341557483493173/pdf/The-Chronology-of-a-Disaster-A-Review-and-Assessment-of-the-Value-of-Acting-Early-on-Household-Welfare.pdf.

Holmes, R. 2019. "Promoting Gender Equality and Women's Empowerment in Shock Sensitive Social Protection." ODI Working Paper 549, Overseas Development Institute, London.

IEG (Independent Evaluation Group). 2011. *Social Safety Nets: An Evaluation of World Bank Support, 2000–2010*. Washington, DC: World Bank.

ILO (International Labour Organization). 2017. *World Social Protection Report 2017–19: Universal Social Protection to Achieve the Sustainable Development Goals*. Geneva: ILO. https://www.ilo.org/wcmsp5/groups/public/---dgreports/---dcomm/---publ/documents/publication/wcms_604882.pdf.

Jorgensen, S., and P. Siegel. 2019. "Social Protection in an Era of Increasing Uncertainty and Disruption: Social Risk Management 2.0." Social Protection and Jobs Discussion Paper 1930, World Bank, Washington, DC. http://documents.worldbank.org/curated/en/263761559643240069/pdf/Social-Protection-in-an-Era-of-Increasing-Uncertainty-and-Disruption-Social-Risk-Management-2-0.pdf.

Kaur, N., D. Steinbach, A. Agrawal, C. Manuel, S. Saigal, A. Panjiyar, C. Shakya, and A. Norton. 2017. "Building Resilience to Climate Change: MGNREGS and Climate-Induced Droughts in Sikkim." IIED Issue Paper. International Institute for Environment and Development, London.

Kuriakose, A., R. Heltberg, W. Wiseman, C. Costella, R. Cipryk, and S. Cornelius. 2012. "Climate-Responsive Social Protection." Social Protection and Labor Discussion Paper 1210, World Bank, Washington, DC. https://siteresources.worldbank.org/SOCIALPROTECTION/Resources/SP-Discussion-papers/430578-1331508552354/1210.pdf.

Leite, P., T. George, C. Sun, T. Jones, and K. Lindert. 2017. "Social Registries for Social Assistance and Beyond: A Guidance Note and Assessment Tool." Social Protection and Labor Working Paper 1704, World Bank, Washington, DC. http://documents.worldbank.org/curated/en/698441502095248081/pdf/117971-REVISED-PUBLIC-Discussion-paper-1704.pdf.

Lindert, K., T. George, I. Rodriguez-Caillava, and Kenichi Nishikawa. Forthcoming. *A Sourcebook on the Foundations of Social Protection Delivery Systems*. Washington, DC: World Bank.

Macours, K., P. Premand, and R. Vakis. 2012. "Transfers, Diversification and Household Risk Strategies: Experimental Evidence with Lessons for Climate Change Adaptation." Policy Research Working Paper 6053, World Bank, Washington, DC. http://documents.worldbank.org/curated/en/275241468340175496/pdf/WPS6053.pdf.

Maher B., C. Fitzgibbon, and A. Solórzano. 2018. "Emerging Lessons in Financing Adaptive Social Protection." Background Paper for the World Bank, Oxford Policy Management, London.

Mansur, A., J. Doyle, J. Gerome, and O. Ivaschenko. 2017. "Social Protection and Humanitarian Assistance Nexus for Disaster Response: Lessons Learnt from Fiji's Tropical Cyclone Winston." Social Protection and Labor Discussion Paper 1701. World Bank, Washington, DC. http://documents.worldbank.org/curated/en/143591490296944528/pdf/113710-NWP-PUBLIC-P159592-1701.pdf.

Manyena, S., G. O'Brien, P. O'Keefe, and J. Rose. 2011. "Disaster Resilience: A Bounce back or Bounce forward Ability?" *Local Environment* 16 (5): 417–24.

Mariotti, C., M. Ulrichs, and L. Harman. 2016. "Sustainable Escapes from Poverty through Productive Inclusion: A Policy Guide on the Role of Social Protection." CPAN Policy Guide 7. Chronic Poverty Advisory Network, London.

O'Brien, C., Z. Scott, G. Smith, V. Barca, A. Kardan, R. Holmes, C. Watson, and J. Congrave. 2018. "Shock-Responsive Social Protection Systems Research: Synthesis Report."

Oxford Policy Management, Oxford, UK. https://www.opml.co.uk/files/Publications /a0408-shock-responsive-social-protection-systems/srsp-synthesis-report.pdf? noredirect=1.

PEI (Partnership for Economic Inclusion). 2016. "Increasing the Income Earning Opportunities of Poor and Vulnerable People." World Bank, Washington, DC. https://www .microfinancegateway.org/sites/default/files/announcement/pei-brochure.pdf.

Pelham, L., E. Clay, and T. Braunholz. 2011. "Natural Disasters: What Is the Role for Social Safety Nets?" SP Discussion Paper 1102, World Bank, Washington, DC. https://www.gfdrr.org /sites/default/files/documents/Social%20Safety%20Nets.pdf.

Robalino, D., L. Rawlings, and I. Walker. 2012. "Building Social Protection and Labor Systems: Concepts and Operational Implications." Social Protection and Labor Working Paper 1202, World Bank, Washington, DC. http://siteresources.worldbank.org/SOCIALPROTECTION /Resources/SP-Discussion-papers/430578-1331508552354/1202.pdf.

Roelen, K., S. Devereux, A. G. Abdulai, B. Martorano, T. Palermo, and L. P. Ragno. 2017. "How to Make 'Cash Plus' Work: Linking Cash Transfers to Services and Sectors." Innoncenti Working Paper 2017-10. United Nations Children's Fund Office of Research, Florence.

Schipper, E., and L. Langston. 2015. "A Comparative Overview of Resilience Measurement Frameworks." ODI Working Paper 422, Overseas Development Institute, London.

Seyfert, K., V. Barca, U. Gentilini, M. Luthria, and S. Abbady. 2019. "Unbundled: A Framework for Connecting Safety Nets and Humanitarian Assistance in Refugee Settings." Social Protection and Labor Discussion Paper 1935, World Bank, Washington, DC. https:// openknowledge.worldbank.org/bitstream/handle/10986/32467/Unbundled-A -Framework-for-Connecting-Safety-Nets-and-Humanitarian-Assistance-in-Refugee -Settings.pdf?sequence=1&isAllowed=y.

Solórzano, A. 2016. "Can Social Protection Increase Resilience to Climate Change? A Case Study of Oportunidades in Rural Yucatan, Mexico." IDS Working Paper 465, Centre for Social Protection and Institute of Development Studies, Brighton, UK.

Tenzing, J. D. 2019. "Integrating Social Protection and Climate Change Adaptation: A Review." *WIREs Climate Change* 11 (2): e626.

Ulrichs, M., and R. Slater. 2016. "How Can Social Protection Build Resilience? Insights from Ethiopia, Kenya and Uganda." Working Paper, Building Resilience and Adaptation to Climate Extremes and Disasters (BRACED), London.

UNDP-UNEP (United Nations Development Programme–United Nations Environment Programme). 2018. *Vulnerability to Climate Hazards Index: Lessons Learned and Systematization of the Design Process and Application of the IVACC Index—Dominican Republic.* Poverty-Environment Initiative. Panama City: Panama.

UNHCR (United Nations High Commissioner for Refugees). 2016. "Global Trends in Forced Displacement." UNHCR, Geneva.

UNICEF. 2018. "Resilience, Humanitarian Assistance and Social Protection for Children in Europe and Central Asia." Social Protection Regional Issue Brief: 2. https://www.unicef.org /eca/media/2671/file/Social_Protection2.pdf.

UNISDR (United Nations International Strategy for Disaster Reduction). 2015. *Making Development Sustainable: The Future of Disaster Risk Management: Global Assessment Report on Disaster Risk Reduction.* Geneva: UNISDR.

UNU-EHS (United Nations University–Institute for Environment and Human Security). 2016. *World Risk Report 2016.* Berlin: Bündnis Entwicklung Hilft.

WFP (World Food Programme). 2015. "Policy on Building Resilience for Food Security and Nutrition." WFP/EB.A/2015/5-C. WFP, Rome. https://documents.wfp.org/stellent/groups /public/documents/eb/wfpdoc063833.pdf?_ga=2.20959473.817428444.1582152603 -752767465.1554223343.

WFP (World Food Programme). 2018. "Scaling Up for Resilient Individuals, Communities and Systems in the Sahel." Fact Sheet. WFP, Rome. https://docs.wfp.org/api/documents/WFP -0000110238/download/?_ga=2.26639604.817428444.1582152603-752767465.1554223343.

Wilkinson, E., L. Weingartner, R. Choularton, M. Bailey, M. Todd, D. Kniveton, and C. Cabot Venton. 2018. "Forecasting Hazards, Averting Disasters: Implementing Forecast-Based Early Action at Scale." Overseas Development Institute, London.

World Bank. 2012. "Resilience, Equity, and Opportunity: The World Bank's Social Protection and Labor Strategy 2012–2022." World Bank, Washington, DC. http://documents.worldbank.org/curated/en/443791468157506768/pdf/732350BR0CODE200doc0version0REVISED.pdf.

World Bank. 2013. *Building Resilience to Disaster and Climate Change through Social Protection: Synthesis Note*. Washington, DC: World Bank. http://documents.worldbank.org/curated/en/187211468349778714/pdf/796210WP0Build0Box0377381B00PUBLIC0.pdf.

World Bank. 2016. "Cash Transfers in Humanitarian Contexts: Strategic Note." World Bank, Washington, DC. http://documents.worldbank.org/curated/en/697681467995447727/pdf/106449-WP-IASC-Humanitarian-Cash-PUBLIC.pdf.

World Bank. 2018. *The State of Social Safety Nets 2018*. Washington, DC: World Bank. https://openknowledge.worldbank.org/bitstream/handle/10986/29115/9781464812545.pdf?sequence=5&isAllowed=y.

World Bank and ILO (International Labour Organization). 2018. *Universal Social Protection: Country Cases. Global Partnership for Universal Social Protection USP2030*. Washington, DC: World Bank and ILO. https://www.social-protection.org/gimi/gess/RessourcePDF.action?id=55072.

1 Programs
DESIGN CONSIDERATIONS FOR BUILDING RESILIENCE

OVERVIEW

To enhance their impact on resilience building, safety net programs need to be explicitly designed to support the capacity of poor and vulnerable households to prepare for, cope with, and adapt to the shocks they face. First and foremost, this requires asking fundamental questions of existing programs—are they reaching those that are most vulnerable to shocks, and does the assistance they provide maximize resilience-related outcomes among beneficiaries? Such appraisals can inform the adjustment of existing programs, or the introduction of new programs to enhance the impact of the social protection system on building resilience to shocks.

An emphasis on encouraging savings can help to enhance people's preparedness by creating a cash or asset based "buffer" to be drawn upon after a shock has hit. Moreover, financial inclusion of beneficiaries can both support saving in this way while also making those beneficiaries more accessible with assistance after a shock has hit. Preparedness can also be supported when beneficiaries are informed about the risks they face and the appropriate strategies and actions they can take, including through even very basic disaster preparedness training and information on the timing of lean or rainy seasons. Now widely utilized, communications sessions that are provided to deliver information on health and education to beneficiaries of safety net programs and their wider communities can provide under-exploited venues for the communication of this pertinent preparedness information.

The continued provision of safety net transfers to beneficiaries who have been affected by a shock can be especially effective in helping them to cope with the impact, smoothing consumption and reducing the need to use negative coping mechanisms. Critically, safety net programs will need to be explicitly prepared to respond after a shock, so that they are more capable of providing timely assistance to help people to cope—in most cases, reaching above and beyond those people typically reached through existing safety net programs delivering in times of acute need and environments of heightened operational complexity.

Lastly, over the long term, cash transfers can be transformative in helping people make the investments needed to adapt. This impact may be enhanced when cash transfers are accompanied by additional measures that encourage income diversification and adoption of more productive livelihoods, reducing the reliance on livelihoods that are at high risk of shocks. When cash transfers also are designed to stimulate human capital investments among poor and vulnerable households, they may better equip the next generation to access opportunity that enables moving away from areas and out of livelihoods of concentrated risk. In complement, public works programs can be designed to enable beneficiaries to implement projects that address some of the sources of vulnerability at the community level, including water insecurity, soil erosion, and frequent flooding.

This chapter draws extensively from the background paper by Barca (2018).

FOCUSING ON THE ROLE OF SAFETY NETS IN BUILDING HOUSEHOLD RESILIENCE

A social protection system comprises multiple programs that can support and sustain the capacity of households to prepare for, cope with, and adapt to shocks. Social protection programs translate government policies and objectives into outcomes among beneficiary households. To date, a significant body of knowledge has accrued on social protection program design and implementation, especially in terms of social safety net programs and their use in the pursuit of poverty reduction and human capital-related objectives, from foundational texts such as Grosh et al. (2008) to more recent treatments such as Subbarao et al. (2012) and Lindert et al. (forthcoming), to name only a select few. Where building resilience to covariate shocks is concerned, however, the knowledge base around program design and implementation is only beginning to emerge (see ADB 2018; McCord 2013; O'Brien et al. 2018a).

Within the social protection system, social safety net programs can be harnessed and enhanced to become increasingly capable of building the resilience of poor and vulnerable households to covariate shocks. The impact of assistance provided through a safety net program can be transformative across a beneficiary's resilience capacities: preparedness, coping, and adaptation. The delivery of a safety net transfer can provide a supplementary source of income which can empower beneficiaries to take critical preparedness measures (such as accumulating savings). In turn, this preparedness can help beneficiaries to cope once a shock hits by smoothing consumption and lessening the need to use negative coping strategies. The continued provision of safety net transfers following a shock can be instrumental in supporting coping capacity, especially when preparedness measures are overwhelmed by a severe shock. Shocks of this nature will invariably generate needs among households beyond core safety net beneficiaries that can also be addressed by temporarily expanding access to safety net programs during and after crises. Over the longer term, safety net transfers that are integrated with productive measures, livelihood diversification, and human capital initiatives also can contribute to the capacity of a vulnerable household to adapt, reducing its exposure and vulnerability.

This chapter highlights an emerging body of knowledge on the role of safety net programs in building resilience to covariate shocks. It begins by reviewing the ways that core design parameters for all safety nets determine their contribution to resilience building outcomes. This includes programmatic objectives and resultant decisions on who is reached and with what kinds of assistance. The chapter then addresses fundamental design considerations for supporting the three capacities—preparedness, coping, and adaptation—with safety net programs.

UNDERSTANDING THE CHALLENGE OF BUILDING HOUSEHOLD RESILIENCE: NO SINGLE PROGRAM CAN "DO IT ALL"

A common thread throughout much of the literature on building household resilience to shocks is that one program cannot "do it all" (ADB 2018; Asfaw and Davis 2018; Bastagli and Holmes 2014; Fallavier 2014; OPM 2017). The social protection system comprises social assistance, social insurance, and labor market programs—each reaching population subsets with unique forms of assistance and each with varying resilience-building utility. As such, a program-specific discussion can be misleading in lieu of a discussion of the wider social protection system, the position of any one social protection program within it, and its comparative advantage in building resilience across the three capacities among which subset of the population.

Evidence suggests that investing in a stronger, more comprehensive social protection system composed of multiple programs provides the requisite foundation for building the resilience of poor and vulnerable households. It is important to take stock of the capacity of a country's existing social protection system to build the resilience of the poor and vulnerable to covariate shocks. As noted in the literature, stronger, more comprehensive systems with a mix of social insurance, social assistance, and labor market programs better position a country when a shock hits. This enables a country to draw from a larger toolbox and facilitates diverse points of access to support vulnerable households to cope with the impacts (Grosh et al. 2011; IEG 2011; Isik-Dikmelik 2012; Marzo and Mori 2012; O'Brien et al. 2018a). In the United States, for example, the wider social protection system has been found to provide substantial assistance across its programs to households affected by hurricanes, implying people are more "insured" against the impacts from these shocks than previously thought (box 1.1).

Beyond the traditional social protection system itself, adaptive social protection (ASP) highlights the need for strong coordination between social protection and the disparate actors and programs each working on building the resilience of vulnerable households to shocks. Take, for example, the many agriculture, human development (health and education), and disaster risk reduction programs that explicitly or implicitly seek to build household resilience to covariate shocks.

For those other nonsocial protection sectors, coordination with social protection actors will often enable increased access among the poorest households, which may otherwise not be reached through their programming. Similarly, after a shock hits, many emergency response and recovery

BOX 1.1

The United States: Role of the social protection system in insuring against disasters

A study by Deryugina found that in the United States, government transfers through the social protection system to areas affected by hurricanes substantially increase in the decade after a hurricane, suggesting that US households are better insured against hurricanes than currently recognized. By extension, the fiscal costs of disasters in the United States have been underestimated because they have not accounted for the transfers through the social protection system in the decade after a hurricane, serving as a form of insurance to the affected households. By extension, the study suggests that victims in developed countries with comprehensive social protection systems are better insured against disasters than previously thought. This also suggests that "expanding social safety nets provides benefits not only to those affected by idiosyncratic shocks and general economic downturns, but also to victims of natural disasters" (Deryugina 2016, 197).

Source: Deryugina 2016.

programs deliver from a multitude of ministries, departments, and agencies as well as from nongovernmental and humanitarian organizations to help people to cope with the impacts. Where such coordination, coherence, and integration of programming among vulnerable households is achieved in practice, household gains in resilience building could be more significant and sustainable; see, for example, the integrated and layered programmatic approaches to building resilience undertaken by the World Food Programme (2015, 2019).

Stress testing the social protection system as a whole and its ability to build resilience to the shocks faced by a country can provide the basis for modifying existing programs or introducing new programs. Much of the literature related to ASP, especially shock-responsive social protection, highlights ex ante stress testing of the social protection system against potential shocks (see, for example, Atkinson 2009; Barca 2018; Kanbur 2009; McCord 2013). Indeed, leveraging the analyses outlined in chapter 2, a risk-informed appraisal of the social protection system can highlight the coverage of social protection programs among the most vulnerable households and the collective impact and effectiveness of the programs on resilience building with regard to the shocks faced by the country. Such analyses could inform the programs that are available to households after a shock hits and elucidate the flexibility and capacity, or lack thereof, of those programs in responding to shocks of varying magnitudes and types. Such analyses also could provide the basis for the needs-based alterations of existing programs and/or for the introduction of new programs.

APPRAISING THE CORE DESIGN FEATURES OF EXISTING SAFETY NET PROGRAMS FOR RESILIENCE BUILDING

Returning to the program level, there are three factors to consider in appraising the core design features of a safety net program and its contribution to building household resilience to covariate shocks: the objectives of the safety net, who it reaches with assistance, and the specific parameters of the benefits it provides.

Programmatic objectives: The right tool for the job?

The objectives of most safety net programs do not explicitly frame the program as an instrument for building resilience to covariate shocks—which can mean that design features are not directly aligned to such outcomes. Most often, safety net programs pursue objectives related to poverty reduction, human-capital accumulation, and the promotion of access to opportunity. These objectives do each themselves tacitly support resilience building, especially for idiosyncratic shocks, often among a subset of the population that is inherently vulnerable to covariate shocks. This has served to elevate the recognition of the potential role of safety nets as instruments to build resilience to covariate shocks. However, without explicit objectives related to such outcomes, the potential for safety nets to build resilience may be constrained, remaining only tacit. For example, the provision of support to the capacity to cope with covariate shocks through the delivery of shock-responsive social protection may contrast with the priorities that underpin social protection development in noncrisis times and have several implications for the design and delivery including the tensions and trade-offs with regular social protection planning and the design and implementation details that facilitate timely, adaptable and adequate social protection programs (Bastagli 2014).

The objectives of existing safety net programs can be reimagined and adjusted, or new programs with explicit objectives introduced, as the basis for building resilience to covariate shocks. Social protection programs that have been specifically designed to build resilience to climate-induced food insecurity, such as Kenya's Hunger Safety Net Program (HSNP) and Ethiopia's Productive Safety Net Programme (PSNP), illustrate that integrating resilience objectives will more explicitly frame the program and its consequent design features in these terms. For example, by design, the PSNP connects to high-level policies on social protection, disaster risk management, and climate change to promote "resilience to shocks and enhance livelihoods, improve food security and nutrition for rural households vulnerable to food insecurity" (Government of Ethiopia 2014, 21). Nevertheless, beyond the importance of possessing explicit resilience-building objectives on paper, consequent design features and, ultimately, the effectiveness of implementation will determine the extent of the program's impact on resilience building (Ulrichs and Slater 2016).

Who is being reached? Are they the most vulnerable to shocks?

Often, safety net programs only reach a subset of those most vulnerable to shocks. The subset of the population reached by different safety net programs is a function of the safety net's objectives and resultant decisions on eligibility criteria and coverage. Low social protection coverage or coverage of those who are not the most vulnerable to covariate shocks inevitably limits the role of social protection in building resilience (Bastagli and Holmes 2014). Uniformly broadening coverage across and within programs widens the safety net, expanding the reach of the safety net system. However, universal access to social protection among the population is a long-term proposition for most countries (Gentilini 2019).

In the mean time, when looking to fill the holes in the safety net that are highlighted by covariate shocks, traditional approaches to beneficiary selection need to be reevaluated. Countries operating narrow poverty-targeted programs with very low coverage are likely to require strategies for expanding access to the poor and vulnerable that are at risk from shocks (Isik-Dikmelik 2012; O'Brien et al. 2018a). While the poor are more vulnerable to shocks, the near-poor and nonpoor also are vulnerable to falling into poverty because of a shock (Grosh et al. 2011; Hallegatte et al. 2016). After a shock, the overlap between the poor, those vulnerable to poverty because of the shocks, and beneficiaries of poverty-targeted programs coexisting also depends on the type of shock. For example, economic shocks and slow-onset (or seasonal) food-security crises tend to affect low-income households disproportionately, while rapid-onset disasters can impact the affected population transversally (O'Brien et al. 2018a). Where there are categorically targeted programs (such as social pensions or child grants) that have broad coverage they also may support resilience building among beneficiaries that are acutely vulnerable to shocks (that is, women, children, the elderly, and the disabled). That said, any single categorical program also will be limited in its reach among the totality of poor and vulnerable households.

As a foundation, risk-informed geographic targeting can increase the reach of a safety net in areas of spatially concentrated risk and high household vulnerability to shocks. To date, geographic targeting for social protection is not typically assessed through a covariate-shock lens. Most often, geographic targeting assesses the depth and breadth of poverty on a subnational basis. It is the first of often multiple targeting mechanisms to select where the program should go, broadly speaking. Within those areas, households are then selected using additional targeting methods such as community-based targeting and the proxy means test. In Bangladesh, social protection is prioritized where poverty and vulnerability to shocks are intertwined, including for the lean season in the Northwest (*monga*), monsoons in the Northeast (*haors*), and tropical storms in the Southwest (Coastal Belt) (Bastagli and Holmes 2014). Similarly, in Niger, a composite index of geographic vulnerability to climate shocks was used as one of the criteria to determine where to target the safety net program (box 1.2).

In addition to geographic targeting, household targeting criteria that include measures of vulnerability to shocks can increase the impact of a safety net program on resilience building. Climate-smart targeting incorporates household-level data in addition to geographic assessments of spatial vulnerability to help identify the specific households that are more vulnerable to natural hazards and climate change risks and that may be, as a result, eligible for programs that can build resilience (ADB 2018; Bastagli and Holmes 2014; World Bank 2013). In the Dominican Republic, the Vulnerability to Climate Hazards Index (IVACC) calculates the probability of a given household being affected by climate shocks using three factors: housing characteristics, estimated income, and proximity to a hazardous natural element (such as a river, stream, or ravine) (Beazley 2017a). In Niger,

BOX 1.2

Niger: Geographic targeting based on spatial vulnerability to climate shocks

In Niger, vulnerability to climate shocks was taken into consideration for the geographical targeting of the safety net program. The selection of departments within each region is based on three geographical targeting criteria: poverty, food insecurity, and vulnerability to shocks. In each region, the departments whose poverty rate is above the regional median as well as departments in which the share of severe and moderate food insecurity exceeds 20 percent are selected. A composite index of geographic vulnerability to climate shocks is then applied. Specifically, the index integrates: indicators of rainfall and Normalized Difference Vegetation Index (NDVI) anomalies to capture the recurrence of drought events; an indicator of price shocks; the ratio of cereal use for consumption to domestic production at the department level; and the vulnerability score given to each department annually by the National Framework for the Prevention and Management of Food Crisis (Dispositif National de Prévention et de Gestion des Catastrophes et des Crises Alimentaires). All the departments whose vulnerability index is found to be above the 80th percentile are included into the program. Having selected the geographic areas at the department level in this way, additional targeting criteria are applied to select the specific communes within them and then, finally, the eligible households.

Source: World Bank 2018b.

in addition to geographically targeting areas that are vulnerable to climate shocks, as outlined above, the proxy means test targeting formula used for selecting beneficiary households was also adjusted to take into account the different factors that contribute to poverty and vulnerability based on a household's location in different agricultural-ecological zones (World Bank 2018b). For example, in a zone where the main livelihood is in agriculture, ownership of land will result in a higher weight in the proxy means test than other variables. In a zone where livestock is the predominant livelihood, livestock will result in a higher weight in the proxy means test than other variables, including versus land. This is done to sensitize the proxy means test to the fact that livelihoods have different effects on a household's level of poverty as well as their vulnerability to climatic shocks based on where they live.

What kind of assistance are beneficiaries receiving? Does it maximize resilience-related outcomes?

When a safety net designed to build resilience to covariate shocks reaches the most vulnerable households, the design parameters of the benefits it provides will play a mediating role in enabling or restraining resilience-enhancing outcomes. Broadly speaking, the design of the benefit package of, say, a cash transfer program can significantly impact resilience building and a program's ability to support a beneficiary household's capacity to prepare for, cope with, and adapt to a covariate shock (Barca 2018).

A program's transfer values can be adjusted and set in relation to resilience-building objectives. Due to the many programmatic objectives pursued by safety net programs, the amount transferred to beneficiaries can vary significantly across interventions. Safety nets tend to cover a small share of a poor person's income/consumption—13 percent on average in low-income countries (World Bank 2018a). An increasing body of evidence from Sub-Saharan Africa indicates programs that include transfers amounting to over 20 percent of per capita income produce more significant results on resilience building (Beazley and Farhat 2016; Daidone et al. 2015; Davis 2014). Conversely, lack of impacts across recent evaluations has often been attributed to modest transfer sizes and erosion of value over time due to inflation (see, for example, Arnold, Conway, and Greenslade 2011; Asfaw et al. 2014; McCord et al. 2016). Beyond the general point on the need for adequate transfer levels, frequent transfers of lesser value tend to favor consumption-smoothing and spending on smaller assets that are beneficial in support of coping with shocks, but which may not stimulate investment in adaptation; less frequent, lump-sum payments tend to increase productive investment in support of adaptation and savings in support of preparedness (Beazley and Farhat 2016; Haushofer and Shapiro 2013) as well as longer-term recovery and the reaccumulation of assets following a large-scale disaster.

The timing of the safety net transfers can enhance their impact on resilience building. Where the needs of poor and vulnerable households are predictable in relation to shocks (such as rainy or lean seasons), the provision of benefits can be timed accordingly to align with this seasonality. This way, beneficiaries receive assistance ahead of the need to resort to negative coping mechanisms materializing, enhancing preparedness and the ability to cope (Barca et al. 2015; Beazley, McCord, and Solórzano 2016).

The duration of time that a household is a beneficiary of a program can impact the resilience-enhancing outcomes. Evaluations of cash transfer programs showcase a "number of improvements in outcomes arising from increased duration [of time spent in a program], including some improvements in health behaviors and child growth outcomes, higher expenditure and food expenditure, lower likelihood of early marriage, pregnancy and greater contraceptive use" (Bastagli et al. 2016, 11). In Ethiopia, Kenya, and Uganda short-term assistance has been found to limit the program's impacts on seasonal and chronic food insecurity (Ulrichs and Slater 2016). Evidence also is increasing on the detrimental effects of households that stop receiving transfers, questioning the longer-term sustainability of impacts and shedding light on the need for responsible "exit" and/or "graduation" strategies to ensure that those who exit do not return to a position of vulnerability[1] (Bastagli et al. 2016).

Predictable transfers are fundamental to building resilience. No matter what the parameters of the transfers—amount, frequency, timing, duration—a regular and predictable benefit is critical to generating resilience-building outcomes. A predictable transfer can be relied upon by a beneficiary to smooth consumption and preempt negative coping; it provides certainty with which to better plan, thus prepare; and it supports risk-taking behavior that contributes to long-term adaptation. In the context of covariate shocks, where a transfer is not predictable and reliable, the resulting uncertainty undermines the ability for beneficiaries to not undertake negative coping strategies. The importance of predictability is extensively discussed across evaluations and reviews of existing social protection interventions (Andrews, Hsiao, and Ralston, 2018; Barca et al. 2015; Bastagli et al. 2016; Daidone et al. 2015; del Ninno, Pierre, and Coll-Black 2016; Fallavier 2014; Solórzano 2016; Ulrichs and Slater 2016).

DESIGN FEATURES TO SUPPORT THE CAPACITY TO PREPARE, COPE, AND ADAPT

In addition to these core design considerations across programs, the impacts of safety nets across the three resilience capacities can be examined more closely. Any one program can provide support across all three capacities, and all three capacities are interlinked. However, the remainder of this chapter disentangles the three capacities and analyzes the design features and types of safety net programs that can serve to support each of the three capacities among identified, at-risk, poor, and vulnerable households (table 1.1).

Support to the capacity to prepare for shocks

Safety nets can support the capacity to prepare for shocks when they reach the most vulnerable households in advance—stimulating savings, financial inclusion, and the communication of information on how to better prepare, cope, and adapt. Safety net beneficiaries often use transfers to save, especially in contexts of recurrent shocks. Evidence indicates that safety nets have significant impacts on increased savings, improved creditworthiness, and reduced debt, though the extent varies based on the context and design (Andrews, Hsiao, and Ralston, 2018; Bastagli et al. 2016; Hidrobo et al. 2018; Ulrichs and

TABLE 1.1 **Adaptive social protection: Supporting the capacity to prepare, cope, and adapt**

	PREPAREDNESS	COPING	ADAPTATION
A more resilient household	• More savings (cash, assets) to draw upon if a shock occurs • Access to public (social protection) and private (insurance) instruments if needed after a shock • Access to information on their own exposure and vulnerability to shocks (including early warning information) to inform action	• Activates coping mechanisms: acting on information (including early warning information), leverages savings, assets, public and private instruments to smooth consumption and to supplement lost income	• Capable of making long-term investments to reduce exposure and vulnerability over time • Adjustment of asset and livelihood portfolios away from sources of risk and vulnerability • Planned movement and migration away from areas of spatially concentrated, chronic risk
Poor and vulnerable households	• Limited savings and assets to draw on if a shock occurs • Limited or no access to public (social protection) and private (insurance) instruments if needed should a shock occur • Limited access to information on their exposure and vulnerability (including early warning information) to inform action	• In the absence of adequate savings and access to social protection and/or private insurance, resort to negative coping strategies—cutting consumption, removing children from school, distress sale of assets, among others	• Fewer resources with which to make long-term investments in adaptation through adjustments in livelihood and asset portfolios that can lead to • Maladaptation and chronic vulnerability • Forced displacement and unplanned migration
Role of safety net programs in supporting preparedness, coping, and adaptation among the poor and vulnerable households	• Increased access to safety nets among the poor and vulnerable, especially those identified as at-risk from shocks • Transfers to at-risk households before shocks occur to support savings and asset accumulation • Safety nets leveraged to transmit information on exposure and vulnerability, enabling the increased anticipation of shocks, and informing actions in support of preparedness, coping, and adaptation	• Support to post-shock coping through continued delivery during and after a shock to existing beneficiaries • Shock-responsive programs capable of adjusting benefit package and temporarily increasing the number of beneficiaries as needed based on post-shock needs	• Support to long-term adjustment of asset and livelihood portfolios, including through cash, cash plus, and productive inclusion interventions • Community asset-building projects through public works programs that address key drivers of community-level vulnerability • Support to human capital accumulation for intergenerational adaptation through increased opportunity

Slater 2016). In Mexico, beneficiaries of the former national conditional cash transfer program (Prospera) who lived in communities highly exposed to droughts and hurricanes use the transfer "to save for the bad times" and their creditworthiness in local markets increases because the communities know the recipient households and the payment intervals (Solórzano 2016). Similar insights were consistent across programs in Ethiopia, Kenya, and Uganda (Ulrichs and Slater 2016). Indeed, in Africa, safety net beneficiary households are 4–20 percentage points more likely to save relative to comparable nonbeneficiary households (figure 1.1). Given the initial low savings rate among poor households, this implies an expansion by a factor of almost two in the incidence of savings (Beegle, Coudouel, and Monsalve 2018).

Safety nets can encourage financial inclusion, which can be instrumental for enhancing the capacity to prepare, cope, and adapt. Financial inclusion seeks to extend financial services to all citizens by ensuring that services are accessible, affordable, and appropriate (ISPA 2017). Access to financial services can help households reduce their vulnerability to shocks by facilitating saving in support of preparedness; enhancing opportunities for income generation, asset accumulation, and consequently adaptation (Cull, Ehrbeck, and Holle 2014); and even making beneficiaries reachable more easily and quickly with assistance in the form of electronic payments after a shock has hit. In the context of social

FIGURE 1.1

Africa: Safety net beneficiaries tend to use the transfers to save

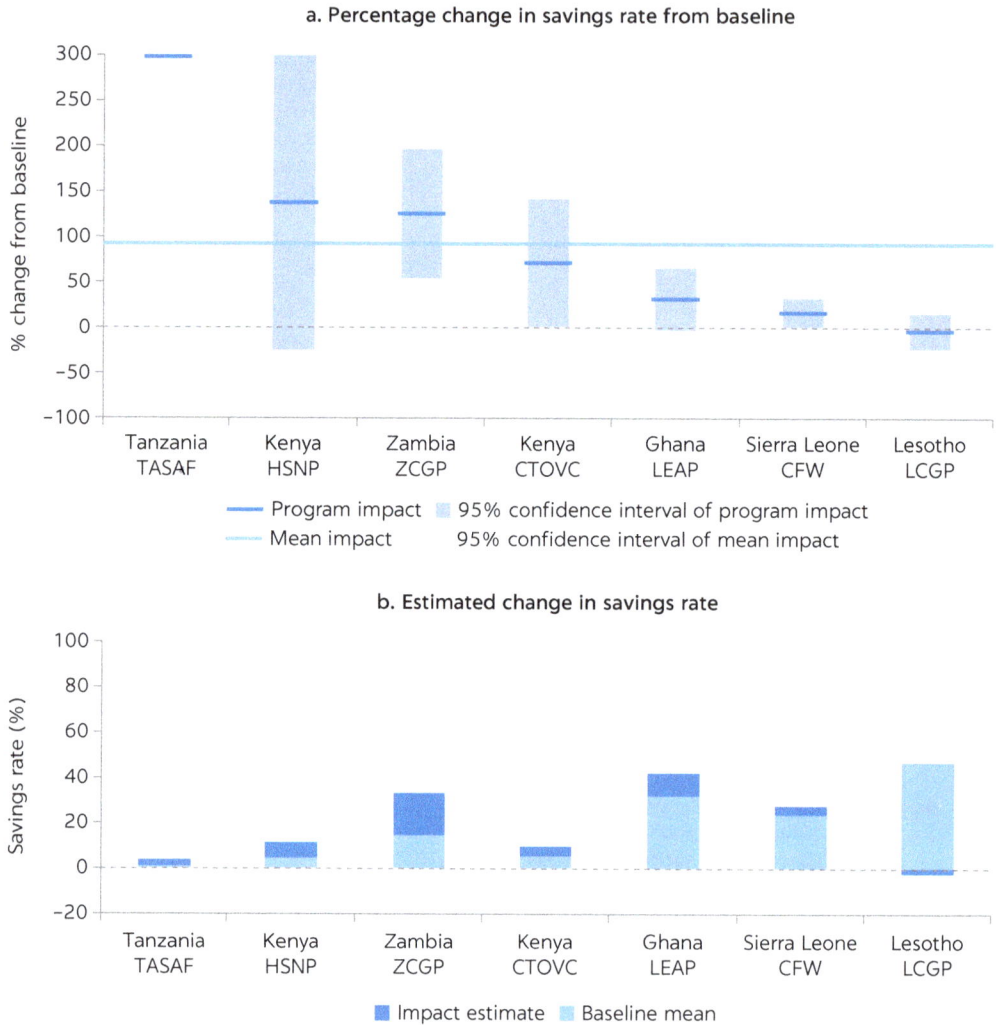

a. Percentage change in savings rate from baseline

b. Estimated change in savings rate

Source: Beegle, Coudouel, and Monsalve 2018.
Note: The mean value of the household transfer (in 2011 US$ purchasing power parity) is Tanzania Social Action Fund $48, Kenya's Hunger Safety Net Program $47, Zambia's Child Grant Program $27, Kenya Cash Transfer for Orphan and Vulnerable Children $71, Ghana's Livelihood Empowerment against Poverty $24, Sierra Leone Cash for Work $83, and Lesotho Child Grants Program $34.

protection, financial inclusion can be explicitly supported where beneficiaries are given access to a "store-of-value" transaction account, encouraged to save, and/or given access to savings groups.

In addition, safety net programs can provide channels for communicating information on exposure and vulnerability to poor and vulnerable households that are hard to reach. Social protection programs rely on a network of implementers who often reach into the community, including social workers and village/community leaders, and may be involved in program implementation. These unique channels into the community level often are used to transmit information to beneficiaries through community that may be mandatory (or not) for cash-transfer beneficiaries. Such "behavioral change communication" sessions can provide venues and conduits for the communication of early warning information to beneficiaries and the wider community that are otherwise hard to reach, as well as broader information on disaster risk, risk reduction, and adaptation measures (ADB 2018). In the Philippines, Family Development Sessions, an integral component of the national conditional cash transfer program (Pantawid Pamilya Pilipino Program), are used as a vehicle and venue to deliver information and practices on disaster risk management to all beneficiaries—including what to pack and where to go (Bowen 2015). In Mexico, the former conditional cash transfer program Prospera and civil protection together provided disaster preparedness training to social protection beneficiaries (Beazley, Solórzano, and Barca 2019).

Support to the capacity to cope with shocks

Safety net programs have well-documented, positive impacts on a household's capacity to cope with shocks, through the delivery of support after a shock has hit. Of the three resilience capacities, safety nets tend to demonstrate the strongest impact on supporting coping capacity: supporting consumption, lessening food insecurity, and providing alternatives to negative coping (Ulrichs and Slater 2016). Complementing a transfer's impact before a shock and its potential to generate a buffer to be leveraged after a shock hits, the continued receipt of transfers during and after a shock supports post-shock coping. Impact evaluations of safety net programs in six African countries describe "unambiguous" increases in the food security of beneficiary households[2] (Asfaw and Davis 2018). In Ethiopia, the PSNP reduced the initial impact of a drought by 57 percent on beneficiaries, eliminating the adverse impact on food security within 2 years (Knippenberg and Hoddinott 2017) (figure 1.2). Relatedly, safety nets can play a role in reducing the need to resort to negative coping strategies that trigger longer-term detrimental effects (Barca et al. 2015; Dammert et al. 2018; Hill, Skoufias, and Maher 2019).

FIGURE 1.2

Ethiopia: PSNP beneficiary and nonbeneficiary recovery trajectories

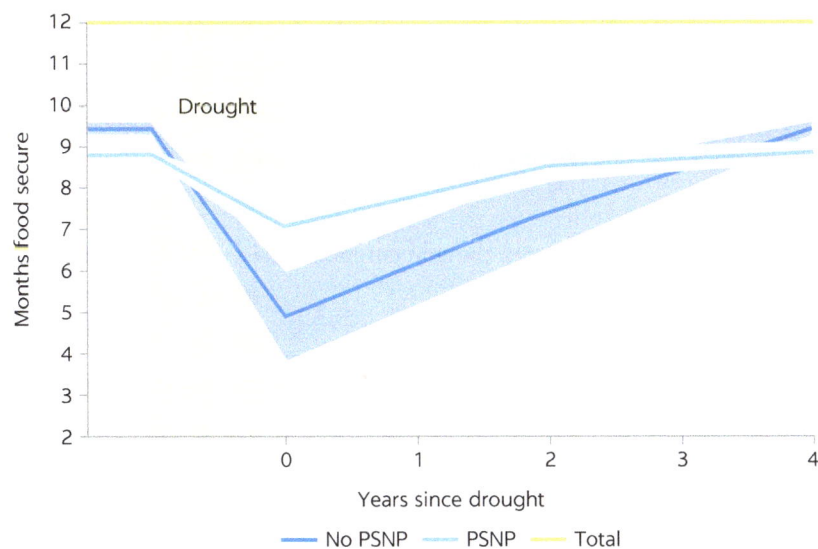

Source: Knippenberg and Hoddinott 2017.
Note: Representative household at mean level of food security. Blue bands represent 95 percent confidence intervals. PSNP = Productive Safety Net Programme.

In the context of covariate shocks, safety net programs with resilience-building objectives need to be shock-responsive to provide extraordinary support to help households cope with often devastating impacts. In their framework for shock-responsive social protection, O'Brien et al. (2018b) outline five potential ways that social protection programs can be leveraged to respond to large-scale shocks:

- **Design tweaks** are small adjustments to a routine social protection program. They can introduce flexibility to maintain the regular service for existing beneficiaries in a shock (for example, by waiving conditionalities). Alternatively, they can address vulnerabilities that are likely to increase in a crisis, through adjustments to program coverage, timeliness, or predictability (for example, by altering the payment schedule), without requiring a flex at the moment of the shock.
- **Vertical expansion** is the temporary increase of the value or duration of a social protection intervention to meet the additional needs of existing beneficiaries. For such vertical expansions to be relevant, the program or programs must have good coverage of the disaster-affected area and also of the neediest households.
- **Horizontal expansion** is the temporary inclusion of new beneficiaries from disaster-affected communities into a social protection program, by extending geographical coverage, enrolling more eligible households in existing areas, or altering the enrollment criteria.
- **Piggybacking** occurs when an emergency response uses part of an established system or program while delivering something new. Exactly which and how many elements of the system or program are borrowed will vary; it could be, for example, a specific program's beneficiary list, its staff, a national database, or a particular payment mechanism.
- **Alignment** describes designing an intervention with elements resembling others that already exist or are planned, but without integrating the two. For example, this could be an alignment of objectives, targeting method, transfer value, or delivery mechanism. Governments may align their systems with those of humanitarian agencies or vice versa, either because an existing intervention is not operational as needed in a crisis or because it may not yet exist.

Where a safety net exists and has a good degree of coverage among affected households, vertical expansion offers a relatively simple method of providing more assistance to existing, affected beneficiaries. Recent examples include the vertical expansion of the social protection system in Fiji following Tropical Cyclone Winston in 2016 and of the national conditional cash transfer program, through additional grants from humanitarian actors (the World Food Programme and UNICEF) following Typhoon Haiyan (Yolanda) and Typhoon Ruby in the Philippines. In the case of Fiji, an impact assessment found that households that received the vertical expansion were more likely to report having recovered from the shock more quickly; for instance, they were 8–10 percent more likely to have recovered from housing damage than nonbeneficiaries (Mansur et al. 2017).

However, vertical expansions generally do not reach nonbeneficiary, shock-affected households that may be in equal or greater need of assistance. As noted, programs with traditional safety net objectives related to poverty reduction, for example, reach subsets of a shock-affected population. Vertical expansions alone therefore risk missing shock-affected households (Barca and O'Brien 2017). In Ecuador, only 15 percent of households within the Registro de Damnificados (the database of affected households established in the aftermath of the 2016 earthquake) received the country's flagship social assistance program, Bono de Desarrollo Humano (Beazley 2017b). In Mozambique, the government estimate on the median population affected by the 2016 droughts was 15 percent across the 71 affected districts. The median coverage of the country's largest social assistance program in these districts was only 9 percent, suggesting that "even if the recipients of the Basic Social Security Program were indeed the population most affected by the drought, there was still a large population in need of support" (Kardan et al. 2017, 43). As such, the ability to temporarily reach additional households that may be equally or more in need of support to their coping capacity but may not be regular beneficiaries of social protection programs is critical for shock-responsive social protection. This can be achieved through horizontal expansion and dedicated emergency programs or through coordination and alignment with non–safety net and/or nongovernmental interventions, including humanitarian assistance.

Horizontal expansion enables a safety net program to temporarily expand its caseload after a shock to include new households based on eligibility from a disaster's impacts. Introducing the ability to scale out in this manner is far more complex than undertaking vertical expansion to existing beneficiaries. Scaling out requires significant investment in the processes and procedures for delivering the program, often in challenging settings. Several countries have invested in the capacity to horizontally expand a safety net program, including most prominently Ethiopia with the PSNP and Kenya with the HSNP; each is prepared to undertake horizontal expansions based on needs generated by drought and related food insecurity. In the United States, the Supplemental Nutrition Assistance Program (SNAP) routinely expands its caseload horizontally in response to economic shocks; Disaster-SNAP (D-SNAP) provides temporary assistance to nonregular participants who have suffered significant losses by relaxing program requirements to ease access and relieve administrative burdens on staff (FNS 2014).

Some countries use a dedicated emergency program with characteristics similar to a safety net (cash, in-kind, and public works), which may piggyback on core safety net delivery systems and capacity. Emergency programs have dedicated response objectives and exist outside of an existing safety net program. Relative to expanding safety net programs, the use of a dedicated emergency program with a singular objective to respond to a shock holds the advantage of ring fencing an existing safety net with its existing, non–disaster response objectives and design features. It enables the development of a dedicated instrument with appropriate design features. It also can reduce confusion around entry and exit decisions for temporary beneficiaries, some of whom may be transitioned into longer-term safety net programs (depending on their longer-term needs following the disaster). Such programs can be located within or outside of the social protection ministries, departments, and agencies and can leverage underlying safety net delivery systems (such as social registries, payment systems, and front-line social protection staff). This process has been referred to as piggybacking (O'Brien et al. 2018a).

In Pakistan, the Citizen's Damage Compensation Program was initially implemented as an emergency flood response that utilized a stand-alone beneficiary registration and payment distribution system in partnership with commercial banks and linked to the national civil registry (World Bank 2013). The cash-based disaster response in Pakistan has since evolved to encompass a combined approach. The Benazir Income Support Program (BISP) is used for vertical expansions to extreme poor households. Horizontal expansion to non-program beneficiaries is undertaken by the National Database and Registration Authority with the use of dedicated one-stop shops (Citizen Facilitation Centers) when support is required by segments of the population over and above the program's poverty cut-off or where tailored responses are required. In the Sahel, with support from the Sahel ASP Program, Mauritania has developed a dedicated emergency response program ("Elmaouna") that piggybacks on existing social protection social registries and payment platforms for its delivery (Mauritania 2019).

Whichever approach to shock-responsive social protection is undertaken, the different phases of postdisaster support generally require multiple programs to reach different households with different kinds of assistance. Where multiple safety net programs exist and cover different subsets of the population, more than one program may need to be used. This includes the use of different programs across the post-shock phases, depending on the relative strengths and weaknesses of each program type, the precise needs generated by a shock, and how they change over time. For example, this may include transitioning from supporting life-saving basic needs in the short term to assistance that supports longer-term recovery of livelihoods and assets (figure 1.3).

Operational processes and contingency plans need to be clearly defined in advance—including who does what when—to better ensure faster implementation. Countries should outline clear processes for the delivery of

FIGURE 1.3

The Philippines: Multiple programs for differing household needs across differing post-shock time periods

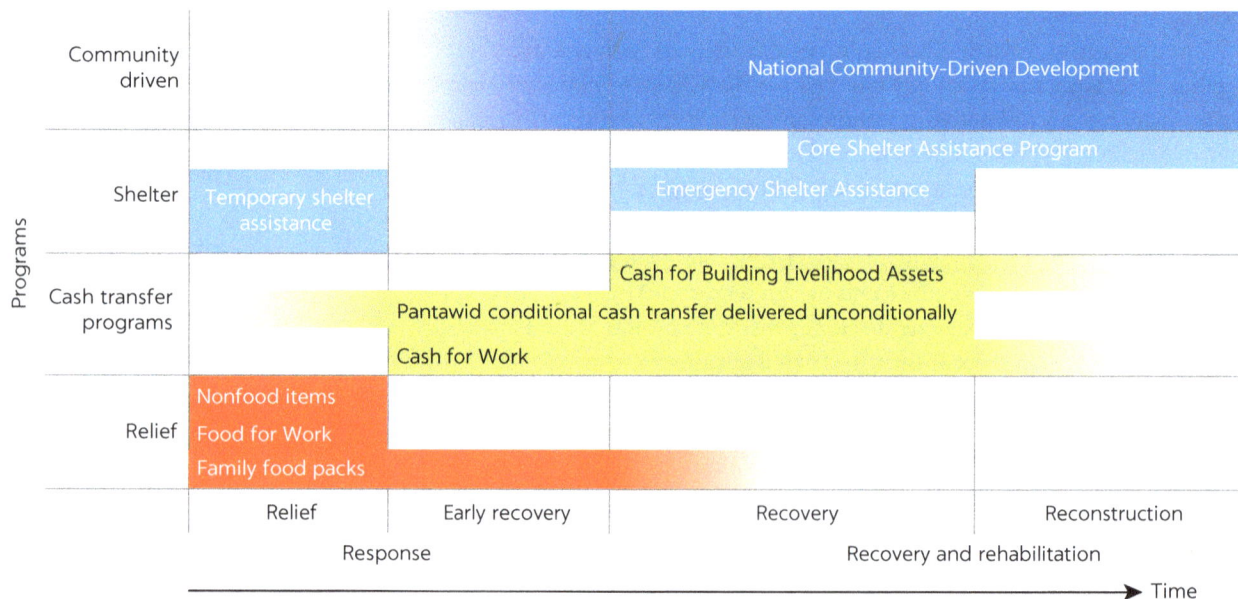

Source: Bowen 2015.

assistance in post-shock environments in operations manuals or contingency plans (as in the case of Ethiopia, box 1.3). These manuals serve as a key guide for implementing staff. After a destructive shock, the often difficult operating environment makes it hard to implement response actions effectively if they are defined in an ad hoc manner only after the fact, contributing to delays. Operational processes can be defined as a subsection of existing program manuals (as in the case of Mexico, box 1.3) or as stand-alone documents. Ideally, they should be as comprehensive as possible, detailing how processes vary from established procedures, among others: time frames for waiving conditions; mechanisms for triggering payments in information systems; rules for taking on and exiting new beneficiaries; grievance redress procedures; and clear details on data management and information sharing protocols.

The social protection delivery chain can help identify the critical implementation processes and contingencies required for shock-response programs, to be captured in contingency plans and protocols, ex ante. The delivery chain,

Ethiopia, Mexico, and Pakistan: Contingency planning

In Ethiopia, the PSNP identified the district (*woreda*) for collecting household information and designed contingency plans to ensure that in the event of shocks, transitory and regular beneficiaries received support in the same manner. The five steps of the PSNP contingency planning include (1) context analysis, based on early warning information, historical data, and community needs; (2) scenario assessment, identifying hazards and their potential impacts on food security and estimating the number of potential additional beneficiaries; (3) response planning, including targeting of transitory beneficiaries, public works activities, and budgeting; (4) operational support planning, including setting up "shelf projects" for public works and identifying the necessary decision makers, resources, systems, and structures; and (5) revising contingency plans, based on new information, early warning systems, and annual updates.

In Mexico, most cash transfer programs, including the former national conditional cash transfer program Prospera, have rules of operation for implementing interventions. These rules are updated annually and broadly define changes in operational processes in the event of a disaster, declared emergency, or epidemic. In the case of the former national conditional cash transfer program Prospera, these changes include, among others, (1) paying cash transfers without verification of co-responsibilities for no more than four consecutive months (unless the National Coordinating Council authorizes an extension) in emergency situations where delivery of education and health services are impeded, (2) adjusting operational processes of the National Coordinating Council, (3) delaying recertification (with prior authorization from the National Coordinating Council) by 1 year for households in affected areas, and (4) deploying Prospera personnel to affected areas.

In Pakistan, the government developed a national strategy for managing catastrophic events, the Federal Disaster Response Action Plan, which outlines contingency plans and the minimum resources and swiftest approval processes required to respond to shocks. The plan clearly defines the cash response model for emergencies and the roles and responsibilities of the respective partner agencies critical for future responses. These include the national and provincial disaster management authorities, the Benazir Income Support Program, the National Database and Registration Authority, the Ministry of Finance, and commercial banks. The processes outlined in the Federal Disaster Response Action Plan have since been implemented during response to floods in Sindh province (2012–13), as well as to internally displaced persons of the conflict-affected Federally Administered Tribal Area regions (2015).

Sources: Coll-Black et al., forthcoming; Mexico 2018.

FIGURE 1.4
Social protection delivery chain

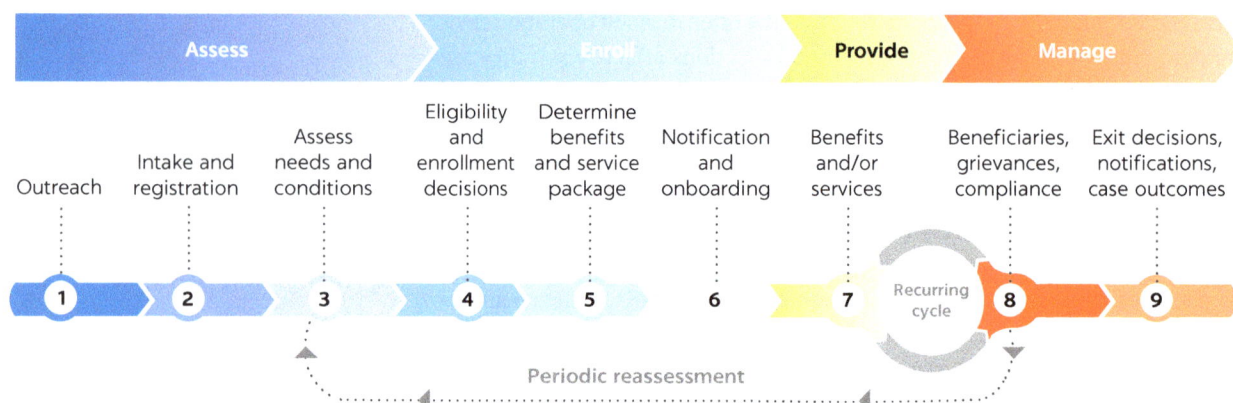

Source: Lindert et al., forthcoming.

pictured in figure 1.4, outlines core steps for the implementation of any safety net program to provide the right amount of benefits and services, to the right households, at the right time. When designing contingency plans for shock-response programs, the delivery chain forms a helpful basis for thinking through the key questions and considerations as well as the ex-ante investments in adapting the delivery chain that are required to undertake those processes and deliver the response program (for further detail, see appendix B).

Support to the capacity to adapt to shocks

Alongside supporting short-term coping after a shock, governments can use safety nets to invest in the capacity for poor and vulnerable households to adapt to shocks over the long term. There has been an increasing and justifiable focus on the role of safety nets in supporting post-shock coping. That said, ASP and the wider definition of resilience used here highlight the central importance of supporting a household's longer-term adaptation in order to reduce its vulnerability to a shock over time. By broadening the focus in this way, safety net programs can also be seen as promising tools for providing pathways toward a more resilient state for poor households that are vulnerable to shocks (see also Tenzing 2019). By extension, where successful, these investments may serve to reduce future post-shock needs over time.

As a foundation for supporting adaptive capacity, the provision of long-term, predictable, and adequate cash transfers can be instrumental in supporting income generation, livelihood diversification, asset accumulation, and human capital accumulation (Asfaw and Davis 2018; Barca 2018; FAO 2019). In Africa, safety net programs enhance the ownership of productive assets and strengthen livelihoods; one of the most striking results is the significant rise in livestock ownership. Across seven programs, livestock ownership improved 34 percent relative to baseline levels (Beegle, Coudouel, and Monsalve 2018). Expenditures on durables (tools and other equipment for farms and businesses) exhibited a smaller, but still significant, improvement: a 10 percent increase relative to the baseline. Ethiopia and Malawi demonstrate improved fertilizer and seed use, which may indicate a shift to higher-risk, higher-return agricultural practices.

Concretely, safety nets can support adaptive capacity when designed to help the poor accumulate and diversify assets and livelihoods (Bahadur et al. 2015; FSIN 2015; Jorgensen and Siegel 2019). The promotion of more productive and resilient livelihoods among poor and vulnerable households is one of the core elements of supporting adaptive capacity. Interventions that promote more productive and resilient livelihoods have the potential to empower beneficiaries to diversify their asset and resilient livelihood portfolios and to reduce their exposure and vulnerability to shocks. For example, a study by Macours, Premand, and Vakis (2012) found that the provision of vocational training or a productive investment grant in addition to a cash transfer to beneficiaries vulnerable to drought in Nicaragua provided full protection against drought shocks 2 years after the end of the intervention (relative to a control group that only received a cash transfer) (figure 1.5). Similarly, safety nets can contribute to livelihood promotion through specific programs that link cash transfer recipients to complementary interventions in other sectors (for example, agricultural inputs, training, and microfinance), leading to positive—yet varied—impacts on production and diversification into on-farm and off-farm opportunities (FAO 2016; Mariotti, Ulrichs, and Harman 2016 as cited in FAO 2019).

For this reason, productive inclusion programs are emerging as potentially powerful instruments for supporting the adaptive capacity of the poorest households by supporting transitions into more productive and resilient livelihoods. Productive inclusion provides an integrated package of assistance, in addition to cash transfers, that is designed to overcome barriers preventing households from moving into more productive and resilient livelihoods. Integrated packages of intervention often include cash transfers plus a mixture of the following: skills and micro-entrepreneurship training tailored to local livelihood opportunities; promotion of and support for saving groups;

FIGURE 1.5

Adaptive capacity: Welfare is less sensitive to shocks for beneficiary households receiving productive grants

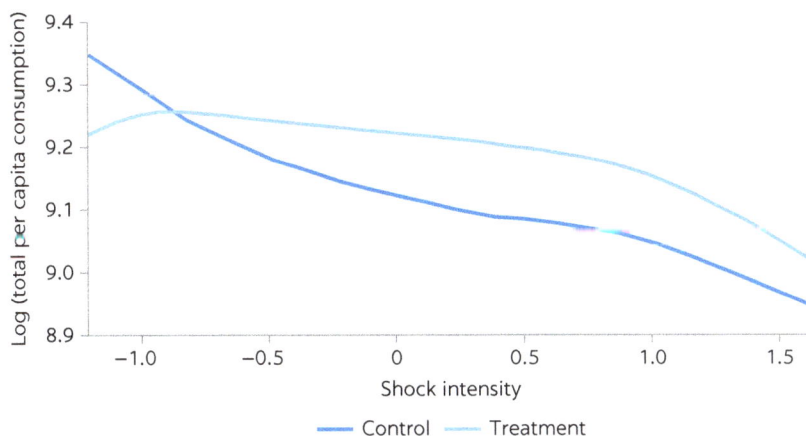

Source: Macours, Premand, and Vakis 2012.
Note: Households eligible for the productive investment package and control only. Shock intensity is standardized by subtracting the mean and dividing by the standard deviation. Estimates exclude shocks more than 1 standard deviation removed from others. Fan regressions with bandwidth of 1.5. Graph trimmed at 5 percent highest and lowest values of shocks intensity. Estimates using fan regressions as in Fan and Gijbels (1996).

provision of seed capital and productive grants; linkage to existing value chains and markets; and mentoring, behavior, and life skills to build confidence and reinforce existing skillsets, among others (Bossuroy and Premand 2016; PEI 2016; Roelen et al. 2017). Impact evaluations over the past 15 years have shown the resilience-enhancing value of such interventions, both in terms of breaking the cycle of chronic poverty and mitigating the risks of "backsliding" into poverty after a shock (Banerjee et al. 2015; PEI 2016; Samson 2015) (figure 1.6 and box 1.4).

In complement to the support for more productive livelihoods, public works programs can be designed to support a community's capacity to adapt to shocks. Through careful design and planning, assets created with public works programs can help build the resilience of communities (ADB 2018; Asfaw and Davis 2018; Steinbach et al. 2017a, 2017b, 2017c; Subbarao et al. 2013). The following channels facilitate community-level adaptive capacity:

- Engaging communities in climate-smart agriculture and integrated natural resource management, including a focus on waste management, reforestation, rainwater harvesting, soil/water conservation, and drought-resistant horticulture, among others.[3]
- Supporting wider disaster-reduction activities and climate-proofing of existing assets (such as building or maintaining local infrastructure to higher standards of resilience). This includes shelter belts and mangrove plantations, building cyclone shelters, and raising embankment heights.
- Enhancing agriculture-based livelihoods by building, among others, irrigation channels, livestock shelters, and water and grain storage structures.

In Ethiopia, the public works component of the flagship safety net invests in building the resilience of communities to climatic shocks. Public works focus on creating community assets to reverse the severe degradation of watersheds and to provide more reliable water supply under different climatic conditions. Its community-based Participatory Watershed Management Planning Process

FIGURE 1.6

Productive inclusion model: Graduation into sustainable livelihoods

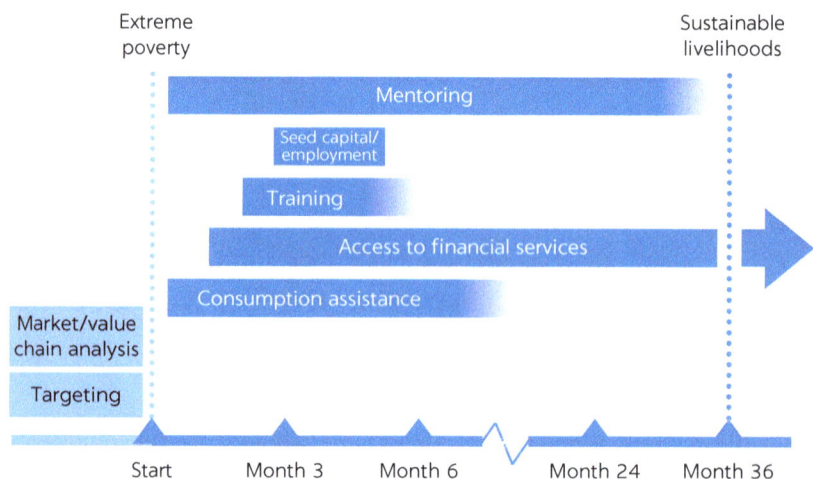

Source: PEI 2016.

Sahel: Productive inclusion to support the adaptive capacity of the extreme poor

In the Sahel, traditional cash transfers are a core component of many social protection systems. However, policy makers in the region are interested in complementing these programs to improve the ability of recipient households to become more productive and by extension more resilient to climatic shocks. Burkina Faso, Chad, Mali, Mauritania, Niger, and Senegal are implementing productive inclusion packages, including the following interventions:

- **Basic consumption support.** Beneficiaries receive regular cash transfers of about $15 per month.
- **Coaching and group formation**. Beneficiaries form groups to meet with coaches on an ongoing basis. Coaches provide support and guidance to the groups, ensure that program components are being implemented effectively, and promote group access to local markets. They also provide individualized follow-up when participants need additional support.
- **Savings groups.** Beneficiaries form groups to pool their savings. The intervention trains and supervises participants to establish and manage Village Savings and Loans Associations for a source of lending funds.
- **Workshops.** Beneficiaries and the wider community attend a screening of a video and engage in a facilitated after-discussion. The aim is to lift aspirations and to address community norms that prevent beneficiaries from making productive investments.
- **Life-skills training.** Beneficiaries are offered a week-long training program designed to promote socio-emotional skills such as self-esteem, effective decision-making, and conflict resolution.
- **Micro-entrepreneurship training.** Beneficiaries receive a week-long training program covering basic business skills for agricultural and nonagricultural activities.
- **Large, lump-sum cash grant.** Beneficiaries receive a one-time grant of $100–$200 meant to promote investment in productive activities.

Source: Karlan et al. 2017.

targets areas and projects. These projects have led to re-greening in previously arid areas and have contributed to the rehabilitation of entire community watersheds. These positive environmental impacts are enhancing agriculture productivity and livelihoods (World Bank 2013b).

Similarly, a series of case studies of India's Mahatma Gandhi National Rural Employment Guarantee Scheme (MGNREGS) found that it can help to build and strengthen resilience to various climate shocks. The MGNREGS was found to do so by providing (1) integrated natural resource management and soil conservation infrastructure, such as check dams, ponds and trenches, afforestation, and land development works; (2) agriculture-based investments, such as irrigation channels; and (3) other local infrastructure. The authors use household surveys to construct both a livelihood vulnerability index and an agriculture vulnerability index, finding that vulnerability falls across the board because of the MGNREGS assets and in particular the natural resource–based assets constructed (Esteves et al. 2013; Kaur et al. 2017). Projects can similarly support wider disaster risk reduction activities and climate-proofing of existing assets. They can be designed to enhance agriculture-based livelihoods by producing irrigation channels, livestock shelters, and water and grain storage structures, among others (ADB 2018; Asfaw and Davis 2018; Steinbach et al. 2017a, 2017b, 2017c; Subbarao et al. 2013). Further results are synthesized in box 1.5.

Lastly, safety net programs that contribute to building human capital can help to equip future generations with the capacity to adapt to shocks. Promoting the accumulation of human capital among poorer households can be critical in terms of connecting those households with the skills to adapt over the long term. Indeed, human capital can empower the next generation

---

BOX 1.5

India: Rural employment guarantee scheme creates assets to manage climate risk

Drawing on field research on India's Mahatma Gandhi National Rural Employment Guarantee Scheme (MGNREGS) and specific climate-related shocks in different states (winter drought in Sikkim, cyclones in Andhra Pradesh, drought in Jharkhand, and flooding and drought in Odisha), the following insights emerge on the assets/infrastructure constructed:

- In **Sikkim**, Dhara Vikas Program (local) and the MGNREGS Springshed Development Program (national) have recharged groundwater, increasing discharge rates from 4.4 to 14.4 liters per minute in 2010/11. This gave households 10–15 percent more water for consumptive and productive use during the lean period. Other private assets created through MGNREGS include cardamom and broom plantations, livestock sheds, water storage tanks, and infrastructure to produce organic fertilizer. The resulting improvements to soil quality and irrigation have increased arable land and enabled the introduction of new crops, while the new structures have contributed to further improving agricultural production. This has led to an average 18 percent increase in crop yields. Public assets such as roads and rural marketing centers, on the other hand, have increased access to markets.

- In **Andhra Pradesh**, most projects focused on irrigation, land productivity improvements, horticulture and sericulture plantations, and developing fallow lands, such as into coconut plantations for landless households. Increased access to water for irrigation and reduced flooding in adjacent farmland during and after cyclones has reduced the sensitivity of farmers' livelihoods to climate impacts. For example, decreased waterlogging in the paddy fields and increased availability of water for irrigation have improved agricultural production from 15–17 to 25–30 bags of rice per acre. Moreover, the amount of land under cultivation for a second paddy crop in the *rabi* (winter) season doubled or tripled from 50 to 100–150 acres.

- In **Jharkhand**, the creation of *dobas* (farm ponds), dug wells, and irrigation pumps resulted in 33 percent of respondents reporting improvements in water availability and irrigation, 29 percent increased availability of agricultural land, 21 percent increased agricultural productivity, and 46 percent increased crop diversity. Mixed results across the region largely depended on program implementation, such as construction of *dobas* that did not adhere to specifications.

- In **Odisha**, a focus on horticultural services, such as the creation of guava, cashew, and mango plantations, and irrigation resulted in 90 percent reporting improvements in agricultural production, 85 percent increased crop diversity, and 40 percent increased irrigation and availability of agricultural land.

Sources: Barca 2018, drawing on Kaur et al. 2017 and Steinbach et al. 2017a, 2017b, and 2017c.

with the means to move out of at-risk areas and toward employment opportunities in lower-risk livelihoods. To encourage the accumulation of human capital among beneficiaries, safety net benefits often come with conditions such as, most prominently, those aligned to conditional cash transfer programs encouraging investments in the health and education of a beneficiary households' children. In cases where the capacity to monitor compliance with "hard" conditions in conditional cash transfer programs may be lower, softer conditions are increasingly being implemented. For example, behavioral change sessions, highlighted for their role in supporting beneficiary preparedness, are increasingly accompanying cash transfer programs, delivered in the community to transmit information on health, nutrition, and education to beneficiaries.

NOTES

1. Program exit refers to exclusion from the program of those who have passed away or no longer qualify (based on predetermined program criteria). Importantly, program exit does not depend on a participant's behavior or economic status, as is the case for graduation (Samson 2015).
2. The six countries are Ethiopia, Ghana, Kenya, Lesotho, Malawi, and Zambia.
3. These are sometimes classified as "soft resilience measures" and typically are low-cost and adaptable to deliver benefits in changing conditions (Cabot Venton et al. 2012).

REFERENCES

ADB (Asian Development Bank). 2018. "Strengthening Resilience through Social Protection Programs." Guidance Note. ADB, Manila.

Andrews, C., A. Hsiao, and L. Ralston. 2018. "Social Safety Nets Promote Poverty Reduction, Increase Resilience, and Expand Opportunities. In *Realizing the Full Potential of Social Safety Nets in Africa*, edited by K. Beegle, A. Coudouel, and E. Monsalve, 87–137. Washington, DC: World Bank.

Arnold, C., T. Conway, and M. Greenslade. 2011. "Cash Transfers." Evidence Paper. Department for International Development, London. https://webarchive.nationalarchives.gov.uk /+/http://www.dfid.gov.uk/Documents/publications1/cash-transfers-evidence-paper.pdf.

Asfaw, S., and B. Davis. 2018. "Can Cash Transfer Programmes Promote Household Resilience? Evidence from Sub-Saharan Africa." In *Climate Smart Agriculture*, edited by L. Lipper, N. McCarthy, D. Zilberman, S. Asfaw, and G. Braca, 227–50. Rome: Food and Agriculture Organization of the United Nations. http://www.fao.org/3/a-i7931e.pdf.

Asfaw, S., B. Davis, J. Dewbre, S. Handa, and P. Winters. 2014. "Cash Transfer Programme, Productive Activities and Labour Supply: Evidence from a Randomized Experiment in Kenya." *Journal of Development Studies* 50 (8): 1172–96.

Atkinson, T. 2009. "A Stress Test for the Welfare State." In *Aftershocks: Economic Crisis and Institutional Choice*, edited by A. Hemerijck, B. Knapen, and E. Van Doorne, 207–11. Amsterdam: Amsterdam University Press.

Bahadur, A., K. Peters, E. Wilkinson, F. Pichon, K. Gray, and T. Tanner. 2015. "The 3As: Tracking Resilience across BRACED." Working Paper, Building Resilience and Adaptation to Climate Extremes and Disasters (BRACED), London.

Banerjee, A., E. Duflo, N. Goldberg, D. Karlan, R. Osei, W. Parienté, J. Shapiro, B. Thuysbaert, and C. Udry. 2015. "A Multifaceted Program Causes Lasting Progress for the Very Poor: Evidence from Six Countries." *Science* 348 (6236): 1260799.

Barca, V. 2018. "Setting the Scene: Building on Existing Systems for Adaptive Social Protection." Background Paper, Oxford Policy Management, Oxford, UK.

Barca, V., S. Brook, J. Holland, and M. Otulana. 2015. *Qualitative Research and Analysis of the Economic Impacts of Cash Transfer Programmes in Sub-Saharan Africa, Synthesis Report.* Rome: Food and Agriculture Organization of the United Nations.

Barca, V., and C. O'Brien. 2017. "Factors Affecting the Usefulness of Existing Social Protection Databases in Disaster Preparedness and Response." Policy Brief. Oxford Policy Management, Oxford, UK. https://assets.publishing.service.gov.uk/media/5a942c50ed915d57d4d0ef98 /Policy-Brief-Factors-affecting-usefulness-existing-social-protection-databases.pdf.

Bastagli, F. 2014. "Responding to a Crisis: The Design and Delivery of Social Protection." ODI Working Paper, Overseas Development Institute, London.

Bastagli, F., J. Hagen-Zanker, L. Harman, V. Barca, G. Sturge, and T. Schmidt. 2016. "Cash Transfers: What Does the Evidence Say? A Rigorous Review of Programme Impact and of the Role of Design and Implementation Features." Overseas Development Institute, London. https://www.odi.org/sites/odi.org.uk/files/resource-documents/11316.pdf.

Bastagli, F., and R. Holmes. 2014. "Delivering Social Protection in the Aftermath of a Shock: Lessons from Bangladesh, Kenya, Pakistan, and Viet Nam." Overseas Development Institute, London.

Beazley, R. 2017a. "Study on Shock-Responsive Social Protection in Latin America and the Caribbean: Dominican Republic Case Study." Oxford Policy Management, Oxford, UK. https://www.opml.co.uk/files/Publications/a1537-shock-responsive-social-protection -latin-america-caribbean/dominican-republic-case-study.pdf?noredirect=1.

Beazley, R. 2017b. "Study on Shock-Responsive Social Protection in Latin America and the Caribbean: Ecuador Case Study." Oxford Policy Management, Oxford, UK.

Beazley, R., and M. Farhat. 2016. "How Can Lump-Sum Cash Transfers Be Designed to Improve Their Productive Potential." Working Paper, Oxford Policy Management, Oxford, UK.

Beazley, R., A. McCord, and A. Solórzano. 2016. "Public Works Programmes for Protection and Climate Resilience: Theory of Change and Evidence in Low-Income Countries." One Pager 335. International Policy Centre for Inclusive Growth, Brasilia.

Beazley, R., A. Solórzano, and V. Barca. 2019. "Study on Shock-Responsive Social Protection in Latin America and the Caribbean: Summary of Key Findings and Policy Recommendations." Oxford Policy Management, Oxford, UK.

Beegle, K., A. Coudouel, and E. Monsalve. 2018. *Realizing the Full Potential of Social Safety Nets in Africa.* Washington, DC: World Bank. http://documents.worldbank.org/curated /en/657581531930611436/pdf/128594-PUB-PUBLIC.pdf.

Bossuroy, T., and P. Premand. 2016. "Boosting Productive Inclusion and Resilience of the Poor: Perspectives from the Sahel Adaptive Social Protection Program." Presentation. World Bank, Washington, DC.

Bowen, T. 2015. "Social Protection and Disaster Risk Management in the Philippines: The Case of Typhoon Yolanda (Haiyan)." Policy Research Working Paper 7482, World Bank, Washington, DC. http://documents.worldbank.org/curated/en/681881468181128752/pdf /WPS7482.pdf.

Cabot Venton, C., C. Fitzgibbon, T. Shitarek, L. Coulter, and O. Dooley. 2012. "The Economics of Early Response and Disaster Resilience: Lessons from Kenya and Ethiopia: Economics of Resilience Final Report." Department for International Development, London.

Coll-Black, S., C. Holmemo, J. Sandford, and W. Soer. Forthcoming. *From Programs to Systems: A Decade of Lessons Learned from Designing and Implementing Ethiopia's Productive Safety Net Program.* Washington, DC: World Bank.

Cull, R., T. Ehrbeck, and N. Holle. 2014. "Financial Inclusion and Development. Recent Impact Evaluation." Focus Note 92. Consultative Group to Assist the Poor, Washington, DC.

Daidone, S., L. Pellerano, S. Handa, and B. Davis. 2015. "Is Graduation from Social Safety Nets Possible? Evidence from Sub-Saharan Africa." *IDS Bulletin* 46 (2): 93–102.

Dammert, A., J. J. de Hoop, E. Myukiyehe, and F. C. Rosati. 2018. "Effects of Public Policy on Child Labor. Current Knowledge, Gaps, and Implications for Program Design." *World Development* 110: 104–23.

Davis, B. 2014. "The Impact of Social Cash Transfers on Labour Market Outcomes: The Evidence from Sub-Saharan Africa." International Seminar and Policy Forum, Instituto de Pesquisa Econômica Aplicada Headquarters, Brasilia, September 2014.

del Ninno, C., F. Pierre, and S. Coll-Black. 2016. *Social Protection Programs for Africa's Drylands.* Washington, DC: World Bank. http://documents.worldbank.org/curated/en/736221 471343475745/pdf/107854-PUB-PUBLIC-PUBDATE-8-9-16.pdf.

Deryugina, T. 2016. "The Fiscal Cost of Hurricanes: Disaster Aid versus Social Insurance." *American Economic Journal: Economic Policy* 9 (3): 168–98.

Esteves, T., K. V. Rao, B. Sinha, S. S. Roy, B. B. Rai, I. B. Rao, N. Sharma, S. Rao, V. Patil, I. K. Murthy, J. Srinivasan, R. K. Chaturvedi, J. Sharma, S. K. Jha, S. Mishra, A. B. Singh, H. S. Rakhroy, S. Rai, R. Sharma, S. Schwan, K. Basu, N. Guerten, I. Porsché, N. Ranjan, K. K. Tripathy, and N. H. Ravindranath. 2013. "Environmental Benefits and Vulnerability Reduction through Mahatma Gandhi Rural Employment Guarantee Scheme (NREGS): Synthesis Report." Ministry of Rural Development, Government of India and Deutsche Gesellschaft für Internationale Zusammenarbeit (GIZ), New Delhi.

Ethiopia, Ministry of Agriculture. 2014. "Productive Safety Net Programme Phase IV, Programme Implementation Manual." Ministry of Agriculture, Addis Ababa. https://www.usaid.gov /sites/default/files/documents/1866/psnp_iv_programme_implementation_manual_14 _dec_14.pdf.

Fallavier, P. 2014. "Social Protection in the Sahel's Drylands: A Review of the Literature on Climate-Adaptive Social Protection for Use in the Sahel." World Bank, Washington, DC.

Fan, J., and I. Gijbels. 1996. *Local Polynomial Modelling and Its Applications.* New York: Chapman and Hall.

FAO (Food and Agriculture Organization of the United Nations). 2016. *Adapting Agriculture to Climate Change. FAO's Work on Climate Change Adaptation.* Rome: FAO. http://www.fao .org/3/a-i6273e.pdf.

FAO (Food and Agriculture Organization of the United Nations). 2019. *Managing Climate Risks through Social Protection, Reducing Rural Poverty and Building Resilient Agricultural Livelihoods.* Rome: FAO.

FNS (Food and Nutrition Service). 2014. "Disaster SNAP Guidance: Policy Guidance, Lessons Learned, and Toolkits to Operate a Successful D-SNAP." U.S. Department of Agriculture, Washington, DC. https://fns-prod.azureedge.net/sites/default/files/D-SNAP_handbook_0.pdf.

FSIN (Food Security Information Network). 2015. "Measuring Shocks and Stressors as Part of Resilience Measurement." Technical Series 5. Resilience Measurement Technical Working Group, FSIN Secretariat, World Food Programme. http://www.fsincop.net/fileadmin/user _upload/fsin/docs/resources/1_FSIN_TechnicalSeries_5.pdf.

Gentilini, U. 2019. "By When Would Universal Social Protection Be Achieved?" Blog post, January 17. Let's Talk Development, World Bank. https://blogs.worldbank.org /developmenttalk/when-would-universal-social-protection-be-achieved.

Grosh, M., C. Andrews, R. Quintana, and C. Rodriguez-Atlas. 2011. "Assessing Safety Net Readiness in Response to Food Price Volatility." SP Discussion Paper 1118, World Bank, Washington, DC. https://www.securenutrition.org/sites/default/files/resources /attachment/english/WBG_Assessing%20safety%20net%20readiness_food%20price%20 volatility.pdf.

Grosh, M., C. del Ninno, E. Tesliuc, and A. Ouerghi. 2008. *For Protection and Promotion: The Design and Implementation of Effective Safety Nets.* Washington, DC: World Bank. https:// siteresources.worldbank.org/SPLP/Resources/461653-1207162275268/For_Protection _and_Promotion908.pdf.

Hallegatte, S., M. Bangalore, L. Bonzanigo, M. Fay, T. Kane, U. Narloch, J. Rozenberg, D. Treguer, and A. Vogt-Schlib. 2016. *Shock Waves: Managing the Impacts of Climate Change on Poverty.* Washington, DC: World Bank.

Haushofer, J., and J. Shapiro. 2013. "Household Response to Income Changes: Evidence from an Unconditional Cash Transfer Program in Kenya." Massachusetts Institute of Technology, Cambridge, MA.

Hidrobo, M., J. Hoddinott, J. Kumar, and M. Oliver. 2018. "Social Protection, Food Security, and Asset Formation." *World Development* 101: 88–103.

Hill, R., E. Skoufias, and B. P. Maher. 2019. *The Chronology of Disaster: A Review and Assessment of the Value of Acting Early on Household Welfare*. Washington, DC: World Bank. http://documents.worldbank.org/curated/en/796341557483493173/pdf/The-Chronology-of-a-Disaster-A-Review-and-Assessment-of-the-Value-of-Acting-Early-on-Household-Welfare.pdf.

IEG (Independent Evaluation Group). 2011. *Social Safety Nets: An Evaluation of World Bank Support, 2000–2010*. Washington, DC: World Bank.

Isik-Dikmelik, A. 2012. "Do Social Benefits Respond to Crises? Evidence from Europe and Central Asia during the Global Crisis." Social Protection and Labor Discussion Paper 1219. World Bank, Washington, DC. http://documents.worldbank.org/curated/en/709131468283465435/pdf/NonAsciiFileName0.pdf.23EDWS

ISPA (Inter-Agency Social Protection Assessments). 2017. *Social Protection Payment Delivery Mechanisms: What Matters Guidance Note*. Washington, DC: World Bank. https://ispatools.org/tools/payments-what-matters.pdf.

Jorgensen, S., and P. Siegel. 2019. "Social Protection in an Era of Increasing Uncertainty and Disruption: Social Risk Management 2.0." Social Protection and Jobs Discussion Paper 1930, World Bank, Washington, DC. http://documents.worldbank.org/curated/en/263761559643240069/pdf/Social-Protection-in-an-Era-of-Increasing-Uncertainty-and-Disruption-Social-Risk-Management-2-0.pdf.

Kanbur, R. 2009. "Systemic Crises and the Social Protection System: Three Proposals for World Bank Action." Cornell University, Ithaca, NY.

Kardan, A., S. Bailey, A. Solórzano, and L. Fidalgo. 2017. "Shock-Responsive Social Protection Systems Research Case Study: Mozambique." Oxford Policy Management, Oxford, UK.

Kaur, N., D. Steinbach, A. Agrawal, C. Manuel, S. Saigal, A. Panjiyar, C. Shakya, and A. Norton. 2017. "Building Resilience to Climate Change: MGNREGS and Climate-Induced Droughts in Sikkim." IIED Issue Paper. International Institute for Environment and Development, London.

Karlan, D. W. Parienté, C. Udry, T. Bossuroy, M. Goldstein, H. Kazianga, P. Premand, and J. Vaillant. 2017. "Promoting Productive Inclusion and Resilience in National Safety Nets: A Four-Country Evaluation in the Sahel." Abdul Lateef Jameel Poverty Action Lab, J-PAL. Cambridge, MA. https://www.povertyactionlab.org/evaluation/promoting-productive-inclusion-and-resilience-national-safety-nets-four-country.

Knippenberg, E., and J. Hoddinott. 2017. "Shocks, Social Protection, and Resilience: Evidence from Ethiopia." Ethiopia Strategy Support Program Working Paper 109, International Food Policy Research Institute, Washington, DC.

Lindert, K., T. George, I. Rodriguez-Caillava, and Kenichi Nishikawa. Forthcoming. *A Sourcebook on the Foundations of Social Protection Delivery Systems*. Washington, DC: World Bank.

Macours, K., P. Premand, and R. Vakis. 2012. "Transfers, Diversification and Household Risk Strategies: Experimental Evidence with Lessons for Climate Change Adaptation." Policy Research Working Paper 6053, World Bank, Washington, DC. http://documents.worldbank.org/curated/en/275241468340175496/pdf/WPS6053.pdf.

Mansur, A., J. Doyle, J. Gerome, and O. Ivaschenko. 2017. "Social Protection and Humanitarian Assistance Nexus for Disaster Response: Lessons Learnt from Fiji's Tropical Cyclone Winston." Social Protection and Labor Discussion Paper 1701. World Bank, Washington, DC. http://documents.worldbank.org/curated/en/143591490296944528/pdf/113710-NWP-PUBLIC-P159592-1701.pdf.

Mariotti, C., M. Ulrichs, and L. Harman. 2016. "Sustainable Escapes from Poverty through Productive Inclusion: A Policy Guide on the Role of Social Protection." CPAN Policy Guide 7. Chronic Poverty Advisory Network, London.

Marzo, F., and H. Mori. 2012. "Crisis Response in Social Protection." Social Protection and Labor Discussion Paper 1205. World Bank, Washington, DC. http://siteresources.worldbank.org/SOCIALPROTECTION/Resources/SP-Discussion-papers/430578-1331508552354/1205.pdf.

Mauritania, Commissariat a la Securite Aimentare (CSA). 2019. "Programme de filets sociaux reactifs aux chocs Elmaouna: Manuel operationnel," Version 2.0.

McCord, A. 2013. "Review of the Literature on Social Protection Shock Responses and Readiness." ODI Shockwatch. Overseas Development Institute, London.

McCord, A., R. Beazley, A. Solórzano, and L. Artur. 2016. "ICF Social Protection and Climate Change in Mozambique with a Focus on the Role of the PASP: Feasibility and Design Consultancy." Final Report. Overseas Development Institute, London.

Mexico, Government of. 2018. "Rules of Operation: Social Inclusion Program PROSPERA (Reglas de operación de prospera programa de inclusión social)." Government of Mexico: Mexico City.

O'Brien, C., J. Congrave, K. Sharp, and N. Keïta. 2018a. "Shock-Responsive Social Protection Systems Research: Case Study—Social Protection and Humanitarian Responses to Food Insecurity and Poverty in Mali." Oxford Policy Management, Oxford, UK.

O'Brien, C., R. Holmes, Z. Scott, and V. Barca. 2018b. "Shock-Responsive Social Protection Systems Toolkit—Appraising the Use of Social Protection in Addressing Largescale Shocks." Oxford Policy Management, Oxford, UK.

OPM (Oxford Policy Management). 2017. *Shock-Responsive Social Protection Systems Research: Literature Review*, 2nd edition. Oxford, UK: OPM.

PEI (Partnership for Economic Inclusion). 2016. "Increasing the Income Earning Opportunities of Poor and Vulnerable People." World Bank, Washington, DC. https://www .microfinancegateway.org/sites/default/files/announcement/pei-brochure.pdf.

Roelen, K., S. Devereux, A. G. Abdulai, B. Martorano, T. Palermo, and L. P. Ragno. 2017. "How to Make 'Cash Plus' Work: Linking Cash Transfers to Services and Sectors." Innoncenti Working Paper 2017-10. United Nations Children's Fund Office of Research, Florence.

Samson, M. 2015. "Exit or Developmental Impact? The Role of 'Graduation' in Social Protection Programmes." *IDS Bulletin* 46: 13–24.

Solórzano, A. 2016. "Can Social Protection Increase Resilience to Climate Change? A Case Study of Oportunidades in Rural Yucatan, Mexico." IDS Working Paper 465, Centre for Social Protection and Institute of Development Studies, Brighton, UK.

Steinbach D., N. Kaur, C. Manuel, S. Saigal, A. Agrawal, A. Panjiyar, and A. Barnwal. 2017a. "Building Resilience to Climate Change: MGNREGS and Drought in Jharkhand." IIED Issue Paper, IIED London.

Steinbach, D., N. Kaur, C. Manuel, S. Saigal, A. Agrawal, A. Panjiyar, and A. Barnwal. 2017b. "Building Resilience to Climate Change: MGNREGS and Cyclones in Andhra Pradesh." IIED Issue Paper, IIED London.

Steinbach, D., N. Kaur, C. Manuel, S. Saigal, A. Agrawal, and A. Panjiyar. 2017c. "Building Resilience to Climate Change: MGNREGS, Drought and Flooding in Odisha." IIED Issue Paper, IIED, London.

Subbarao, Kalanidhi, Carlo del Ninno, Colin Andrews, and Claudia Rodríguez-Alas. 2013. *Public Works as a Safety Net: Design, Evidence, and Implementation*. Washington, DC: World Bank. https://openknowledge.worldbank.org/handle/10986/11882.

Tenzing, J. D. 2019. "Integrating Social Protection and Climate Change Adaptation: A Review." *WIREs Climate Change* 11 (2): e626.

Ulrichs, M., and R. Slater. 2016. "How Can Social Protection Build Resilience? Insights from Ethiopia, Kenya and Uganda." Working Paper, Building Resilience and Adaptation to Climate Extremes and Disasters (BRACED), London.

WFP (World Food Programme). 2015. "Policy on Building Resilience for Food Security and Nutrition." WFP/EB.A/2015/5-C. WFP, Rome. https://documents.wfp.org/stellent/groups /public/documents/eb/wfpdoc063833.pdf?_ga=2.20959473.817428444.1582152603-7527 67465.1554223343.

WFP (World Food Programme). 2018. "Scaling Up for Resilient Individuals, Communities and Systems in the Sahel." Fact Sheet. WFP, Rome. https://docs.wfp.org/api/documents/WFP -0000110238/download/?_ga=2.26639604.817428444.1582152603-752767465.1554223343.

World Bank. 2013. *Building Resilience to Disaster and Climate Change through Social Protection: Synthesis Note.* Washington, DC: World Bank. http://documents.worldbank.org/curated /en/187211468349778714/pdf/796210WP0Build0Box0377381B00PUBLIC0.pdf.

World Bank. 2018a. *Fundamentals of Disaster Risk Finance. Disaster Risk Financing and Insurance.* Washington, DC: World Bank, Open Learning Campus.

World Bank. 2018b. "Second Niger Adaptive Safety Net Project: Project Appraisal Document." World Bank, Washington, DC. http://documents.worldbank.org/curated/en/77793 1546830037773/Niger-Second-Niger-Adaptive-Safety-Net-Project.

2 Data and Information
UNDERSTANDING RISK AND HOUSEHOLD VULNERABILITY

OVERVIEW

Data and information strengthening are at the core of the adaptive social protection (ASP) agenda. That is, fundamentally, there is a need to invest in a stronger understanding of risk and household vulnerability to shocks within the social protection (SP) sector in order to understand who is likely to be most at-risk to which kinds of shocks, as a basis for designing appropriate programs.

This will require a multisectoral approach to the collection, sharing, and analysis of data. Concretely, the insights provided from the analyses typically undertaken by the disaster risk management (DRM) community can contribute to an improved understanding of spatial disaster risk as a function of the historical hazard incidence and the exposure and vulnerability of assets and people. Integrating these analyses with the data on household-level poverty and vulnerability routinely undertaken as the basis for safety net program design and held in SP information systems promises to provide a more complete picture of household-level vulnerability to shocks.

To this end, the information systems that inform the delivery of SP programs require strengthening for ASP. In turn, these information systems themselves will become more capable of generating increasingly relevant data to refine analyses of household risk and vulnerability and programs that are more capable of building resilience.

First and foremost, social registries that hold valuable information on beneficiaries and non-beneficiaries will enable safety net programs to identify those most vulnerable to shocks when they expand into, and deepen their coverage within high-risk areas. Moreover, the closer integration of social registries with those information systems leveraged by the DRM and humanitarian sectors will further sensitize the SP information system, informing ASP programs. Critically, fostering operational linkages with early warning systems alongside tools that enable the rapid assessment of post-shock needs will be transformative in predicting household needs and assessing them after a shock.

To do so, considerable investment in and coordination with actors and information systems from outside of the SP sector will be required to strengthen information for ASP.

This chapter draws extensively from a background paper by Beazley and Barca (2018).

INVESTING IN AN IMPROVED UNDERSTANDING OF RISK AND HOUSEHOLD VULNERABILITY

Information on household vulnerability to disasters is crucial for the design and implementation of ASP programs. What kinds of hazards does the country face? How frequently? Where? Which assets and population groups are exposed, and among them which are the most vulnerable? What is their capacity to cope? The analysis of disaster risk is a core pillar of operational work conducted in the DRM sector. ASP programs will need to draw on these analyses and assessments of disaster risk and to integrate them with assessments of household poverty, vulnerability to poverty, and the relative ability for households to cope with shocks.

Household risk and vulnerability analyses attempt to better understand the impact of shocks on poverty. Recent studies have used weather data as objective measures of shocks and have analyzed impacts on poverty (Gao and Mills 2018; Hill and Porter 2017; Skoufias et al. 2019). Risk and vulnerability analyses carried out under the first phases of the Sahel ASP Program in Burkina Faso, Chad, Niger, and Senegal focused on developing such analyses to identify the populations most vulnerable to climatic shocks. At the same time, resilience to shocks often has been measured as the ability to not become poor or food insecure in the face of adverse shocks based on factors such as distance from the poverty line, probability of exposure to shocks, and the impact of shocks on consumption-based measures of household well-being (see, for example, Gao and Mills 2018). Such analyses provide an informed, needs-based foundation for ASP policy dialogue and program design. (For a discussion of information needs for targeting assistance following shocks, see, for example, del Ninno and Mills 2015.)

Risk and vulnerability analysis represents a clear point of intersection and complementarity for both SP and DRM. Traditionally, the DRM sector has focused on analyzing the vulnerability of assets and physical structures (such as buildings and roads) to disasters, whereas the SP community has focused on the analysis of household poverty (often as a proxy for vulnerability to shocks) and vulnerability to poverty as an outcome from shocks. Integrated SP and DRM analyses hold the potential for generating a deeper understanding of disaster risk, household exposure, and household impacts which are often highly heterogenous. As an example, in emphasizing the vulnerability of poor households to disasters, Hallegatte et al. (2017) developed a variable for measuring disaster risk called "socioeconomic resilience" that encompasses the effects of asset losses on household income, consumption, and well-being. Based on estimates of socioeconomic resilience in 117 countries and including in the analysis how poverty and lack of capacity to cope with disasters magnify losses in well-being, the authors suggest that the effects of floods, wind storms, earthquakes, and tsunamis on well-being are equivalent to a $520 billion drop in consumption—60 percent more than the widely reported assessment of asset losses. The measure also accounts for increases in household resilience that accompany the introduction and expansion of ASP in a country (see box 2.1).

BOX 2.1

Analyzing socioeconomic resilience and the potential impact of ASP

Socioeconomic resilience models the effects of asset losses on income, consumption, and well-being at the household level. It also measures the expected increases to household resilience that accompany the development (introduction and expansion) of social protection in a country. Socioeconomic resilience demonstrates the value of joining vulnerability analyses related to social protection and disaster risk management (DRM), and it may be a useful starting point for a social protection–DRM engagement looking to quantify the vulnerability and resilience co-benefits of social protection systems.

Socioeconomic resilience complements and extends traditional DRM analyses. Hazard, exposure, and physical vulnerability quantify asset losses but do not allow DRM interventions or social protection systems to incorporate the fact that poor households experience and recover from a given amount of asset losses differently than do wealthy households. Nor do they decode the complex factors that determine how

likely a household is to recover from its losses without assistance.

Socioeconomic resilience links directly to the co-benefits of ASP engagements. Traditional DRM analyses measure the costs of interventions relative to the benefits of avoided asset losses, and therefore cannot quantify the real benefits of ASP programs—which help households to smooth income and consumption losses, accelerate recovery, and prepare for future hazards, though they do not affect asset losses. Conversely, the design and budgeting of ASP programs will in most cases need to incorporate DRM inputs—especially geographical and socioeconomic heterogeneity in asset and well-being risk—in order to deliver targeted, timely assistance. Sample applications of the socioeconomic resilience model in Sri Lanka and the Philippines can be found in Walsh and Hallegatte (2019a, 2019b), including the modeled impact of ASP on well-being outcomes.

Source: Hallegatte et al. 2017.

SOCIAL REGISTRIES AT THE HEART OF THE ASP INFORMATION AGENDA

Beyond foundational analyses of risk and vulnerability, the global expansion of social registries is framing much of the current discussion around the ASP information agenda (Barca 2017; Bastagli 2014; Bastagli et al. 2016; IEG 2011; Kuriakose et al. 2012). Social registries are information systems that support outreach, intake, registration, and the determination of potential eligibility for inclusion in one or more social programs. Ultimately, social registries provide a "gateway" for potential inclusion of intended populations into SP programs (figure 2.1). Social registries can serve as a gateway to one or many programs. When multiple programs use a common social registry or integrated social registry, they can play an important social policy role in helping coordinate efforts to reach intended populations. This facilitates synergies across programs aiming to deliver complementary benefits and services to common groups. Recent estimates suggest that at least 60 countries have social registries, while 18 countries have beneficiary

FIGURE 2.1

Social registry as a gateway for multiple programs

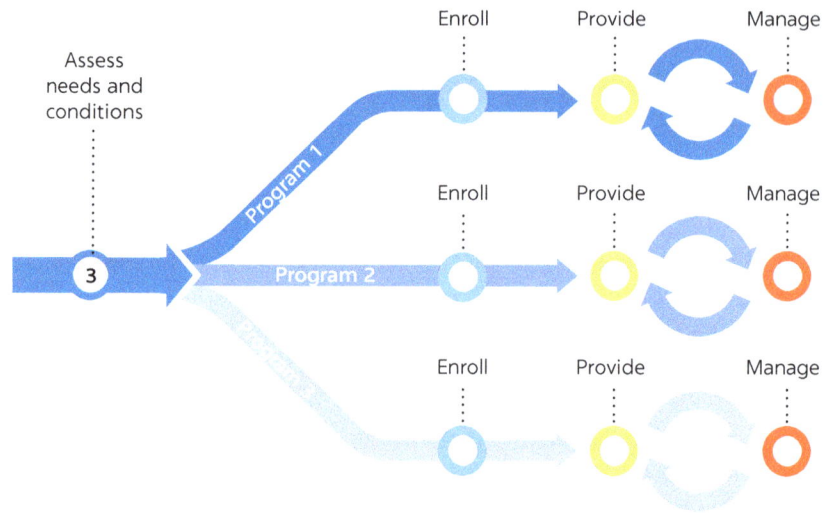

Source: Lindert et al., forthcoming.

TABLE 2.1 Beneficiary and social registries: Terminology

TERM	DEFINITION
Beneficiary registry	• Track beneficiary/benefit(s) to support program management and implementation • A household is referred to as a "beneficiary"
Integrated beneficiary registry	• Monitor and coordinate benefits • Support identification of intended/unintended duplications across programs • Better-integrate services across programs
Social registry	• Support outreach, intake, registration, and assessment of needs and conditions to determine eligibility for social programs • Contain and maintain information on all registered households regardless of beneficiary/nonbeneficiary status • A household is referred to as a "registered household"
Integrated social registry	• Monitor and coordinate across programs

Sources: Based on Barca 2017; Leite et al. 2017.

registries (table 2.1). Social registries play a key role in providing necessary information to operate ASP programs, such as the information base for building resilience and scaling up after a shock.

However, the expansion of social registries alone may not meet the information requirements for ASP. Many countries operate registries with "fixed lists" of registrants and program beneficiaries, and they generally update the lists every four to five years based on a census sweep approach (figure 2.2). Thus, many static registries operating fixed lists often comprise dated information along with partial coverage. Box 2.2 compares the coverage of social registries in four countries to demonstrate the varying population shares that are more or less easily identified and reached with assistance after a shock.

FIGURE 2.2

Social registries: Global coverage and registration processes

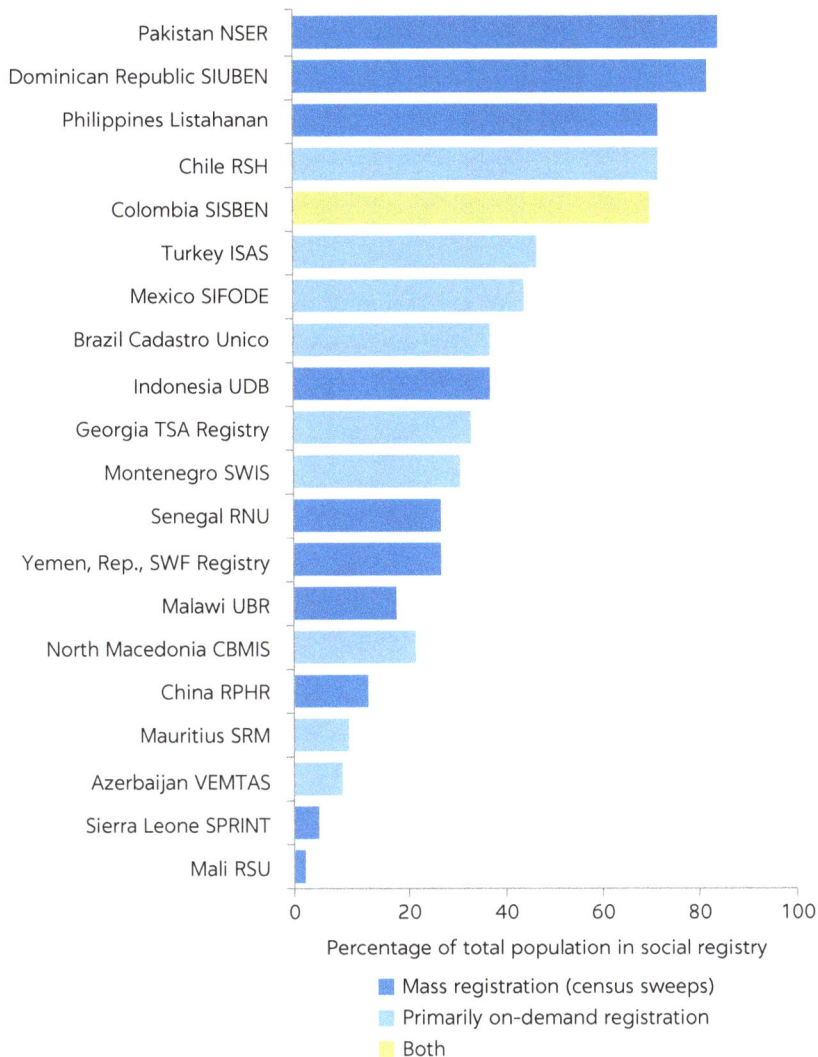

Source: Leite et al. 2017.
Note: CBMIS = Cash Benefits Management Information System; ISAS = Integrated Social Assistance System; NSER = National Socio-Economic Registry; RNU = Unified National Registry; RPHR = Rural Poor Household Registry; RSH = Households Social Registry; RSU = Unified Social Registry; SIFODE = Integrated System for Development; SISBEN = Beneficiary Identification System; SIUBEN = Unique Beneficiary Identification System; SPRINT = Social Protection Registry for Integrated National Targeting; SRM = Social Registry (Mauritius); SWF = Social Welfare Funds; SWIS = Social Welfare Information System; TSA Targeted Social Assistance; UBR = Unified Beneficiary Registry; UDB = Unified Data Base; VEMTAS = Electronic Application and Appointment Subsystem.

The data collected for social registries often do not differ substantially from that required for identifying households that are vulnerable to shocks. A recent study from the World Bank (Schnitzer 2018) compares two of the most widely used approaches to target poor and vulnerable households: proxy means testing, which is designed to identify the chronic poor, and the household economy approach, which is a livelihoods analysis framework. The paper finds that proxy means testing better identifies the chronic poor, and the household economy approach better identifies households suffering from seasonal food insecurity. Most importantly, it highlights that both rely largely on the same household

BOX 2.2

Lesotho, Mozambique, Pakistan, and the Philippines: Social registry coverage and utility for shock response

The panels in figure B2.2.1, developed by Oxford Policy Management, compare and contrast social protection databases in four of the research countries, showcasing completeness of social registry data where a registry exists (the dark blue oval) and completeness of beneficiary data for one or more noncontributory social protection program(s) (the green oval). It also introduces an arbitrarily sized group of households potentially affected by any given shock to show how existing data can be used for vertical expansion (temporary increase of the value/duration for existing beneficiaries) of the social protection scheme, horizontal expansion (temporary expansion of the caseload), or piggybacking on the social protection database to provide an emergency response.

FIGURE B2.2.1

Coverage of selected social protection databases in four countries

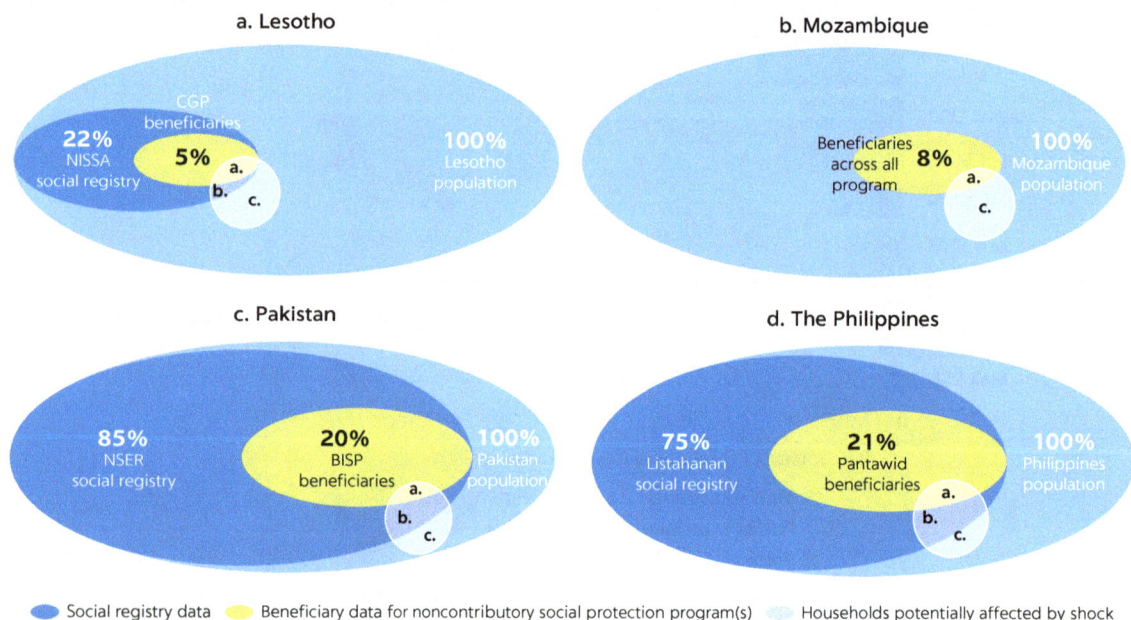

a. Lesotho

b. Mozambique

c. Pakistan

d. The Philippines

Social registry data   Beneficiary data for noncontributory social protection program(s)   Households potentially affected by shock

Source: Barca and O'Brien 2017.
Note: BISP = Benazir Income Support Program; CGP = Child Grants Program; NISSA = National Information System for Social Assistance; NSER = National Socio-Economic Registry. Figures do not represent the totality of social protection databases in each country.
a = households that can be reached through vertical expansion or piggybacking (on the beneficiary databases); b = households that can be easily reached through horizontal expansion or piggybacking (on the social registry); c = households less easily reached through horizontal expansion or piggybacking (not covered by existing social protection databases).

information. As a result, small tweaks to the data collected for a social registry can enable easier and more accurate estimation not only households in chronic poverty but also those vulnerable to shocks and their capacity to cope.

The additional data required for social registries depend on the shocks that affect a country, the predominant household livelihoods in high-risk areas, and the coping mechanisms utilized by poor and vulnerable households. In the case of seasonal droughts, for example, data on food insecurity and livelihoods can help to identify vulnerable households. In relation to livelihoods, high reliance on agricultural activities can imply high vulnerability in regions prone to floods and droughts. In the case of seasonal floods, typhoons, or hurricanes, the additional data could relate to the location of households, such as living in coastal locations, or to the proximity to rivers, streams, or ravines as areas at risk of flooding as identified by DRM models. Social registries that contain geo-referenced household data can be more effective and precise in assessing household exposure to shocks, in coordination with hazard data from the DRM sector. When this information is overlaid with data from risk and vulnerability assessments and hazard risk mappings, the government will have a powerful tool to help determine who should be supported and where. In the Philippines, the Disaster Response Management Bureau utilized the social registry, Listahanan, to estimate the number of households that would be affected by a disaster given its location/path (Bowen 2015).

Expanding the coverage of social registries in high-risk areas may be particularly effective in contexts of recurrent or seasonal shocks where household needs may be more predictable. In Mauritania, the government developed a methodology to determine the ideal coverage (number of households) the social registry should have in each commune to ensure it was capable of informing shock response to drought. The analysis of vulnerability to food insecurity from drought recommended including an additional 50,000 households (distributed proportionally across communes considering hazard vulnerability and exposure indexes). Kenya's Hunger Safety Net Program (HSNP) is commonly cited in the literature as the prime example of collecting operationally relevant data in advance of a shock, allowing horizontal expansions to preidentified vulnerable households in times of need. The program has registered almost all of the households in the four participating high-risk counties—nearly 300,000—and preenrolled them, giving them bank accounts into which post-shock payments can be deposited. A key component of the consolidation process was the launch of a computerized management information system, the Single Registry, in 2016.

DATA QUALITY CONSIDERATIONS FOR ASP

Ultimately, ASP requires a clear vision for improving data quality. Barca and O'Brien (2017) provide a useful framing to consider the five main dimensions of data quality in a shock-responsive setting: completeness, relevance, currency, accessibility, and accuracy. Given no data can perfectly cover all these dimensions, it is very context-specific whether ASP programs can rely on available data and information. In some contexts, data that are not completely relevant or up-to-date or do not cover the whole population affected by the shock can still be the best vehicle for providing timely support. In other contexts, the opposite may be true, with incomplete and outdated data undermining a response. Table 2.2 analyzes the five main dimensions of data quality—completeness, relevance, currency, accessibility, and accuracy (Barca and O'Brien 2017).

The data quality of existing SP information systems for shock response can be determined by a number of factors. In line with the literature, "data quality" is here defined as data fit for use by users (Wang and Strong 1996). In this particular case, the users are the government (or humanitarian actors) involved in preparedness and response to shocks. Whereas for data from the SP sector, "the nature and quality of SP [social protection] databases and information systems is

TABLE 2.2 Implications of the different dimensions of data quality for adaptive social protection

DIMENSION	DEFINITION	IMPLICATIONS FOR USE OF EXISTING SOCIAL PROTECTION DATA	IMPLICATIONS FOR DIFFERENT SHOCKS
Completeness	Number of records compared with what would be perceived as a full set of records	• Depends on the overlap (if any) of households that are currently beneficiaries of a program and those affected by the shock. • Higher coverage and uniform coverage across geographic areas (regions, urban/rural) is desirable.	• Extensive coverage in regions affected by recurrent shocks. • Overlap of poverty and vulnerability depends on the shock; such as rapid-onset shocks, economic crises, pandemics, and conflicts are more likely to affect the nonpoor (who often are not covered by existing databases) than other shocks.
Relevance	Contains the requisite variables for the intended purpose	• More useful if the data include variables that can help predict vulnerability to shocks. • More useful if the data include operational information; such as location, contacts, and bank-account details. • In the case of nonbeneficiaries, inclusion of socioeconomic data can help prioritize post-shock support.	• Operational data are relevant for any shock. • Socioeconomic data may be more relevant for certain shocks; such as economic, slow-onset, and recurrent.
Currency	Degree to which data are up to date	• Data will never reflect the situation after a shock but the more up-to-date the better. • The status depends on the underlying approach to data collection (on-demand approaches are more flexible) and information management.	• Conflict or rapid-onset disasters may cause widespread internal displacement, split up households, and significantly change their material circumstances.
Accessibility	Refers to the ease for potential users	• Digital data (maintained/stored) can increase accessibility. • Data-sharing agreements need to be defined in advance. • While accessibility is critical, provisions for data security are important to ensure privacy of beneficiary data.	• The challenges of accessing a database are compounded in a conflict or rapid-onset natural disaster. • In conflicts, security concerns around the sharing of personal information are particularly acute.
Accuracy (integrity)	Data are considered to be accurate if free of errors and omissions; meaning, trustworthy	• Accuracy increases with processes to verify and validate existing data; such as supervision and cross-checks with other databases. • A function of the perceived trustworthiness of the institution responsible for collecting and housing the data. • In poverty-targeted programs, high errors of inclusion and exclusion affect perceived accuracy and may affect the usability of data for responses.	• Accuracy is relevant for all shocks. • Accuracy is particularly problematic where trust between actors is already undermined; such as conflicts.

Source: Beazley and Barca 2018.

so varied that it is meaningless to ascribe a generic role to their use in shock responses, and inappropriate to assert that they will always be of use: such a role can only be identified with reference to the particularities of the database(s) in the country and context under review" (Barca and O'Brien 2017, 5).

A major challenge for improving data quality is that high-frequency data are required to properly monitor and assess risk and vulnerability. This can be a challenge in low-capacity and dynamic contexts where new risks are unfolding (such as refugee inflows). For example, in Turkey, the government, with financial support from the European Union, responded to the Syrian refugee influx by scaling up the existing SP system. Although facing a language issue for registration and placing additional burdens on local officials, its strong delivery infrastructure allowed for the inclusion of refugees for emergency social assistance. This process was undertaken with substantial support from the Turkish Red Crescent, a local nongovernmental organization with a strong field network.

Rapid progress in the SP sector with the use of biometrics, identification, and e-payments is providing a game-changing backdrop to the ASP information agenda. Technology can broaden the potential reach of SP programs and cash transfers—a strategy that works to raise productivity and resilience among beneficiaries in times of shock (box 2.3). In India, the Aadhaar Program uses biometric technology to make it easier for the poor to prove their identity and to authenticate the beneficiaries of dozens of social programs. The program, which covers 1.2 billion people, has provided government cost savings by improving efficiency, reducing transaction costs, and providing the infrastructure for reform—as in the case of the Pahal/LPG subsidy program (Mittal et al. 2017). Despite ongoing difficulties and concerns related to beneficiary privacy that remain to be addressed, the program has enjoyed a high rate of satisfaction (92 percent) and trust in the system and has been responsible for increasing financial inclusion (72 percent of adults have linked their bank accounts to Aadhaar) (Sonderegger et al. 2019). In Lebanon, electronic smart cards support 125,000 Syrian refugee households; the program was such a success that the government of Lebanon now uses smart cards for its social programs.

There are other important opportunities to leverage technology for low-income, fragile, and conflict-affected areas. In recent years, for example, there has been growing interest in the use of remote sensing, geographic information system data, and cell phone data as potential sources to predict poverty across time and space and to improve program performance. Box 2.4 unpacks some of these innovations, their relevance, and their constraints going forward.

Pakistan: National Database and Registration Authority

In Pakistan, the National Database and Registration Authority (NADRA) is responsible for civil registration. To date, the NADRA has issued a computerized national identity card in-country and abroad to nearly two-thirds of Pakistan's 150 million citizens.

NADRA provides other information technology solutions for identification, e-governance, and program implementation, with a key strength being biometric verification. Its project management unit provides a platform to integrate different systems. Over the years, it has facilitated and implemented cash transfer and social protection programs. Services provided to governmental and nongovernmental agencies outside of NADRA's core business come at a cost.

NADRA's involvement in disaster response started with the 2005 earthquake. Five years later, the NADRA responded to flooding by supporting rapid computerized national identity card registration for the *Watan* card and delivered cash to internally displaced persons.

NADRA employs more than 11,000 technical and management personnel. It has developed 365 multibiometric Interactive Registration Centers and deployed 189 mobile vans to register citizens living in remote areas.

Source: Watson et al. 2017.

Big data and technology leapfrogging: Power and limitations

Policy makers in the poorest countries are often forced to make decisions based on limited data or overriding political interests. In situations where reliable data are missing, dated, or cost-prohibitive, an area of increased focus is the use of "big data" and the role of technology.

Central to the discussion of big data is the potential for machine learning to inform policy making. Machine learning is the process of instructing computers to learn. It exists at the intersection of computer science, statistics, and linear algebra, with insights from neuroscience and other fields. Traditionally, machine learning has focused on making predictions and creating structure out of unstructured data. A recent example includes the World Bank's new partnership with the United Nations, the Red Cross, Microsoft, Google, and Amazon on the Famine Action Mechanism. The group will use artificial intelligence and machine learning to predict famine and mobilize early funding to mitigate its effects.

In this context, big data have the potential to become a disruptive technology, changing traditional approaches to survey-based data collection and shifting ways of doing business on many levels. Country experience for ASP in this area is thus far limited, but a few important initiatives are relevant.

- In Rwanda, an individual's past history of mobile-phone use can be applied to infer his or her socioeconomic status, and the predicted attributes of millions of individuals can, in turn, accurately reconstruct the distribution of wealth of an entire nation or infer the asset distribution of micro-regions composed of just a few

households (Blumenstock, Cadamuro, and On 2015). Another approach uses high-resolution satellite imageries to predict poverty (World Bank 2016).

- In Sri Lanka, the poverty estimation by the machine learning techniques using key information from the satellite imagery (such as building density, vegetation, road types, and roof types) tracks regional differences in poverty extremely well comparing with the estimation from the census. The predictions derived from satellite data generate much more plausible estimates of changes in subdistrict poverty rates than the traditional method of using household characteristics in the model.

The potential applications for this technology are promising. In resource-constrained environments where censuses and household surveys are rare, this approach creates an option for gathering localized and timely information at a fraction of the cost of traditional methods. Improved data can inform program performance through improved monitoring and response.

Although promising, these nontraditional methods have caveats. One of the strongest concerns relates to privacy, and how individual, proprietary information can be misused in the process of machine learning. While rigid data protection procedures are an important mitigating factor at the program level, it is harder to control privacy practices in the public and private sectors. So too, the proliferation of different information sources and the risk of manipulation by governments and donors is a concern.

Source: Beazley and Barca 2018.

Ensuring data security and privacy are fundamental considerations that are only heightened in a crisis context. For example, sensitive information on a country's citizens such as information stored for SP purposes—potentially including their ethnicity, religion, and more—could be swiftly put to wrong uses in cases of conflict and violence. Examples include the Rwandan genocide and the Holocaust (Seltzer and Anderson 2001). Crises require rapid decision-making and often involve multiple actors with little prior experience in coordinating (for example, there are no memorandums of understanding in place for data sharing). These situations can easily lead to significant breaches of standard protocols for the secure collection, transfer, and storage of information (such as non-encrypted sharing of personal information via email), especially where country laws do not adhere to international data transfer and information privacy protocols. The reverse can also be true, with existing data privacy and security legislation constraining timely sharing of data across institutions. For example, in the Philippines, a new privacy law created barriers for sharing personal data in the national social registry, Listahanan, with external agencies.

FILLING THE GAPS: LINKING ASP TO EARLY WARNING INFORMATION AND POST-SHOCK NEEDS ASSESSMENTS

Given the cross-sectoral nature of ASP, data and information gaps straddle across programs and systems within and outside the SP sector. Considerable ex ante work is required to set in place rules, system requirements, and approaches to design and scale up SP programs in response to a shock. This requires careful delineation of information priorities in assessing, deciding on, and implementing a shock response. It also requires the preagreement of mechanisms to determine a shock response, prominently as related to early warning systems and predefined triggers that initiate action, along with post-shock assessments of household needs.

Early warning systems continue to play a critical role in providing and monitoring information for response and in triggering early action, especially in a context of growing climate-related risks.[1] Early warning systems for drought–food security hybrid systems typically use a range of information on food production, access, and livelihood outcomes from national agencies and international assessments (such as the Famine Early Warning Systems Network and the Integrated Food Security Phase Classification) and merge the information into an assessment of the food-security status and likely risk (Wilkinson et al. 2018). More recently, forecasts have started using a growing range of climate information. Systems using probabilistic forecast information typically draw on products from international, regional, and national forecasting centers. Products from international and regional forecasting centers are most common, as these are freely available and considered reliable. Where appropriate, these are complemented with products from national hydrological and meteorological services.

Countries are already linking SP responses to early warning information and developing index-based triggers for response, particularly for slow-onset shocks. In the Dominican Republic, the Vulnerability to Climate Hazards Index (IVACC) generates household-level information that supports the assessment of vulnerability to shocks and climate change and which can provide estimations of post-shock needs (box 2.5). In Uganda, satellite data and a Normalized Difference Vegetation Index anomaly provide the basis for triggering earlier response to drought (box 2.6).

Triggers for rapid response can be built using the data generated by existing early warning systems and climate forecasts (Bastagli and Harman 2015; O'Brien et al. 2018). Triggers are typically designed to release funds and initiate early actions when preestablished thresholds are met. These triggers can lead to automatic responses; this implies front-loading the decision-making process and directly linking climate forecasts to their potential consequences.

BOX 2.5

Dominican Republic: Leveraging the social registry for early warning information

The Dominican Republic developed the Vulnerability to Climate Hazards Index (IVACC) to quantify the likelihood of a household being vulnerable to hurricanes, storms, and floods. The index uses data from the country's national social registry, the Sistema Unico de Beneficiarios, which covered approximately 85.5 percent of the population in 2015. The IVACC produces a vulnerability score for all households in the social registry and can be aggregated to larger administrative areas (such as towns and municipalities). It has a scale of 0–1, where households with values close to 0 are the least vulnerable and those with values close to 1 are the most vulnerable. The score is based on three variables: (1) the physical characteristics of the dwelling, (2) average household labor income, and (3) proximity of the house to a source of danger (such as river, waterbody, or stream).

Using the index, figure B2.5.1 simulates the most vulnerable neighborhoods and the characteristics of vulnerable households in such areas.

FIGURE B2.5.1

Hurricane simulation using IVACC to identify households that may be most affected

María Trinidad Sanchez **river**

Household head: Altagracia Martínez
0.5 to 1 km from the river
1 child (from 5 to 9 years of age)
1 adolescent (10–14 years of age)
Spouse
Concrete roof
Cinder block walls
IVACC: 0.524

Household head:
María Gómez
0.5 km from
the river
2 children (from
0 to 4 years of age)
1 adult
Zinc roof
Concrete walls

Household head:
Juan Pérez
0.5 km from the river
3 children (from 5 to
9 years of age)
Spouse
Zinc roof
Palm-thatched walls

Source: SIUBEN (Sistema Único de Beneficiarios/Unified Beneficiary Identification System).

Source: UNDP-UNEP 2018.

Uganda: Establishing satellite-based triggers for drought response

In Karamoja, Uganda, the Northern Uganda Social Action Fund has a cash-for-work program that is designed to respond to drought. The government has identified an objective and automatic satellite indicator as the trigger to scale up the number of households accessing the cash-for-work program.

The Normalized Difference Vegetation Index (NDVI) was selected as the indicator to determine when to respond, as it simply and quickly identifies vegetated areas and their "condition" over time. The NDVI is observed on a 14-day basis, and an average score assigned for each district in Karamoja is calculated for each calendar month.

An NDVI anomaly is an early indicator of drought but is not by itself enough to declare a drought emergency. However, it does mean cash-for-work payments are triggered well before any late-onset indicators (for example, livestock mortality and malnutrition rates) reach emergency levels. This has the effect of mitigating these late-onset negative impacts and ultimately saves money in the long term. A perceived risk in responding early is that funds will be released incorrectly to situations that turn out not to be a disaster (for example, a payout is triggered; it then rains; and no drought occurs). However, the benefits of scaling social protection programs in response to very early warning indicators in the spirit of "no regrets" are becoming increasingly clear.

Sources: Cabot Venton et al. 2012; Government of Uganda 2016.

TABLE 2.3 **Early warning systems: Triggers for rapid action**

ADVANTAGES	PREREQUISITES
• Enables quick, even automatic, shock response • Helps secure financing • Increases transparency (actual or perceived) • Can minimize moral hazard and adverse selection risks • Technological triggers can be less time consuming	• The trigger's effectiveness depends on correlation between the index and the household's needs • Indexes should be easily measured, objective, transparent, independently verifiable, and available in a timely manner • If based on proxies rather than on observed measures, effectiveness also depends on the correlation between the proxy and the main indicator • To turn early warning into early response, contingency planning and predictive analysis are required so that early warning system data can lead to better decisions

Sources: Beazley and Barca 2018, based on Bailey 2012; Bastagli and Harman 2015; and Levine, Crosskey, and Abdinoor 2011.

Otherwise, they can be used to inform ex post, decision-making processes to trigger early action (Wilkinson et al. 2018). The use of early warning systems to trigger SP responses is promising, predicated on a number of prerequisites (table 2.3).

Ultimately, data collected before a shock cannot provide an exact assessment of needs after a shock. As noted, in a post-shock environment, those most in need are not necessarily the beneficiaries of existing programs (Bastagli 2014; McCord 2013; O'Brien et al. 2018). Multiple programs will be needed (implemented by SP, DRM, and/or humanitarian actors) to provide response alongside a vertically expanded SP program (O'Brien et al. 2018). Horizontal expansion to new households based on prepositioned SP data or piggybacking on those data for a response can help enable timely response to a shock but will often need to be complemented by additional post-shock data collection.

Post-shock data collection can play a key role in reflecting the socioeconomic and damage condition of potential beneficiaries, especially after fast-onset, less predictable, and destructive disasters. Postdisaster household assessments often are employed to collect information on the level of damage and needs of affected households after natural disasters. Existing SP information systems such as social registries can be a valuable resource that can help to inform such assessments. At the same time, with sufficient planning, data from postdisaster household needs assessments can be incorporated into social registries to support their expansion and updating. Several Latin American and Caribbean countries apply postdisaster needs assessment instruments to households after disasters, informing the provision of SP–related support. These instruments are at times formalized through standardized processes with strong legal foundations, such as Chile's Basic Emergency Sheet (Ficha Básica de Emergencia—FIBE) (box 2.7); operate as formalized processes without associated legislation, such as Jamaica's Household Disaster Impact and Needs Assessment— JHDINA (box 2.8); or may be developed from scratch following a disaster event, as in the case of Dominica's Vulnerability Needs Assessment following Hurricane Maria in 2017. In the Philippines, the Department of Social Welfare and Development utilizes the paper-based Disaster Assistance Family Access Card containing basic information pertaining to whether the beneficiary's house was damaged (partially or totally), whether they are existing beneficiaries of social programs (that is, the conditional cash transfer program Pantawid), and whether they belong to a vulnerable group (such as women, children, the elderly, and the disabled).

Where post-shock assessments are concerned, the trade-off between a timely versus accurate shock response must be balanced. Inclusion errors can and should be tolerated in the short term (that is, those included who do not warrant support based on predetermined eligibility criteria).

BOX 2.7

Chile: A postdisaster data collection tool to assess shock-impacted households

In Chile, the FIBE collects detailed information on shock-impacted households in response to emergency. FIBE is part of the Damages and Needs Assessment System for emergencies, disasters, and catastrophes. FIBE consists of a questionnaire that is administered to impacted households and individuals in the immediate aftermath of an event.

An app version of FIBE links to the Household Social Registry, replacing the paper-based questionnaire. The FIBE app is downloadable for smartphones to guarantee easy access for users, and users can enter their information into the app. The FIBE app can then verify and validate information on the registrant's education, health, housing conditions and characteristics, and level of vulnerability to the shock.

All validated information is transmitted to the Ministry of Interior and subsequently to the other relevant ministries, including the Ministries of Health and of Education. Based on the information, the Ministry of Interior determines the nature and magnitude of the social programs (cash transfers and/or housing subsidies) that should be triggered to support affected households. This integrated system ensures that Household Social Registry registrants who are not eligible for social programs based on their socioeconomic characteristics receive assistance in the case of disaster under FIBE's criteria.

Source: Beazley and Barca 2018.
Note: FIBE = Ficha Básica de Emergencia (Basic Emergency Sheet).

BOX 2.8

Jamaica: Household Disaster Impact and Needs Assessment

Jamaica's Household Disaster Impact and Needs Assessment (JHDINA) instrument is the main tool used to assess post-shock needs of households affected by disasters, assist in quantifying post-shock social protection needs, and inform social protection shock response by a range of government and nongovernment actors. The JHDINA is an instrument of the Humanitarian Assistance Committee of the National Disaster Risk Management Council. The committee is chaired by the Ministry of Labour and Social Security, which is responsible for social protection; also serving on the committee are representatives of Jamaica's national DRM agency, other government agencies, and nongovernmental organizations such as Food for the Poor and the Adventist Development and Relief Agency. The JHDINA is applied by multisector teams from the committee, led by ministry social workers. Communities to be assessed are prioritized following an initial damage assessment at the national level.

The JHDINA was redesigned in 2017 to help address gaps identified in the previous version. Challenges included a reliance on paper-based data collection, limited variables to inform appropriate social protection response across a range of actors, and limited coordination in the postdisaster household assessment process. The new instrument is available in multiple formats to enable quick decision-making and integration of the multiple agencies engaged in disaster response in the country. Variables captured by the questionnaire included disaster type, location, demographics and family composition, health of household members, receipt of social assistance, damage and losses, and immediate needs.

Jamaica has not experienced a national-level disaster event since the JHDINA's redesign. However, the instrument's predecessor informed vertical expansion of the Programme of Advancement Through Health and Education (PATH) conditional cash transfer program and National Insurance pensions, and horizontal expansion to non-PATH affected households following Hurricane Dean in 2007.

Source: World Bank 2018.

Exclusion errors should be addressed expeditiously through a sound grievance redress process and coordination with other programs (in the SP system and by nongovernmental actors) to swiftly reach larger shares of affected households. As the response evolves and refocuses on longer-term recovery, more precise targeting of losses and needs helps identify those eligible for longer-term support.

CONSIDERATIONS FOR INSTITUTIONALIZING INFORMATION FOR ASP

The drive toward strengthening and integrating information for ASP depends substantially on mechanisms to institutionalize and operationalize information systems. Before the onset of any shock, it is essential to invest in preparatory measures to improve data quality, based on a strong policy vision and national commitments to strengthen the adaptive capacities of SP systems. This brings into focus the importance of capacities to collect, store, manage, and share these data, as well as the institutional structures that will underpin these arrangements. In shock-prone environments, this can vary significantly across countries.

As a starting point, information requirements for ASP involve a more diverse range of stakeholders, compared to traditional SP programming. The breadth of data requirements implies a multisectoral engagement, with significant information often coming from outside of the SP sector. Table 2.4 provides an illustrative framework to consider the different information functions at the policy and program levels, and how this may look based on the maturity of a given information structure within a country.

The development of ASP information systems can also promote institutional coordination among SP, DRM, and humanitarian actors. Ultimately, this can lead to improved targeting accuracy, reduced duplication of efforts, and potentially cost-saving (for example, administrative costs of data

TABLE 2.4 The maturity of ASP information systems and the roles of different actors in strengthening them

KEY FUNCTIONS	SYSTEM MATURITY		
	LOW (NASCENT)	(EMERGING)	HIGH (ESTABLISHED)
Policy setting			
Coordination and management	Fragmented approaches to social protection, DRM, and humanitarian information systems. Social protection information often focused around a single-user program, requiring heavy engagements of development partners.	Collaboration across social protection, DRM, and humanitarian information actors. Clear identification of stakeholders. Social protection information more streamlined, across multiple programs, with increasing engagement of government.	Clear arrangements in place within government for cross-sector coordination and leadership. Social protection information spans multiple programs, with clear sector links. Role of stakeholders formalized through agreements, terms of reference.
Financing	External financing is key to allow start up. Data initiatives separately resourced.	Combination of nongovernment and government financing, with increasing synergies of financial resources.	Largely government financed. Nongovernment financing is required only when the magnitude of a shock is significant.
Frameworks, standards, and ethics	General information protocols are often poorly defined, outsourced to nongovernment providers.	Increased attention to formalizing protocols, privacy, and data sharing, with implications for engaging in shock response.	Mechanisms in place, with national laws adhering to international data transfer and privacy protocols.
Program delivery aspects			
Data collection/update modalities	Infrequent (en masse registration), partial across the country. Data collected by development partners may supplement the gap.	Open registration (dynamic inclusion). Nongovernment partners encouraged to use the same ID for postdisaster data collection.	Open registration and capable of post-shock open registration.
Citizen interface (point of contact) for registration	Limited, temporary site and heavy engagements of partners required.	Online or local office.	Online and local office, mobile team.
Data verification, quality assessment	Limited, manual cross-check among government and nongovernment partners.	Automatic cross-checks available for government-led social protection, but manual cross-check of social protection data with nonsocial protection and nongovernment data (DRM, humanitarian database).	Automatic cross-checks among government and nongovernment partners.
Data interoperability	Limited, information based at program level.	Same ID used in multiple social protection programs.	National ID used for social protection, DRM, and humanitarian database.

Source: World Bank.
Note: DRM = disaster risk management; ID = identification.

collection, recurring costs of data management, and private costs to citizens) (Pelham, Clay, and Braunholz 2011). There is increasing evidence on countries that have been able to reap such benefits in one way or another. In Turkey, refugees benefiting from the Emergency Social Safety Net are being enrolled in SP programs (social assistance programs and employment services) through the country's existing information management platform. In Mali, development partners have invested in establishing a solid information system for Jigisèmèjiri, with the aim of improving coordination of targeting and sharing the costs of data collection and analysis with other interventions (government and nongovernment) (O'Brien et al. 2018). In the Philippines, the Cash Working Group has piloted a process for humanitarian agencies to coordinate with the Listahanan, digitizing the information on their beneficiaries by submitting it to the National Household Targeting Office for verification and/or inclusion into the database. This process was intended to help digitize the Disaster Assistance Family Access Cards process of tracking which households were receiving which benefits from humanitarian agencies (Bowen 2015).

A key implication is the need to anchor the information strengthening agenda around a government vision and a set of institutional commitments. While a combination of national and international expertise often will be needed to undertake different information functions, efforts need to be harnessed in a central way. In Mexico, for instance, a parliamentary act requires the ministries involved in disaster response to share a common database and information system (World Bank 2013). The country's social registry, Sistema de Focalización para el Desarrollo, supports targeting of social assistance. It is shared by the Ministry of Social Development with other ministries/DRM actors and is layered with any additional postdisaster data collection and information on who is receiving emergency programs. Similarly, SP actors can incorporate tools used by the DRM sector in formulating their programs, such as contingency planning, early warning systems, and postdisaster needs assessments.

Over time the quality of administrative and staffing structures also will become important to institutionalize. As information systems become more relevant for ASP, mechanisms will need to evolve to allow for their decentralized implementation while maintaining centralized control functions (for example, verifying and validating data). This will require a network of staff at various levels to support implementation. These networks will allow the government to dispatch staff horizontally (for example, across different departments or ministries), vertically (for example, through higher tiers of government), or through collaboration with nonstate actors (for example, humanitarian actors and voluntary groups) to address the gap of beneficiary caseload and the capacity of the government's departments that manage the relevant information systems.

The challenges of financing and costing information systems for ASP should not be overlooked. Progressing from nascent to emerging or mature information systems takes time and continuous effort, and entails many different types of financing and costs (Leite et al. 2017). The first set of costs include "back-office" costs to develop information technology system capabilities and "front-office" costs such as administrative costs for outreach, intake, and registration. Costs for individuals and households should also be acknowledged, such as for their travel to citizen interface points and for participating in the intake and registration interview.

Lastly, it will be critical to ensure that this information can be easily communicated to and interpreted by decision makers involved in ASP policy and implementation. Potentially, important lessons can be introduced to SP programs from crisis-related information systems. For example, the Integrated Food Security Phase Classification is a common global scale for classifying the severity and magnitude of food insecurity and malnutrition. The scale is a "big-picture" classification focusing on providing information that is consistently required by stakeholders around the world for strategic decision-making. It focuses on actionable, easily interpretable information for strategic decision-making in a manner that is simple and accessible (FAO 2016).

NOTE

1. The United Nations International Strategy for Disaster Reduction defines early warning systems as "an integrated system of hazard monitoring, forecasting and prediction, disaster risk assessment, communication and preparedness activities systems and processes that enables individuals, communities, governments, businesses and others to take timely action to reduce disaster risks in advance of hazardous events" (www.unisdr.org/we /inform/terminology).

REFERENCES

Bailey, R. 2012. *Famine Early Warning and Early Action: The Cost of Delay*. London: Chatham House.

Barca, V. 2017. *Integrating Data and Information Management for Social Protection: Social Registries and Integrated Beneficiary Registries*. Canberra: Commonwealth of Australia, Department of Foreign Affairs and Trade. https://dfat.gov.au/about-us/publications /Documents/integrating-data-information-management-social-protection-full.pdf.

Barca, V., and C. O'Brien. 2017. "Factors Affecting the Usefulness of Existing Social Protection Databases in Disaster Preparedness and Response." Policy Brief. Oxford Policy Management, Oxford, UK. https://assets.publishing.service.gov.uk/media/5a942c50ed915d57d4d0ef98 /Policy-Brief-Factors-affecting-usefulness-existing-social-protection-databases.pdf.

Bastagli, F. 2014. "Responding to a Crisis: The Design and Delivery of Social Protection." ODI Working Paper, Overseas Development Institute, London.

Bastagli, F., J. Hagen-Zanker, L. Harman, V. Barca, G. Sturge, and T. Schmidt. 2016. "Cash Transfers: What Does the Evidence Say? A Rigorous Review of Programme Impact and of the Role of Design and Implementation Features." Overseas Development Institute, London.

Bastagli, F., and L. Harman. 2015. "The Role of Index-Based Triggers in Social Protection Shock Response." Overseas Development Institute, London.

Beazley, R., and V. Barca. 2018. "The Role of Data and Information for Adaptive Social Protection." Background paper for the World Bank, Oxford Policy Management, Oxford, UK.

Blumenstock, J., G. Cadamuro, and R. On. 2015. "Predicting Poverty and Wealth from Mobile Phone Metadata." *Science* 350 (6264): 1073–76.

Bowen, T. 2015. "Social Protection and Disaster Risk Management in the Philippines: The Case of Typhoon Yolanda (Haiyan)." Policy Research Working Paper 7482, World Bank, Washington, DC. http://documents.worldbank.org/curated/en/681881468181128752/pdf /WPS7482.pdf.

Cabot Venton, C., C. Fitzgibbon, T. Shitarek, L. Coulter, and O. Dooley. 2012. "The Economics of Early Response and Disaster Resilience: Lessons from Kenya and Ethiopia: Economics of Resilience Final Report." Department for International Development, London.

del Ninno, C., and B. Mills, eds. 2015. *Safety Nets in Africa: Effective Mechanisms to Reach the Poor and Most Vulnerable*. Washington, DC: World Bank. http://documents.worldbank.org /curated/en/869311468009642720/pdf/Safety-nets-in-Africa-effective-mechanisms-to -reach-the-poor-and-most-vulnerable.pdf.

FAO (Food and Agriculture Organization of the United Nations). 2016. *Resilience Index Measurement and Analysis–II (RIMA-II)*. Rome: FAO.

Gao, J., and B. F. Mills. 2018. "Weather Shocks, Coping Strategies, and Consumption Dynamics in Rural Ethiopia." *World Development* 101 (January): 268–83.

Government of Uganda. 2016. "Third Northern Uganda Social Action Fund (NUSAF3) Project— Disaster Risk Financing Sub-Component Handbook." Government of Uganda, Kampala.

Hallegatte, S., A. Vogt-Schilb, M. Bangalore, and J. Rozenberg. 2017. *Unbreakable: Building the Resilience of the Poor in the Face of Natural Disasters*. Washington, DC: World Bank. https:// www.gfdrr.org/sites/default/files/publication/Unbreakable_FullBook_Web-3.pdf.

Hill, R., and C. Porter. 2017. "Vulnerability to Drought and Food Price Shocks: Evidence from Ethiopia." *World Development* 96: 65–77.

IEG (Independent Evaluation Group). 2011. *Social Safety Nets: An Evaluation of World Bank Support, 2000–2010*. Washington, DC: World Bank.

Kuriakose, A., R. Heltberg, W. Wiseman, C. Costella, R. Cipryk, and S. Cornelius. 2012. "Climate-Responsive Social Protection." Social Protection and Labor Discussion Paper 1210, World Bank, Washington, DC. https://siteresources.worldbank.org/SOCIALPROTECTION /Resources/SP-Discussion-papers/430578-1331508552354/1210.pdf.

Leite, P., T. George, C. Sun, T. Jones, and K. Lindert. 2017. "Social Registries for Social Assistance and Beyond: A Guidance Note and Assessment Tool." Social Protection and Labor Working Paper 1704, World Bank, Washington, DC. http://documents.worldbank.org/curated /en/698441502095248081/pdf/117971-REVISED-PUBLIC-Discussion-paper-1704.pdf.

Levine, S., A. Crosskey, and M. Abdinoor. 2011. "System Failure? Revisiting the Problems of Timely Response to Crises in the Horn of Africa." Humanitarian Practice Network Paper 11, Overseas Development Institute, London.

Lindert, K., T. George, I. Rodriguez-Caillava, and Kenichi Nishikawa. Forthcoming. *A Sourcebook on the Foundations of Social Protection Delivery Systems*. Washington, DC: World Bank.

McCord, A. 2013. "Review of the Literature on Social Protection Shock Responses and Readiness." ODI Shockwatch. Overseas Development Institute, London.

Mittal, Neeraj, Anit Mukherjee, and Alan Gelb. 2017. "Fuel Subsidy Reform in Developing Countries: Direct Benefit Transfer of LPG Cooking Gas Subsidy in India." CGD Policy Paper. Center for Global Development, Washington, DC.

O'Brien, C., Z. Scott, G. Smith, V. Barca, A. Kardan, R. Holmes, C. Watson, and J. Congrave. 2018. "Shock-Responsive Social Protection Systems Research: Synthesis Report." Oxford Policy Management, Oxford, UK. https://www.opml.co.uk/files/Publications/a0408-shock -responsive-social-protection-systems/srsp-synthesis-report.pdf?noredirect=1.

Pelham, L., E. Clay, and T. Braunholz. 2011. "Natural Disasters: What Is the Role for Social Safety Nets?" SP Discussion Paper 1102, World Bank, Washington, DC. https://www.gfdrr.org /sites/default/files/documents/Social%20Safety%20Nets.pdf.

Schnitzer, P. 2018. "How to Target Households in Adaptive Social Protection Systems? Evidence from Humanitarian and Development Approaches in Niger." *Journal of Development Studies* 55 (Supplement 1): 75–90.

Seltzer, W., and M. Anderson. 2001. "The Dark Side of Numbers: The Role of Population Data Systems in Human Rights Abuses." *Social Research* 68 (2): 481–513.

Skoufias, E., Y. Kawasoe, E. Strobl, and P. Acosta. 2019. "Identifying the Vulnerable to Poverty from Natural Disasters. The Case of Typhoons in the Philippines." Policy Research Working Paper 8857, World Bank, Washington, DC. http://documents.worldbank.org/curated /en/326941558453867995/pdf/Identifying-the-Vulnerable-to-Poverty-from-Natural -Disasters-The-Case-of-Typhoons-in-the-Philippines.pdf.

Sonderegger, Petra, Swetha Totapally, Jasper Gosselt, Adityendra Suman, James Goh, Devvart Poddar, Surya AV, and Mahesh Vyas. 2019. "State of Aadhaar, 2019." Harvard Dataverse. https://dataverse.harvard.edu/dataset.xhtml?persistentId=doi:10.7910/DVN/M9RWZN.

UNDP-UNEP (United Nations Development Programme–United Nations Environment Programme). 2018. *Vulnerability to Climate Hazards Index: Lessons Learned and Systematization of the Design Process and Application of the IVACC Index—Dominican Republic*. Poverty-Environment Initiative. Panama City: Panama.

Walsh, B., and S. Hallegatte. 2019a. "Measuring Natural Risks in the Philippines: Socioeconomic Resilience and Wellbeing Losses." Policy Research Working Paper 8723, World Bank, Washington, DC. http://documents.worldbank.org/curated/en/482401548966120315/pdf/WPS8723.pdf.

Walsh, B., and S. Hallegatte. 2019b. "Socioeconomic Resilience in Sri Lanka: Natural Disaster Poverty and Wellbeing Impact Assessment." Policy Research Working Paper 9015, World Bank, Washington, DC. http://documents.worldbank.org/curated/en/173611568643337991/pdf/Socioeconomic-Resilience-in-Sri-Lanka-Natural-Disaster-Poverty-and-Wellbeing-Impact-Assessment.pdf.

Wang, R., and D. Strong. 1996. "Beyond Accuracy: What Data Quality Means to Data Consumers." *Journal of Management Information Systems* 12 (4): 5–33.

Watson, C., T. Lone, U. Qazi, G. Smith, and F. Fashid. 2017. "Shock-Responsive Social Protection Systems Research: Case Study: Pakistan." Oxford Policy Management, Oxford, UK.

Wilkinson, E., L. Weingartner, R. Choularton, M. Bailey, M. Todd, D. Kniveton, and C. Cabot Venton. 2018. "Forecasting Hazards, Averting Disasters: Implementing Forecast-Based Early Action at Scale." Overseas Development Institute, London.

World Bank. 2013. *Building Resilience to Disaster and Climate Change through Social Protection: Synthesis Note*. Washington, DC: World Bank. http://documents.worldbank.org/curated/en/187211468349778714/pdf/796210WP0Build0Box0377381B00PUBLIC0.pdf.

World Bank. 2016. *Big Data Innovation Challenge: Pioneering Approaches to Data-Driven Development*. Washington, DC: World Bank. http://documents.worldbank.org/curated/en/396861470905612761/pdf/107751-REVISED-PUBLIC-BigData-Publication-e-version-FINAL.pdf.

World Bank. 2018. *Post-Disaster Damage Assessment and Targeting Mechanisms in Jamaica*. Washington, DC: World Bank.

3 Finance
APPLYING A DISASTER RISK FINANCING APPROACH

OVERVIEW

Adaptive social protection implies different financing burdens for governments to address. Resilience-building interventions tend to generate outcomes among beneficiaries over the long term, meaning that sustainable-financing commitments to support such initiatives are critical. More generally, adaptive social protection (ASP) will benefit from increased fiscal space for the extension of social protection access to vulnerable households and the strengthening of the overall social protection system.

At the same time, for ASP programs to become more responsive to shocks, risk financing strategies will need to be developed with appropriate risk financing instruments prepositioned and linked to responsive safety net programs. In doing so, funding will be made more readily available for quick disbursement through shock-responsive safety net programs—a key determinant in the timeliness of response, and by extension its effectiveness in protecting the well-being of affected households.

Emerging evidence highlights three core lessons for applying a disaster risk financing approach to ASP. First, investment is needed to understand the potential cost of response, leveraging a variety of data sources including historical hazard data to shed light on the anticipated contingent liability of using a safety net to respond to shocks. Second, building from these costing models, appropriate funding should be preplanned. However, no single financial instrument should cover the entire contingent liability created through the development of a shock-responsive safety net program. Rather, a risk financing strategy that layers multiple instruments according to the frequency and severity of the shock will be required. Third, robust payment mechanisms that are capable of absorbing the funding made available after a shock and delivering it to households are critical to enable the disbursement of these risk financing instruments to households. Building from the payment conduits used for safety net programs, the requisite rules and capacity among payment service providers should be established ex ante. Doing so after the shock will often cause severe delays in disbursement and delivery.

This chapter draws extensively from a background paper by Maher, Fitzgibbon, and Solórzano (2018).

DISASTER RISK FINANCING: FROM REACTIVE TO PROACTIVE RESOURCE MOBILIZATION

The prevailing model for financing disaster response poses challenges to responding in a timely manner, at the expense of the well-being of those who have been affected and are in urgent need of support. Historically, the humanitarian response system has been the first responder to covariate shocks, especially in poorer countries, with national governments and international partners mobilizing resources after the shocks hit to meet estimated needs. Today, this system is buckling under the weight of growing demand, as illustrated in figure 3.1 (see also IASC 2016). Indeed, an "ad hoc postdisaster funding model...is too slow, leads to a fragmented and under-funded response, and encourages underinvestment in risk reduction and preparedness, thereby increasing the economic and human costs of catastrophes" (Clarke and Hill 2016, 10). For poorer countries, this can have significant impacts where spending is already constrained, borrowing is more costly, and reallocations can affect the continuity of basic government functions. In such instances, these countries often turn to global humanitarian agencies and development partners for support, which leads not only to delays but recurring, large funding gaps relative to needs on the ground. In such cases, funding can come late and can be insufficient (Clarke and Dercon 2016).

Disaster risk financing is part of a global shift in thinking from seeing disasters as unpredictable humanitarian crises to predictable events that can be planned for and managed to minimize their impact. This involves moving from a reactive approach that addresses the impact of shocks once they happen to a more proactive approach, putting in place the required systems and financing to respond to shocks before they take place. A proactive approach highlights the need for governments to develop risk financing strategies that enable funding to flow in the event of a shock and, thus, to enable a faster response to disasters.

FIGURE 3.1

Humanitarian response: Trend in requirements and funding gaps, 2007–17

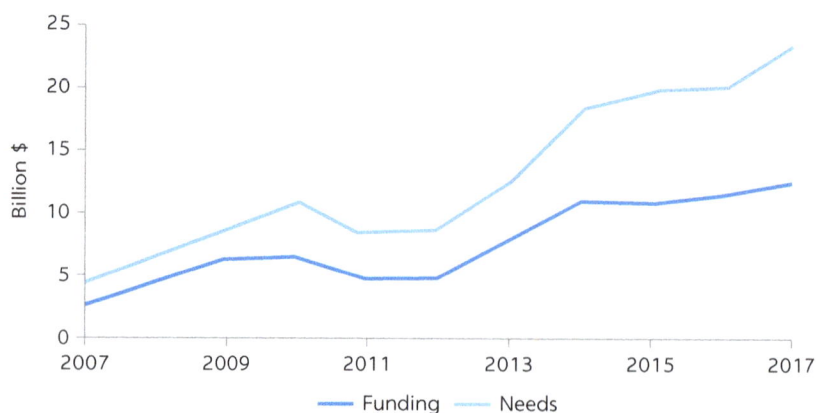

Source: UN OCHA 2018.

This chapter documents emerging lessons on applying these same principles to the financing of ASP, specifically. In doing so, the need for and value in proactively planning for how to finance shock-responsive social protection for timely support becomes clear. Indeed, this highlights a strong synergy: when disaster risk financing strategies are established, a shock-responsive safety net represents a preprepared mechanism whereby risk financing instruments can disburse directly to affected households. Conversely, the availability of the kinds of risk financing instruments outlined in this chapter will be instrumental in enabling fast response through a safety net. In that way, they are both critical components to building the resilience of poor and vulnerable households.

The disaster risk financing approach outlined here enables the delivery of shock-responsive programs to support short-term coping after a shock. This approach can be complemented by safety net interventions that also support a household's preparedness and longer-term adaptation for a holistic approach to resilience building along the pre- and post-shock continuum. Long-term investments in preparedness and adaptation could help to reduce future household needs, and by extension, lower response costs over time—but more evidence is needed. The kinds of interventions discussed in chapter 1 to support household adaptation over the longer term can be costly at scale (for example, in contexts of widespread chronic and severe poverty in high-risk areas). Yet, initial evidence indicates that more expensive investment scenarios are broadly offset by the avoided cost of humanitarian response (Cabot Venton 2018; Wilkinson et al. 2018). In Bangladesh, the Chars Livelihoods Program focused on building an annual contingency budget into its project design for disaster response, but the need for this contingency fund decreased over time because of the program's specific focus on reducing vulnerabilities and supporting the adaptation of poor households living in the chars to regular flooding (ADB 2018). Where resources are limited, more evidence is needed on the cost-effectiveness of and trade-offs between resilience-building interventions in support of adaptation and risk reduction at the household level over the long term versus the cost of ex post shock response to support short-term coping.

WHY IS A DISASTER RISK FINANCING APPROACH IMPORTANT FOR ASP?

A disaster risk financing approach in support of an early response can lower the overall cost of a disaster, relative to a scenario in which the response arrives late. In Ethiopia in 2016, the timeliness of funding that was made available to respond to the drought created savings of over $6 million. The longer-term economic cost of responding later could have been $47.9 million (Cabot Venton and Sida 2017). Similar estimates including Kenya and Somalia alongside Ethiopia also suggest that an early response saves $1.6 billion over 15 years in comparison to a late response. When avoided losses are incorporated, an early response saves $2.5 billion, or an average of $163 million per year (Cabot Venton 2018).

Cost savings are realized when faster assistance dissuades affected people from engaging in negative coping strategies. As outlined previously in this report, negative coping strategies can have long-term, intergenerational, and irrevocable impacts on household welfare. In Ethiopia, the cost of a drought to poor households increased exponentially over time: $0–$50 for a 4-month delay versus $1,300 for a 6–9-month delay (Clarke and Vargas Hill 2013). Acting early is critical to prevent the use of negative coping mechanisms, and the availability of financing is a key factor determining the ability to do so.

Where risk financing encourages predictable assistance among households, the reduced uncertainty in the face of potential disasters also can enable households to invest in preparedness and adaptation. As noted in chapter 1, in cases where households understand that they are protected by predictable, shock-responsive programs, evidence indicates they adopt higher-yield, higher-risk livelihood investments. This can enable beneficiaries to grow their household income and ultimately leads to a pathway of a more resilient state. In Mexico, municipalities participating in the drought index insurance program Component for the Attention of Natural Disasters (CADENA)—with similar properties to a shock-responsive safety net—increased expenditure per capita by 27 percent and income per capita by 38 percent, which is about $284–$378 in additional income (Clarke and Hill 2016).

Preplanning and prepositioning financing (with clear rules for its use) also can reduce uncertainty in government budgets around the role of social protection in responding to shocks. In Uganda, a $10 million contingent line of credit finances drought response through the social protection system. The preestablished line of credit means the shock-responsive safety net does not introduce any budget uncertainty to the Ministry of Finance, Planning, and Economic Development. It also precludes more expensive ex post financing options such as budget reallocations, which divert resources from high-yield investments (Clarke and Dercon 2016).

Financial planning for shock-responsive social protection also can increase country ownership and government leadership. While for now this is less tangible than the other benefits, it holds the promise of being the most transformative. Using ASP programs for disaster response places governments in the driving seat, with the ownership and (importantly) the responsibility to deliver emergency resources to their citizens. This is a paradigm shift from the status quo, which relies predominantly on nongovernment actors to deliver said resources. Empowering governments to invest in their systems and capacities to manage shock response ultimately leads to a more sustainable shock-response system in the country. It also can serve to strengthen the social compact between citizens and their governments.

A CLOSER EXAMINATION OF THE DISASTER RISK FINANCING APPROACH FOR ASP

This section outlines the key lessons for applying a disaster risk financing approach for ASP. Three emerging lessons are (1) estimate the cost of response before a shock, (2) preplan the funding required to ensure timely response, and (3) establish and link the plan to effective disbursement mechanisms. Each lesson is examined below and illustrated with reference to relevant country examples.

Lesson 1: Estimate the cost of response before the shock

Financial planning for shocks *before* they occur requires a very different set of skills and information than planning responses *after* the event. Pre-shock planning requires the data and analysis to understand the magnitude, frequency, and impact of potential shocks as well as a decision on the scale and duration of support. Without this, it is impossible to calculate the costs of responding with social protection and its financial feasibility.

The first good-practice principle involves estimating in advance the impact of a shock on a target population and the resulting losses. Developing a realistic estimation of the scale and range of required funding involves establishing, based on existing data sources from the disaster risk management, humanitarian, and social protection sectors, the following:

- What major shocks are likely to affect the target population?
- How frequently do these shocks occur?
- For each risk, can its scale and magnitude be quantified?
- Which areas of the country or parts of the population are most likely to be affected?
- What response is required to enable the identified populations to cope in or overcome the immediate impacts?
- How long will this assistance be required?

Natural disaster shocks have well established technical definitions, quantification metrics, and historical data. Droughts and hurricanes draw on meteorological indicators around rainfall and wind speed. An earthquake's strength, or magnitude, is measured using the Richter scale. Information on past shocks (including the cost of response) exists in publicly available databases (O'Brien et al. 2018c). This is not the case for anthropogenic hazards such as conflict where the potential impact of any given risk is much more complex to predict and quantify.

However, these metrics and data are not always sufficient to understand how a target population will be impacted by the same level of shock. Nor do they provide an acceptable level of accuracy when assessing impact in specific geographical areas (subnational) given the complex relationship between vulnerability and risk. Some hazards (floods) can only be defined locally in relation to long-term norms. Understanding the risk of a subpopulation involves calibrating standard definitions or measurements to the local context. These definitions serve to trigger payment mechanisms and other response interventions.

A household's vulnerability to shocks can be difficult to assess ex ante. Typical factors in the calculation include the following:

- Poverty and vulnerability to poverty—levels and sources of income, assets, and savings, among others
- Livelihood issues—food security (rise in food prices) and reliance on livelihood activities highly affected by shocks, such as rain-fed subsistence agriculture (drought)
- Location—proximity to coastal areas, waterways (floods and hurricanes), and conflict areas
- Infrastructure—construction standards, disaster-proof roads, bridges, and wells, among others
- Timing—the point at which a shock hits can vary impact, such as just before or just after a harvest
- Preparedness systems—community early warning strategies

Previous shocks can provide proxies for gaps in information, using postdisaster needs assessments and funding appeals. In Kenya, the Hunger Safety Net Program (HSNP) preassessed the additional proportion of the population to receive cash transfers for different levels of drought. The HSNP used an existing quantification metric (twice yearly post-rains assessment) and past historical data and information (a maximum of 77 percent of the population needed support for high-magnitude drought, with 50 percent of households in the affected areas in need of food aid) to assess the proportion of the population in need of humanitarian support (a maximum of 75 percent). Assessments during previous high-magnitude drought had never put needs above 77 percent of a population and, on average, the affected areas had identified 50 percent of households in need of food aid in drought years. Hence, the guideline for shock response adopted these rates.

When designing a shock-responsive safety net program of the kind highlighted in chapter 1, key questions can help to determine its potential cost, as outlined in chapter 2. Key questions to ask in designing the component include:

- When should the social protection program respond? To what shocks? How are the shocks defined and measured? Using what data or indicators? Before or only after the shock?
- Where should the shock response happen? What is the geographic coverage of the expanded transfers? At a regional, district, or ward level, for example? Should the geographic coverage depend on the shock?
- Who should benefit from the shock response? Existing beneficiaries, other members of the population, or both?
- What should be the value of any additional transfers? Should there be a standard transfer amount or should it vary according to the shock and the needs? Should existing beneficiaries receive the same, more, or less than nonroutine beneficiaries?
- How long should beneficiaries receive a scaled-up benefit? Should payments or transfers be a one-off or continue for several months after the disaster trigger has been hit (such as until the rains arrive or the floods subside)?

The answers to these questions can inform a matrix to support decision-making. Tables 3.1 and 3.2 provide examples of decision support matrices for drought in Uganda and Kenya, respectively. This in turn can be used to develop a costing model which automatically calculates the long-term cost implications of permutations.

In order to assist policy makers, it is useful to link the variables in the framework to a financial model that calculates the cost impact of changes to any parameter. A model can show the cost implication of changes in a matrix, and thus facilitate decision-making. The financial model should calculate the cost of

TABLE 3.1 **Uganda: A framework to scale up the NUSAF cash-for-work program**

LOCATION	PRIMARY TRIGGER	DROUGHT CONDITIONS	HOUSEHOLDS COVERED BY LABOR-INTENSIVE PUBLIC WORKS PROGRAM	DAILY WAGE FOR PUBLIC WORKS	NUMBER OF DAYS PER MONTH	DURATION OF WORKS AND PAYMENT
By district	NDVI anomaly value ≥ −0.02	No drought	Routine NUSAF households (currently 4 percent of households)	U Sh 4,000	15	4 months
	NDVI anomaly value < −0.02	Drought	Routine NUSAF households (currently 4 percent of households)	U Sh 4,000	15	4 months
			Additional households to cover a maximum of 15–20 percent of households in each district	U Sh 4,000	15	4 months

Source: Government of Uganda 2016.
Note: NDVI = Normalized Difference Vegetation Index; NUSAF = Northern Uganda Social Action Fund; U Sh = Uganda shilling.

TABLE 3.2 **Kenya: A framework to scale up the Hunger Safety Net Program**

LOCATION	TRIGGER OF VCI	DROUGHT-PHASE EQUIVALENT	MAXIMUM COVERAGE OF HOUSEHOLDS TO RECEIVE CASH TRANSFER	AMOUNT OF TRANSFER	FREQUENCY OF TRANSFER	DURATION OF TRANSFER
Subcounty	≥ 50 and 35–50	Wet or no drought	1. Normal	Routine HSNP households	Standard payment (K Sh 5,100)	Every 2 months	Ongoing
	20–35	Moderate drought	2. Alert	Routine HSNP households	Standard payment	Every 2 months	Ongoing
	10–20	Severe drought	3. Alarm	Routine HSNP households	Standard payment	Every 2 months	Ongoing
				Households beyond routine, up to 50 percent coverage in each sublocation	Emergency payment (K Sh 2,550)	Every month	For each month VCI is at severe drought status
	< 10	Extreme drought	4. Emergency	Routine HSNP households	Standard payment	Every 2 months	Ongoing
				Households beyond routine, up to 50 percent coverage in each sublocation	Emergency payment (K Sh 2,550)	Every month	For each month VCI is at extreme drought status

Source: Fitzgibbon 2016.
Note: HSNP = Hunger Safety Net Program; K Sh = Kenya shilling; VCI = Vegetation Condition Index.

FIGURE 3.2

Kenya: Modeling the cost of responding to drought

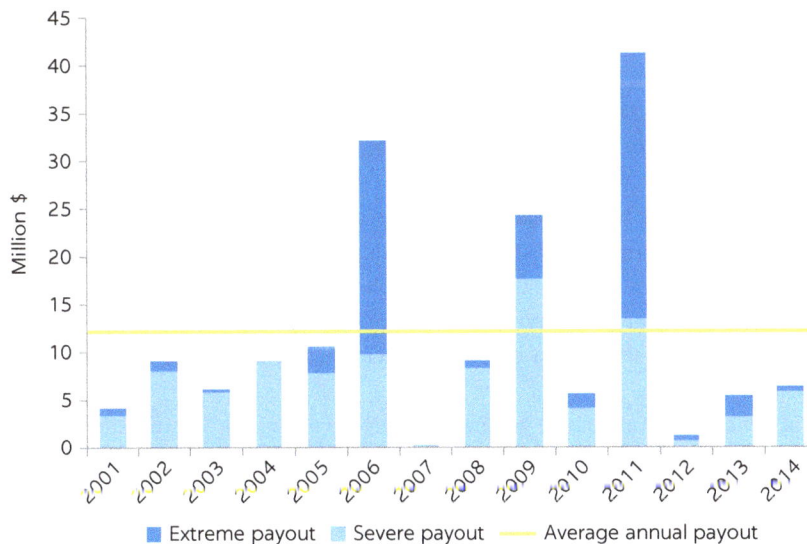

Source: Maher, Fitzgibbon, and Solórzano 2018.
Note: Annual scalability costs are totaled across the four Hunger Safety Net Program counties.

a one-off response and also the long-term cost of scaling a shock-responsive approach over 10–20 years. Figure 3.2 shows the result of modeling Kenya's HSNP. The bars illustrate how much the approach would have cost over the last 14 years using an agreed drought-response trigger. The model shows the cost in very severe years and nondrought years and provides an average over all years. This enables policy makers to see that scaled-up payments would be required almost every year in response to severe drought while a scale up that only triggers in response to extreme drought would be far less frequent (and hence less expensive). This information is valuable to policy makers in making decisions about what scale and level of shock-responsiveness is financially feasible in the long term.

Risk analysis can inform the trigger point(s) at which a safety net program responds or modifies its response. Programs can be designed to trigger an earlier response, or even before a disaster occurs, by linking responses to early warning systems (as discussed in chapter 2). When preagreed thresholds are breached, programmatic responses are triggered as are the requisite, prepositioned financial resources.

Lesson 2: Preplan the financing required to ensure timely response

Ensuring funds are available when needed is critical for effective risk financing. Once a clearer picture of the potential costs of responding through social protection emerges, governments are far better placed to examine their risk financing options.

Postdisaster response, recovery, and reconstruction phases require different financial instruments and disbursement rates/durations. The immediate response operation requires the most instantaneous funding, whereas recovery and reconstruction take time to get under way. These later costs can be much larger than initial relief assistance. For example, monsoons or earthquakes destroy infrastructure that is costly to replace. That said, droughts may result in larger immediate support costs through food aid or cash payments during the event, in the relief phase, which may persist for a longer period of time.

Funding constraints can slow the response even if systems are in place. In Lesotho, "the fact that the mechanism for the top-up [vertical expansion] was designed at the time of the crisis—not an integral part of the Child Grant Program—meant that it was slow to start and disburse and had to hunt for funds." The program "only started providing top-ups [vertical expansions] in June 2016, 6 months after the declaration of the drought emergency" (and only for two quarterly payments), with delays partly due to the program waiting for the scheduled quarterly payment date (Kardan, O'Brien, and Masasa 2017, 26).

Humanitarian response generally involves waiting until a disaster has hit before securing financing for the response, recovery, and reconstruction phases. As noted, these responses typically undertake a needs/loss assessment and use the results to launch a global funding appeal; few funding appeals are ever fully funded. Consequently, funds for emergency response arrive piecemeal and often months after the crisis.

A disaster risk financing strategy that layers instruments according to the frequency and severity of the risk can be developed based on the potential costs for shock-responsive social protection. No single financial instrument can or should cover all risk financing requirements. Risk-layering considers how to meet the financial cost of response using a menu of financial instruments (figure 3.3). Each instrument has its own terms and conditions and, therefore, advantages and disadvantages (see table 3.3). When assessing how to finance contingent liabilities using a safety net, assessing which instruments are the most appropriate,

FIGURE 3.3
Disaster risk financing: Visualizing risk layering

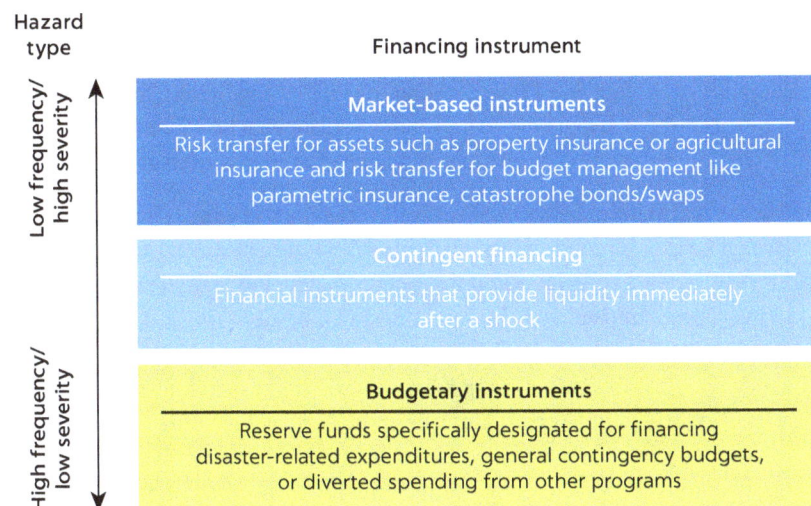

Source: Financial Protection Forum 2018.

TABLE 3.3 Disaster risk financing: A comparison of instruments

TYPE	ADVANTAGES	DISADVANTAGES	BEST SUITED
Ex ante			
Contingency/ reserve funds	• Can be cheap, particularly for frequent shocks • Fast to disburse • Allows implementers to plan ahead for their use • Approach has been used in many contexts; thus, experience is available for countries to build upon	• Requires fiscal discipline • High opportunity cost of funds, given high rates of return on other government investments • Can be hard to justify given the opportunity cost	Low risk layer such as frequent low-level events (annual flooding, localized drought, conflict)
Contingent credit	• Can be cheap, particularly for midfrequency shocks • Fast, when conditions for disbursement are met • Allows implementers to plan • Can incentivize proactive actions to reduce risk (for example, policy actions in disaster risk reduction and disaster risk management)	• Has conditionality • Opportunity cost of loan • Adds to country's debt burden, must be repaid • Current low (but growing) uptake of Cat DDOs as some countries prefer investment projects guaranteed resources over contingent instruments	Mid-risk layer such as higher-magnitude, less frequent events whose damages exhaust the resources of national contingencies (widespread flooding, hurricanes)
Market-based risk transfer instruments	• Can be cheap, particularly for extreme shocks • Can be fast • Allows implementers to plan • Supports fiscal discipline • Risk diversification	• Can be expensive for frequent shocks • Can be vulnerable to criticism and "regret" • Can miss need • Need a level playing field to negotiate • Trade-off between the cost of premiums and the frequency or scale of the pay-out	High-risk layer such as extreme, less frequent events, less than every 5–10 years (severe droughts, hurricanes, earthquakes)
Ex post			
Humanitarian assistance	• Flexible—can respond to need • Doesn't have to be repaid	• Can be slow to be mobilized • Can be unreliable • Undermines preplanning	Only as a last resort
Other ex post instruments	• Approach has been used in many contexts; thus, experience is available for countries to build upon	• Can be slow • Can have negative impact on long-term development/investment programs • Can be expensive	Only as a last resort

Source: Maher, Fitzgibbon, and Solórzano 2018.
Note: Cat DDO = Catastrophe Deferred Drawdown Option.

adequate, and cost-effective alongside the frequency and severity of the antici-pated shocks is critical. In most cases, multiple financial instruments will be required to meet the financial cost of the response.

There are three main financial instruments for designing a risk financing strategy for ASP. Budgetary instruments, contingent credit, and market-based instruments are discussed in detail below. They can be directly linked to shock-responsive safety net programs. Looking at each instrument, in turn:

- **Budgetary instruments (contingency/reserve funds).** These are rela-tively cheap and immediately available following a covariate shock, allow-ing ministries, departments, and agencies to develop realistic contingency plans. These funds may be included in shock-responsive ASP financing in the form of flexible budget lines or contingency budget lines, allocating funds for shocks and avoiding bureaucratic delays such as verification, administrative accounting, and disbursement scheduling (box 3.1). Of critical importance are the rules under which such funds disburse. In many countries contingency funds exist; however, the conditions under which they disburse are vaguely written and often broad. In such instances, it can be a challenge to ensure sufficient funds are available when a shock occurs, especially when shocks occur later in the budgetary cycle, as the funds can be depleted. The main disadvantage is the oppor-tunity cost when there is no disaster because of competing needs for funds. In addition, when a shock hits, the sums rarely cover all costs; thus, they need to be complemented with other financial instruments (World Bank 2017). Budgetary reallocations, though these are not an ex ante instrument, also fall under this category, but in contrast are used in the aftermath of a shock, usually in the absence of financial planning (dis-cussed further below).
- **Contingent credit (mainly ex ante loan agreements).** Such credit provides immediate liquidity in the aftermath of a covariate shock, often at highly con-cessional terms (long duration with low interest rates). Ex ante loan agree-ments typically are offered by multilateral development banks and international financial institutions (box 3.2). These agreements have the potential to assure financing beyond a government's own reserve funds

BOX 3.1

Mexico: The Natural Disasters Fund

In Mexico, the federal government established the Natural Disasters Fund (Fondo de Desastres Naturales—FONDEN) in 1996 as a mechanism to finance the postdisaster recovery and reconstruction of Mexico's public assets and low-income housing. The fund consists of three primary financial accounts: the FONDEN Program for Reconstruction, the FONDEN Trust, and the Revolving Fund.

Collectively, these instruments assist the govern-ment in its efforts to respond quickly to natural disas-ters by providing funding for emergency relief, rehabilitation, and reconstruction. These instruments are continuously updated to enhance their efficiency and effectiveness.

FONDEN has a mandatory annual budget alloca-tion of at least 0.4 percent of total expenditure.

Source: World Bank 2017.

(World Bank 2017). The main drawbacks are (1) the funds are often provided as budget support, so there is no guarantee that they will be used to finance ASP programs; and (2) it is still a loan and so adds to the country's debt (O'Brien et al. 2018a). Contingent credit is most cost-effective for high-impact, low-frequency shocks.

Contingent credit instrument: Catastrophe Deferred Drawdown Option

The World Bank developed the Catastrophe Deferred Drawdown Option (Cat DDO) in 2008 as a development policy loan for countries that have the financial ability to borrow from the International Bank for Reconstruction and Development (that is, International Bank for Reconstruction and Development countries).

- Cat DDOs incentivize proactive action to reduce risk. Governments must demonstrate the capacity to manage natural risks to be eligible.
- Cat DDOs may be drawn upon declaration of a state of emergency in the borrower's territory, as a result of a natural disaster.
- Cat DDOs act as a fiscal buffer that reduces disaster impact.
- Cat DDOs can be used to back up existing insurance pools.

Cat DDOs have been effective liquidity instruments, providing countries with needed cash in the immediate aftermath of a disaster. The World Bank has approved 16 Cat DDOs for a total value of $3.1 billion. It also, in 2018, expanded the instrument to countries with low per capita incomes that lack the financial ability to borrow from the International Bank for Reconstruction and Development (that is, International Development Association countries).

Kenya is the first African country to develop a disaster risk financing strategy and the first International Development Association country to receive Cat DDO financing ($220 million). Cat DDOs are under preparation in Benin, Madagascar, and Malawi. Catastrophe risk pools are emerging as useful mechanisms to support country access to cost-effective risk transfer solutions. Regional risk pools can facilitate (1) building regional reserves to finance losses from small and medium events; (2) attracting donor support to capitalize a fund; (3) pooling country-specific disaster risks into one diversified portfolio; (4) accessing international reinsurance markets on competitive terms, diversifying risk across multiple countries with different risk profiles; and (5) building a more robust foundation of risk information and management (World Bank 2017).

For example, the Caribbean Catastrophe Risk Insurance Facility has 17 members (primarily small Caribbean island states). It allows member governments to purchase insurance coverage to finance immediate postdisaster recovery needs. The facility acts as a risk aggregator by enabling participating countries to pool their country specific risks into one, better-diversified portfolio. This diversification should result in a substantial reduction in premium cost of 45–50 percent. Claims payments are based on parametric triggers, which means they are index-based insurance instruments that pay claims based on the occurrence of a predefined event, (such as hurricanes, earthquakes, flooding) rather than on an assessment of actual losses on the ground. This measurement, made remotely by an independent agency, allows for transparent, low-settlement costs and quick-disbursing contracts.

Insured countries pay an annual premium commensurate with their own specific risk exposure. Parametric insurance products are priced for each country based on their individual risk profile. Annual premiums typically vary from $200,000 to $4 million, for coverage ranging from $10 million to $50 million. The Caribbean Catastrophe Risk Insurance Facility has made 38 payouts between 2007 and 2018 totaling $135 million, including payouts to 10 Caribbean countries following the 2017 hurricane season.

Sources: CCRIF SPC n.d.; Ghesquière et al. n.d.

FIGURE 3.4

Ethiopia: PSNP integrates ex post humanitarian assistance within a risk financing strategy

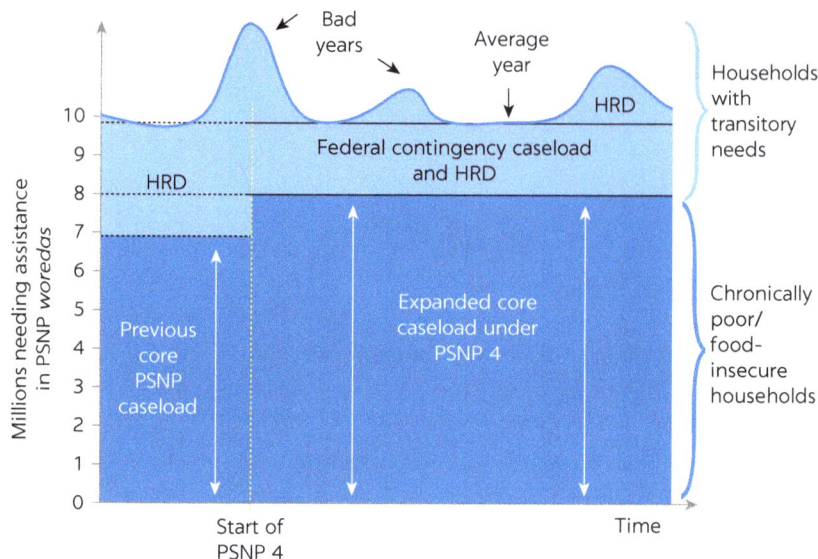

Source: Woldemichael 2018.
Note: HRD = Humanitarian Requirement Document. PSNP = Productive Safety Net Programme. Federal contingency budget can also be used in non-PSNP *woredas* within PSNP regions.

- **Other common ex post financing instruments.** Some governments fund part of the response ex post, usually through budget reallocations. This was the case in Fiji after Tropical Cyclone Winston in 2016. The government financed relief and recovery activities through the social protection system by reallocating budgeted resources from lower-priority expenditures. Countries also may have scope for borrowing (depending on market access and existing levels of domestic and external debt) as well as tax increases or private sector investments, but these ex post measures are not cheap and come with other drawbacks. Humanitarian assistance remains a prevalent ex post instrument for response, as discussed at the outset of this chapter. When developing a comprehensive risk-layering strategy, humanitarian assistance can be integrated alongside other instruments, especially for shocks of low frequency, limited predictability, and high intensity. In Ethiopia, if needs exceed 8 million people in Productive Safety Net Programme (PSNP) *woredas* (districts), a combination of contingency budgets and humanitarian assistance is utilized to cover up to an additional 2 million people. When needs surpass 10 million people, the additional people are reached through the humanitarian system (figure 3.4).

It is advisable to consider a suite of options rather than to rely on a single financing instrument, as each type of funding has advantages and disadvantages, relative to the frequency, severity, and predictability of the disaster. This is the core principle of risk layering, the core considerations of which are outlined in table 3.3. Examples of risk layering from five countries are depicted in table 3.4.

TABLE 3.4 **Ethiopia, Kenya, Mexico, the Philippines, and Uganda: Financial layering for adaptive social protection programs**

COUNTRY	RESERVE FUND	CONTINGENT CREDIT	RISK TRANSFER	BUDGET REALLOCATION	DONOR FINANCE	HUMANITARIAN RESOURCES
Ethiopia	●			●	●	●
Kenya	●				●	
Mexico	●		●	●		
Philippines	●			●	●	
Uganda		●				

Source: Maher 2018.

Lesson 3: Establish and link the financing to effective disbursement mechanisms

Establishing effective disbursement mechanisms (that is, how funding reaches beneficiaries) and linking disaster risk financing instruments to them is as important as securing funds in the first place. Having funds available in-country is of limited benefit if they cannot be timely transferred to the relevant institutions and to the shock-affected communities. One reason there has been so much interest in shock responsive social protection is that this is very often the only government service already regularly transferring cash (or other in-kind benefits) to large numbers of households.

A key factor affecting the disbursement of funds to affected households is the existence of effective safety net payment systems. Countries can select different approaches in the use of social protection payment mechanisms for the delivery of cash-based emergency responses. These may include manual systems or electronic transfer to bank accounts or new technologies such as mobile phone payments. Scaling up manual systems tends to increase costs in line with the number of people assisted; it also can prove difficult in the aftermath of some disasters where roads and other key infrastructure prevent the physical distribution of cash. E-payment systems are emerging as the preferred option to deliver aid, as they have the advantages of speed, accuracy in targeting, and flexibility, even in challenging environments.

Establishing such payment systems can be very costly and delay assistance if the infrastructure is only set up during or in response to a crisis. The registration of households for bank accounts can take months, even years. The adoption of e-payment systems takes time and faces challenges, including the coverage of agents and vendors, their financial liquidity, and unreliability of the technology. Nonetheless, e-payment systems are increasingly being introduced to channel private payments and remittances as well as social protection payments. Depending on the institutional arrangements, payments to the affected population can be conducted by the implementing agency, decentralized to a local government, or outsourced to a financial service provider (which may be a private or state-owned company) (O'Brien et al. 2018b).

Once established, automatic payment systems provide a faster and much more efficient mechanism to disburse cash for both regular and emergency programs. Kenya's HSNP is one of the best examples of putting a payment mechanism in place in advance of any disaster. Likewise, in Ecuador, the robust payment system of the social protection system allowed a timely response to the 2016 earthquake. Expanding e-payment systems also has the positive side-effect of substantially increasing financial inclusion (which, as noted in chapter 1, is a key component for enhancing a household's capacity to prepare and become more resilient). In Kenya, the coverage of households with bank accounts in the four poorest counties rose from being negligible to over 90 percent as part of the HSNP second phase.

Core factors determining the effectiveness of safety net payment mechanisms are explored below, including their implication for disbursing postdisaster financing to beneficiaries.

- **Release of funds.** Delays in the disbursement of upstream funding can cause delays to the beneficiaries receiving transfers. This is a common challenge for routine social protection delivery, and countries have tackled it in a variety of ways, including: minimizing the number of accounts for transferring resources; automating transfer procedures where possible; ensuring timely approval of budgets and monitoring availability of funds; defining a strategy for liquidity and cash management, as well as contingency planning for delays; (where feasible) utilizing the country's single treasury account system; exploring the feasibility of classifying social protection expenditures as personnel emoluments rather than general expenses in the national budget (Barca et al. 2017).[1]

- **Absorptive capacity within the disbursement mechanism.** In shock-affected contexts, standard delays are inherently exacerbated, partly as tried and tested financing arrangements for routine programming need to be complemented by new ad hoc processes, depending on the country's strategy. Both Lesotho and Mali, for instance, have faced challenges in releasing the funds pledged to interventions after disasters occurred. In the Philippines, too, despite the existence of contingency financing mechanisms for disaster response, there were administrative delays in releasing the emergency funding allocated to the department overseeing disaster response after Typhoon Haiyan. Therefore, robust processes need to be put in place for anticipating and releasing funds (O'Brien et al. 2018b), in line with the contingency planning highlighted in chapter 2.

- **Transfer of funds to the local level.** The delays in upstream funding can be further exacerbated if processes for ensuring liquidity at the local level are not in place. In practice, this will depend on the overarching payment modality of any existing social protection programs in the country and the selected payment mechanism for shock response (if not piggybacking on existing systems). E-systems pose some advantages but may be disrupted by shocks themselves. Evidence from existing experiences maintaining the routine delivery schedule in the aftermath of a shock has shown that liquidity can be a major constraint for payment agents—stressing, again, the need for preparedness measures and contingency plans to ensure liquidity is rapidly available down to the local level. In terms of over-the-counter payments to beneficiaries, this may include plans for moving currency from headquarters and regional hubs to provincial and district distribution networks (such as local automated teller machines or pay agents).

- **Reconciliation.** In the reconciliation process of routine social protection payments, the amount paid to the payment provider (whether a private contractor or a government counterpart) is reconciled with the amount disbursed by the provider to beneficiaries. If data management is electronic (for example, using a program management information system), a reconciliation statistics report is drafted and analyzed to identify to whom transfers were paid and whether any inconsistencies emerge (Barca et al. 2017). Robust processes for postdisaster reconciliation of payments can better ensure limited leakage and corruption. Moreover, when funding comes from separate budget envelopes, such as from development and humanitarian partners, the underlying financial procedures outlining the source and flow of funds, including reconciliation requirements, are often different. This poses challenges for a timely response due to differing donor accountability requirements. In such instances, establishing common processes with key nongovernmental partners in advance of a shock will be important to encourage alignment and ultimately expedite the processing of payments to beneficiaries after a shock.

NOTE

1. These are prioritized government expenses that are honored and predictable.

REFERENCES

ADB (Asian Development Bank). 2018. "Strengthening Resilience through Social Protection Programs." Guidance Note. ADB, Manila.

Barca, Valentina, Thea Westphal, and Veronica Wodsak. 2017. "Administration of Non-Contributory Social Protection: Delivery Systems—Manual for a Leadership and Transformation Curriculum on Building and Managing Social Protection Floors in Africa." Transform (Transformation Curriculum on Building and Managing Social Protection Floors in Africa).

Cabot Venton, C. 2018. "Economics of Resilience to Drought in Ethiopia, Kenya and Somalia: Executive Summary." Center for Resilience, U.S. Agency for International Development, Washington, DC.

Cabot Venton, C., and L. Sida. 2017. "The Value for Money of Multi-Year Humanitarian Funding: Emerging Findings." Department for International Development, London.

CCRIF SPC. n.d. *2017–18 Annual Report*. Grand Cayman: CCRIF SPC. https://www.ccrif.org /sites/default/files/publications/CCRIF_Annual_Report_2017_2018_0.pdf.

Clarke, D., and S. Dercon. 2016. *Dull Disasters? How Planning Ahead Will Make a Difference.* Oxford, UK: Oxford University Press.

Clarke, D., and R. Hill. 2016. "Disaster Risk Financing as a Tool for Development." Report. World Bank and Disaster Risk Financing and Insurance Program, Washington, DC. https://www .gfdrr.org/sites/default/files/publication/DisasterRisk.pdf.

Clarke, D., and R. Vargas Hill. 2013. "Cost-Benefit Analysis of the African Risk Capacity Facility." IFPRI Discussion Paper 01292. International Food Policy Research Institution, Washington, DC.

Financial Protection Forum. 2018. "Disaster Risk Finance: A Primer, Core Principles and Operational Framework." World Bank, Washington, DC. https://financialprotectionforum .org/publication/disaster-risk-finance-a-primercore-principles-and-operational -framework.

Fitzgibbon, C. 2016. "Shock-Responsive Social Protection in Practice: Kenya's Experience in Scaling up Cash Transfers." Humanitarian Policy Group, Overseas Development Institute, London. https://odihpn.org/blog/shock-responsive-social-protection-in-practice-kenyas -experience-in-scaling-up-cash-transfers/.

Ghesquière, F., O. Mahul, M. Forni, and R. Gartley. n.d. "Caribbean Catastrophe Risk Insurance Facility." *International Aid + Trade* IAT03-13/3. World Bank, Washington, DC. http://siteresources.worldbank.org/PROJECTS/Resources/Catastrophicriskinsurancefacility.pdf.

IASC (Inter-Agency Standing Committee). 2016. "Too Important to Fail—Addressing the Humanitarian Financing Gap: High-Level Panel on Humanitarian Financing Report to the Secretary-General." United Nations Office for the Coordination of Humanitarian Affairs, Geneva.

Kardan, A., C. O'Brien, and M. Masasa. 2017. "Shock-Responsive Social Protection Systems Research Case Study: Lesotho." Oxford Policy Management, Oxford, UK.

Maher, B. 2018. "Financing Adaptive Social Protection Financial Tools and Approaches for Adaptive Safety Nets." Presentation at World Bank South–South Learning Forum, Frankfurt. http://pubdocs.worldbank.org/en/827871520537561050/SSLF18-Financing-ASP-Framing.pdf.

Maher B., C. Fitzgibbon, and A. Solórzano. 2018. "Emerging Lessons in Financing Adaptive Social Protection." Background Paper for the World Bank, Oxford Policy Management, London.

O'Brien, C., J. Congrave, K. Sharp, and N. Keïta. 2018a. "Shock-Responsive Social Protection Systems Research: Case Study—Social Protection and Humanitarian Responses to Food Insecurity and Poverty in Mali." Oxford Policy Management, Oxford, UK.

O'Brien, C., R. Holmes, Z. Scott, and V. Barca. 2018b. "Shock-Responsive Social Protection Systems Toolkit—Appraising the Use of Social Protection in Addressing Largescale Shocks." Oxford Policy Management, Oxford, UK.

O'Brien, C., Z. Scott, G. Smith, V. Barca, A. Kardan, R. Holmes, C. Watson, and J. Congrave. 2018c. "Shock-Responsive Social Protection Systems Research: Synthesis Report." Oxford Policy Management, Oxford, UK. https://www.opml.co.uk/files/Publications/a0408-shock-responsive-social-protection-systems/srsp-synthesis-report.pdf?noredirect=1.

Uganda, Government of. 2016. "Third Northern Uganda Social Action Fund (NUSAF3) Project—Disaster Risk Financing Sub-Component Handbook." Government of Uganda, Kampala.

UN OCHA (United Nations Office for the Coordination of Humanitarian Affairs). 2018. *Global Humanitarian Overview 2018*. New York: UN OCHA. https://www.unocha.org/sites/unocha/files/GHO2018.PDF.

Wilkinson, E., L. Weingartner, R. Choularton, M. Bailey, M. Todd, D. Kniveton, and C. Cabot Venton. 2018. "Forecasting Hazards, Averting Disasters: Implementing Forecast-Based Early Action at Scale." Overseas Development Institute, London.

Woldemichael, B. 2018. "New Ways of Working: Linkages between Humanitarian Assistance and the Productive Safety Net Program in Ethiopia." Presentation at World Bank South–South Learning Forum, Frankfurt. http://pubdocs.worldbank.org/en/304641520538162620/SSLF18-Humanitarian-Assistance-Ethiopia.pdf.

World Bank. 2017. *Sovereign Climate and Disaster Risk Pools: World Bank Technical Contribution to the G20*. Washington, DC: World Bank.

4 Institutional Arrangements and Partnerships
MULTISECTORAL COORDINATION AND HUMANITARIAN LINKAGES

OVERVIEW

Adaptive social protection (ASP) is an inherently multisectoral undertaking, requiring coordination across a broad range of actors who are engaged in building the resilience of vulnerable populations, and whose expertise and resources will be critical to the advancement of ASP in any country. This includes, most prominently, those in the disaster risk management (DRM) sector as well as those operationalizing climate change adaptation initiatives.

Institutional
arrangements and
partnerships

To promote the required coordination, ASP needs to have coherence and complementarity across the policies and strategies of these sectors. Concretely, social protection strategies and frameworks can provide the foundation for pursuing objectives related to ASP. However, an exclusive focus on articulating the function of social protection in building resilience within its own sectoral strategies can result in overlapping mandates, competition for resources, and a limited impact on resilience building. Clear policy commitments that align the overall objectives of these different sectors along with the specific mandates, roles, and responsibilities of the actors involved will help to provide the policy framework to encourage increased coordination. At the same time, policy commitments will need to be backed by appropriate financial resources and investments in the required capacity for those tasked with delivery to be credible.

Moreover, as the role of safety net programs in response to previously humanitarian crises and shocks increases, the closer integration of social protection actors and programs within the humanitarian system, particularly in settings of limited national capacity and/or particularly severe shocks, increasingly comes to the fore. Evolutions in the humanitarian system enshrined in the World Humanitarian Summit's Grand Bargain (2016) promote the expanded use of cash transfers and, in doing so, a commitment to "increase SP [social protection] programs and strengthen national and local systems to build resilience in fragile contexts." Operationally, unbundling a clear delineation of roles and responsibilities for the delivery of resilience-building programs between government and humanitarian actors, based on the specific context and relative comparative advantages, will help to create actionable, strategic partnerships for the advancement of ASP across the government–humanitarian divide.

This chapter draws extensively from background papers by Bailey (2018) and Kardan (2018).

MULTISECTORAL COORDINATION FOR ASP

A defining feature of ASP is the many actors within government that may be involved in its implementation. The inherent multidisciplinary and interagency nature of resilience building across the three capacities of preparedness, coping, and adaptation requires diversified expertise and coordination among actors. Indeed, the number of potential actors and complementary programs aligned to ASP objectives calls for institutional arrangements to anchor the planning, management, and delivery of this assistance. In practice, the development of ASP in many countries has shifted attention from a singular focus on national social protection systems, the policies that guide them, and the organizations that deliver social protection programs to a wider focus inclusive of the policies, organizations, and programs involved in DRM and climate change adaptation.

Strong government leadership is necessary to ensure the coordination of the often disconnected actors, based on a clear articulation of respective roles and responsibilities. Concretely, governments lead by setting resilience-related objectives in policies and strategies, inclusive of social protection, DRM, and climate change adaptation, among other sectors. Policy commitments can work to instill the necessary budgetary allocations for national ministerial structures to translate objectives into outcomes among vulnerable households. In practice, government leadership also includes establishing the standards and procedures to guide the integration of nongovernmental organizations (NGOs) and humanitarian actors in ASP implementation. This chapter begins with an overview of the key considerations around the requisite institutional arrangements among national actors before moving to focus more squarely on the creation of strategic partnerships with nongovernmental actors.

Establishing policy coherence for adaptive social protection

National social protection policies and strategies can provide the foundation for ASP. Most countries have social protection policies and strategies that set out the government's vision. The extent to which these policies and strategies are rooted in legislation varies (see, for example, Beegle, Coudouel, and Monsalve 2018). The functions of social protection often are equity, which provides protection against deprivation; resilience, which is insurance against shocks; and opportunity, which seeks to promote human capital and access to income earning opportunities (World Bank 2012; see also Devereux and Sabates-Wheeler 2004, who set a similar framework of protection, prevention, promotion, and transformation). Articulated in this manner, these policies and strategies provide a foundation for the aims of ASP.

The strategies of other sectors such as—prominently—DRM also may support the advancement of ASP. For example, the ASP objective of building the resilience of poor and vulnerable households to shocks overlaps with the objectives set out in national DRM policies and strategies. This is particularly true given the ongoing shift from response to disaster preparedness within the DRM community.[1] In Kenya, ASP emanated out of the government's resolve to address poverty and vulnerability as a cause of and outcome from drought emergencies; a framework developed by the government (Ending Drought Emergencies) laid the policy foundation for the Hunger Safety Net Program which scales and retracts vertically and horizontally for drought emergencies. Where the political appetite for social protection is low, national DRM policies, and the DRM sector more broadly, can provide a foundation for introducing ASP. This suggests a government's commitment to ASP can come from sectors other than social protection itself (boxes 4.1 and 4.2). Beyond the DRM sector, ASP commitments are found in climate change adaptation policies aiming to promote the livelihoods of the poorest households. For example, social protection has been singled out as a key component to climate-change adaptation (Stern 2006) and thus countries seeking to adapt to climate change may opt to invest in ASP.

Ultimately, policy coherence within individual sectors provides the basis for coordination across sectors. A starting point to improve cross-sectoral coordination is to improve policy coherence within each sector. A more internally consistent sector provides clearer opportunities for cross-sectoral collaboration (O'Brien et al. 2018). Sectoral policy frameworks provide the space to articulate roles and responsibilities within and across sectors and enable the establishment of appropriate platforms for coordination. A key challenge of coordinating social protection and other sectors is that each sector often is itself multisectoral and in need of coordination (OPM 2017).

Covariate shocks themselves can create momentum for policy reform in support of ASP. For example, the evolution in Japan's legal framework for DRM can be traced to specific shocks (figure 4.1). The Basic Act was enacted in 1961 after major typhoons caused extensive damage in a southwestern part of Japan in 1959. The Act has since been amended several times, with at least 10 specific amendments in the last 5 years, following the East Japan Great

Pacific Island countries: Disaster risk management (DRM) institutions can help to drive the ASP agenda

The commitment to ASP objectives may be located in a DRM policy and driven forward by a DRM agency, particularly in regions or countries where exposure to disasters is a key determinant of poverty.

In the Pacific Region, there appears to be an appetite for this type of institutional arrangement for ASP. All recognize the importance of DRM and have put in place DRM legislation and plans since the mid-1990s. By contrast, no Pacific Island countries have legislation governing social protection and few have agencies explicitly tasked with managing social protection programs.

As a result, some countries have expressed interest in embedding elements of the ASP agenda in Natural Disaster Management Acts and having the equivalent National Disaster Management Office in charge of coordinating a response.[a] This is particularly the case for such countries as Vanuatu, the Solomon Islands, and Samoa which are reluctant to allocate funding for regular social safety net programs (due to financing constraints or concerns around the impact on informal support networks) but clearly recognize the importance of having the delivery systems in place required to target transfers following large-scale disasters. While this type of institutional arrangement has not yet been fully tested, it could prove to be suitable in regions where social protection institutions have limited capacity or are nonexistent.

a. These priorities were formally set out during the inaugural Pacific Shock-Responsive Social Protection Conference, which was held in Nadi, Fiji, in 2018.

BOX 4.2

The Philippines: Social protection embedded in disaster risk management (DRM) frameworks

The Philippines has a well-developed social protection system and a comprehensive legislative and institutional arrangement governing DRM. The social protection sector uses a common definition of social protection that is understood by all actors and is spearheaded by the Department of Social Welfare and Development (DSWD). The respective policies of each sector explicitly recognize the role of social protection in disaster response.

The DRM sector has a well-established and strong institutional framework articulated through the Disaster Risk Reduction and Management Act of 2010. The National Disaster Risk Reduction and Management Framework of 2011 and the National Disaster Response Plan, developed in 2015 based on the lessons learned from Typhoon Haiyan, elaborate the structures, roles, and responsibilities at different levels of government and across different departments. Within this framework, the DSWD is the lead on disaster response. The social welfare and development officers at the regional, provincial, and municipal levels are part of the action teams responsible for supporting disaster response. Beyond immediate response, DSWD also plays an important role

during the rehabilitation and recovery phases following a disaster, with interventions and services that contribute to longer-term recovery. At the same time, the DSWD is the co-lead of the international humanitarian cluster system designed to coordinate government and humanitarian actors, and is the government's lead agency for the protection, food, and shelter clusters.

As such, social protection and DRM have become more closely interlinked over time in the Philippines through an iterative process that has captured learning from each emergency response. Central to this policy coherence and coordination is high-level political commitment, strong legislative and regulatory backing, clear roles and responsibilities, and well-established coordination structures. Having the DSWD as the lead agency for social protection as well as emergency response has provided a seamless link between the DRM, humanitarian, and social protection actors. However, this has not been without its challenges, with capacity constraints straining the DSWD's ability to effectively manage all its obligations during large shocks such as Typhoon Yolanda in 2013.

Sources: Bowen 2015; Smith et al. 2017.

Earthquake in 2011, to refine the roles and responsibilities across actors and ultimately the effectiveness of DRM. In Ethiopia, the government launched the Productive Safety Net Programme (PSNP) in 2005 in response to persistent drought in rural areas and associated food insecurity, which had plagued the country over an extended period of time.

From policy coherence on paper to coordination in practice

Multisectoral coordination for ASP requires clear institutional guidelines for program delivery. National social protection systems already include a range of service providers to support program implementation. For example, the data that inform program participation can be generated by government systems or contracted out. Payments are often made by banks or telephone companies (for e-payments) through a contractual arrangement with the government. Additional services, such as livelihood support, may be provided by local government institutions or by NGOs. NGOs or communities may operate a program's grievance redress mechanism.

FIGURE 4.1

Japan: History of postdisaster DRM reforms and ASP legislation

Background		Evolution of legislation (summary)	
1946 Earthquake	Necessity of swift response, defining the role of national/local governments	1947	Disaster Relief Act
1959 Typhoon	Necessity of comprehensive DRM system (both physical and social)	1961	Disaster Countermeasures Basic Act
	Necessity of consistent and swift approach to severe disasters	1962	Act on Special Financial Support to Deal with the Designated Disaster of Extreme Severity
1964 Earthquake	Fire insurance (private) could not cover exceptional large-scale disasters; necessity of public intervention	1966	Act on Earthquake Insurance
1967 Heavy rain	Discussions: Difficulty to support individuals versus heavier damage to vulnerable people (took 6 years) → As condolence grant	1973	Act on Provision of Disaster Condolence Grant (cash transfer)
1995 Earthquake	Necessity of institutional arrangement and collaboration after severe disasters → HQs in national and local governments	1995	(Amendment) Disaster Countermeasures Basic Act
	Civic movement complaining about the necessity of safety net (firstly to target by income, but eliminated at amendment 2007)	1999 2004	(Amendment) Act on Support for Reconstructing Livelihoods of Disaster Victims
2011 Earthquake tsunami	Various lessons, i.e., necessity to support people requiring support for evacuation and at a shelter, breakdown of local governments	2013	(Amendment) Disaster Countermeasures Basic Act

Source: Kawasoe, forthcoming.
Note: DRM = disaster risk management.

The choice of the ministry responsible for coordinating social protection tends to determine the level of government oversight. Social protection programs are often housed in central ministries (Ministry of Finance, Office of the Prime Minister), social ministries (Ministry of Social Welfare), and other sectoral ministries. Management by central ministries situates social protection close to the locus of power and authority, which can result in secured (and possibly increased) financing and advancement of the agenda but oversight by staff who may be less supportive to the program's aims than are dedicated social protection staff. Management by a social ministry can result in staff delivering the program or advancing the agenda who are supportive of social protection objectives but may not have the direct access to the resources of central ministries (Beegle, Coudouel, and Monsalve 2018).

The overall effectiveness of ASP rests on government-led coordination among and delivery modalities within programs. A number of factors can contribute to more effective programmatic coordination in responding to shocks, including the existence of and support through a single central agency that coordinates response and works closely with other national agencies and subnational authorities; the presence of dedicated, multisectoral technical working groups; existence of DRM strategies and response plans with clearly identified roles and responsibilities; and advanced planning for coordination of implementation during crises and its incorporation within the program's standard operating procedures (operational manual) (OPM 2017). Importantly, coordination across programs (and even across sectors) requires strong, sustained government leadership through oversight agencies.

The introduction of national standards or a coordination framework can help to facilitate the required coordination. Because ASP spans a number of sectors and involves a number of ministries and/or NGOs, each of these organizations will have its own management systems as well as incentives and accountabilities. While these differences may lead to fragmentation (and even competition), the creation of national standards or frameworks may be able to bring coherence and consistency across ASP programs, while also drawing on the strengths of different organizations.[2] Examples of the application of harmonized approaches or frameworks for various aspects of ASP design and delivery exist across a range of countries. For example, common transfer guidelines were developed in the Philippines and Lesotho. Such frameworks aim to introduce similar accountability across services as well as flows of information, both to the government and citizens. Box 4.3 describes the framework that Ethiopia has put in place to create a national, shock-responsive safety net.

Determining the roles and functions of each ASP program (or providers of each function within a program) in advance of any shock is vital. Such an approach is critical given the large number of organizations involved in delivering different aspects of ASP programming and the overriding need for speed in response to most shocks. In Pakistan, the Citizen Damage Compensation Program established partnerships with private sector commercial banks through a memorandum of understanding implemented as part of disaster preparedness plans (World Bank 2013). The Federal Disaster Response Action Plan was developed following the Citizen Damage Compensation Program's response to flooding in 2010, defining the cash-based response model for future shocks as well as the roles and responsibilities of the respective agencies critical for implementation, including the national and provincial disaster management authorities, the Benazir Income Support Program, the National Database and Registration Authority, the Ministry of Finance, and commercial banks. In Niger, the government implemented a national contingency plan for responding to weather-related shocks that includes ensuring access to food through social assistance, protection of household assets, and developing early warning indicators (Bastagli 2014). Beyond establishing roles in advance, ensuring stakeholders' active participation in joint planning can strengthen the knowledge and skills of each partner. Such participation also can contribute to creating a common understanding of the problems.

National standardized guidelines for program implementation can facilitate vertical coordination from national to local actors. The degree of vertical coordination within a government from national to regional to local actors is determined by the broader government structure and the extent of its decentralization (see below). In Lesotho, for example, social protection is managed centrally, while emergency is the responsibility of district DRM teams. Regardless of the precise government system, vertical coordination from central to local levels is strengthened by clear roles and responsibilities for each

Ethiopia: Framework of a national, shock-responsive safety net

In Ethiopia, the government needed an instrument with the capacity to respond to chronic and transitory food insecurity in rural areas of the country. It turned to social protection and DRM policies to create a framework for a scalable safety net program.

In 2018, the government of Ethiopia recognized that bringing the PSNP and Humanitarian Food Assistance (HFA) together into a common framework could help putting a scalable safety net system into practice. It operates based on the following guidelines: (1) the rural safety net is a government-led framework that allows three delivery modalities: the government, the United Nations (World Food Programme), and NGOs; (2) these three delivery modalities share a set of common procedures and common monitoring and evaluation mechanisms; (3) the procedures distinguish a "normal year" from an "emergency" situation for safety net transfers to be used (that is, a distinction which is required to trigger humanitarian assistance); and (4) financing includes developmental and humanitarian funds.

Within this system:

- The National Disaster Risk Management Commission is responsible for conducting needs assessments and the allocation of resources for all transitory food needs. This includes humanitarian resources pledged in response to the Humanitarian Appeal and the geographic allocation of any resources channeled through the PSNP federal contingency budget. Through

this process, any transitory needs of core PSNP clients will be considered in the needs assessment and contingency planning and met through humanitarian financing.

- All implementing stakeholders use a common set of core procedures and structures to deliver both core PSNP transfers and HFA. This includes (1) procedures for targeting, (2) software to keep track of beneficiary lists and transfers, and (3) using common delivery structures at the district and community level. All transfer values will be set for "normal" periods and increase to the Sphere standards when an emergency is identified.[a]

- All resources channeled through the government are managed by the ministry with the appropriate mandate and skills. Therefore, (1) all cash transfer resources (whether for the PSNP or HFA) channeled through the government flow through the Ministry of Finance, while cash payments are the responsibility of District Finance Offices; and (2) all food transfer resources (whether for the PSNP or HFA) channeled through the government flow through the National Disaster Risk Management Commission's Logistics Department with the relevant disaster management desk at the district level responsible for overseeing the appropriate storage and distribution of food at the subdistrict level.

a. The Sphere movement was started in 1997 by a group of humanitarian professionals aiming to improve the quality of humanitarian work during disaster response. With this goal in mind, they framed a Humanitarian Charter and identified a set of humanitarian standards to be applied in humanitarian response. The Sphere Handbook outlines common principles and universal minimum standards in humanitarian response.

level of government as well as clear lines of accountability and resourcing. (For a general discussion of vertical coordination for social protection, see Beegle, Coudouel, and Monsalve 2018; Barca et al. 2017.)

Investing in the capacity to deliver ASP programs

For national actors to deliver ASP, significant investments in capacity are required at both the national and local levels. The extent to which the organizations responsible for program delivery have an effective local presence influences their ability to deliver program benefits. ASP programs require front-line ASP staff to carry out a range of tasks, including coordination with other sectors to ensure that households receive complementary services. For example, this includes the delivery of training to households or the provision of information or "accompanying measures" to strengthen nutrition. In Peru, the Haku Winay Program utilizes *Yachachiq* (trained local productive community leaders) to provide technical assistance, capacity building, and accompaniment of households to implement the program and build resilience to food insecurity. In Brazil, the Social Assistance Center (Centro de Referencia de Assistencia Social—CRAS) provides social assistance at the municipal level; households that are beneficiaries of Bolsa Familia and registered in the social registry are assisted by the Social Assistance Center and can be included in the other services, policies, and programs delivered by the Brazilian Unified Social Assistance System (WWP 2019).

The degree of governmental decentralization affects the central–local relationship and the capacity to respond to shocks with ASP. In a devolved, decentralized setting where the state transfers authority for decision-making and management from central government to autonomous units of subnational, local government, any reliance on local financing, variations in needs and resources are likely to lead to inconsistencies in service provision between areas unless equalization mechanisms are put in place (Barca et al. 2017). These may be mitigated if they are understood and reflected in the legislative and policy frameworks of the country and where the relationships of the different actors at different tiers of government are clearly defined. In Ecuador, DRM has been decentralized to the local level; yet, the national guidelines stipulate that when a shock exceeds capacities at the local level, higher levels of government provide support. This was the case in 2016, when severe capacity constraints at the local level triggered a centralized response to a major earthquake (Beazley 2017).

When responding to shocks, the delivery capacity of ASP programs also needs to expand and contract. Most simply, to expand coverage in response to shocks, social protection programs will require more staff, vehicles, and equipment, for example, to serve more people often across a greater geographic area. Often, government systems and resources are required to respond at a time when these systems themselves may be under strain and further constrained (O'Brien et al. 2018). Identifying surge capacity to support the response processes is critical. This surge capacity may be obtained, for instance, horizontally across departments and ministries, vertically through higher tiers of government, or collaboratively with nonstate actors.

The relative roles and responsibilities at each level of government, as well as how staff access information and resources, have an impact on the effectiveness of ASP programming. Semi-autonomous or autonomous central government agencies often have the mandate, and resources, to deliver services through field offices. In contrast, delivery through devolved national structures requires vertical coordination that may demand significant investments in systems and procedures in advance of any shock, as well as coordination among decision makers at different levels of government. In El Salvador, Indonesia, and Mozambique, strengthening subnational DRM committees has been identified as a key strategy for strengthening the DRM systems (Harkey 2014). In the Philippines, local government units lead disaster response with reserve funds (5 percent of their revenue), although national resources supplement this local-level financing in the case of large disasters. In Pakistan, in 2011, the federal structure devolved the responsibility for social protection and DRM to provincial governments; however, the Benazir Income Support Program (national cash transfer program) remained federal because it was established before the devolution.

CREATING STRATEGIC PARTNERSHIPS ACROSS THE GOVERNMENT-HUMANITARIAN DIVIDE

At the same time, given the nature of covariate shocks, ASP highlights the importance of deepening linkages with humanitarian actors. In lower-capacity environments and contexts where there is no functioning, legitimate state with access to populations affected by a shock, the international humanitarian system often leads the provision of assistance. When states lack the capacity or willingness to ensure that the basic needs of its population are met, international humanitarian assistance often complements and sometimes substitutes for national and local capacity. When protracted crises that result from intractable political instability and conflict are the norm, the leadership role of the humanitarian system often becomes longer term in nature. Some of the primary features of the international humanitarian systems are summarized in table 4.1 along with their implications for ASP, which are explored in further detail, in turn.

TABLE 4.1 International humanitarian system: Features and implications for adaptive social protection

FEATURE	CHARACTERISTICS	IMPLICATIONS
Policy commitments and the Grand Bargain	High-level policy support for building resilience and increasing the role of social protection	Opportunities to advance aims of ASP but need to be translated into more concrete and strategic actions
Bifurcation of humanitarian/ development and rise of resilience building	Humanitarian and development assistance often underpinned by different financing channels, coordination structures, mandates, and principles	Divide between humanitarian and development systems may remain an obstacle; need for specificity on "resilience building"
Humanitarian financing	Very little direct funding goes to national governments; significant flows to fragile and conflict settings, and year-on-year to the same places Shares of humanitarian financing go to some areas and populations supported by national safety nets	Limited potential for humanitarian financing to be channeled to governments for national safety nets; scope to fund NGOs operating within national frameworks for ASP in some countries
Humanitarian principles	Humanitarian assistance is guided mainly by the four principles of humanity, impartiality, independence, and neutrality Differing views on flexibility of principles exist, but they are not incompatible with working with governments	Humanitarian principles should inform the response function of ASP to shocks; can be referenced to advocate for a principled engagement around ASP with governments by humanitarian agencies
Coordination	Established mechanisms for coordination (see the cluster system) but varying coordination approaches because of differing levels of national involvement in those mechanisms	Need for engagement of ASP at various levels of humanitarian operational and strategic coordination and for bilateral engagement with major donors and aid agencies
Increasing shift to cash transfers	Cash transfers increasingly accepted as mainstream tool of humanitarian response, but programs often fragmented and still represent only a small share of total assistance	Offers an entry point for engagement of national ASP programs with humanitarian system

Source: Bailey 2018.

The Grand Bargain: High-level commitment in support of government–humanitarian integration

The 2016 World Humanitarian Summit, and the resulting Grand Bargain, created high-level policy support to strengthen linkages with social protection. More than 50 donors and aid agencies committed to the Grand Bargain, which is a series of 10 commitments to improve assistance to crisis-affected populations. Among others, the donors commit to increasing the routine use of cash and to enhancing the engagement between humanitarian and development actors. This includes a commitment to "increase social protection programmes and strengthen national and local systems and coping mechanisms in order to build resilience in fragile contexts" (Grand Bargain 2016, 14). However, the challenge remains to move from endorsements to concrete actions.

In parallel, increased policy attention to building household resilience within the humanitarian community is highly favorable to advancing the aims of ASP. The increasing focus on building resilience within the humanitarian community (see also appendix A) aims to promote adaptation and to respond to the interaction between chronic poverty and acute needs. In Somalia, for example, efforts are under way to improve the continuity of activities across preparedness, relief, rehabilitation, and development. This includes providing a minimum level of social protection in response to chronic and seasonal food insecurity (Bailey 2018).

"Humanitarian principles": What are they and what are their implications for ASP?

The provision of humanitarian assistance is informed by a set of principles. Primarily, these principles include humanity (alleviating suffering wherever it is found), impartiality (assisting solely on the basis of need), neutrality (not taking sides in a conflict), and independence (operating freely from political and military agendas). In some instances, commitment to humanitarian principles can create tensions with supporting governments to assist and protect people in their territory if the government is not working in the interest of its people, in opposition to the principles of neutrality and impartiality (FAO 2016; Harvey 2009). In other instances, humanitarian principles can be invoked by humanitarian actors to justify not engaging with governments when there may be many possible—and necessary—relations with states and governments in a given context (Harvey 2009; Levine and Mosel 2014).

Humanitarian principles should play a role in guiding the design and implementation of ASP. Engaging with humanitarian actors necessitates speaking the language of humanitarian principles and understanding how these inform actions. The principles exist to help ensure that organizations can access people affected by crisis and support those most in need, which is ultimately at the heart of the ASP resilience-building objectives. At the same time, the humanitarian community will need to continue aligning with, leveraging, and complementing efforts to support national systems where appropriate and consistent with humanitarian principles (World Bank 2016). While tensions exist, it is possible to remain committed to principles underpinning both humanitarian and development-oriented ASP initiatives (Harvey 2009). That is, the humanitarian principles should provide a basis for deepening linkages and coordination as opposed to a roadblock.

Coordination mechanisms: Streamlining government and humanitarian interventions

Coordination is a perennial challenge with the humanitarian system itself. Recent estimates reveal that international humanitarian assistance involves some 4,480 actors drawing from international and national NGOs, civil society, and others (Development Initiatives 2018). Numerous organizations provide similar and different types of aid in the same locations and thus must coordinate to minimize gaps and overlap in meeting needs (Clarke and Campbell 2018). To address these issues, the United Nations system has a well-institutionalized, country-level "cluster" coordination system articulated by sectors and an array of institutional governing arrangements. Clusters are groups of humanitarian organizations, both UN and non-UN, in each of the main sectors of humanitarian action (such as water, health, and logistics). They are designated by the Inter-Agency Standing Committee and have clear responsibilities for the coordination of aligned actors[3] (figure 4.2).

FIGURE 4.2

United Nations cluster system: Overview

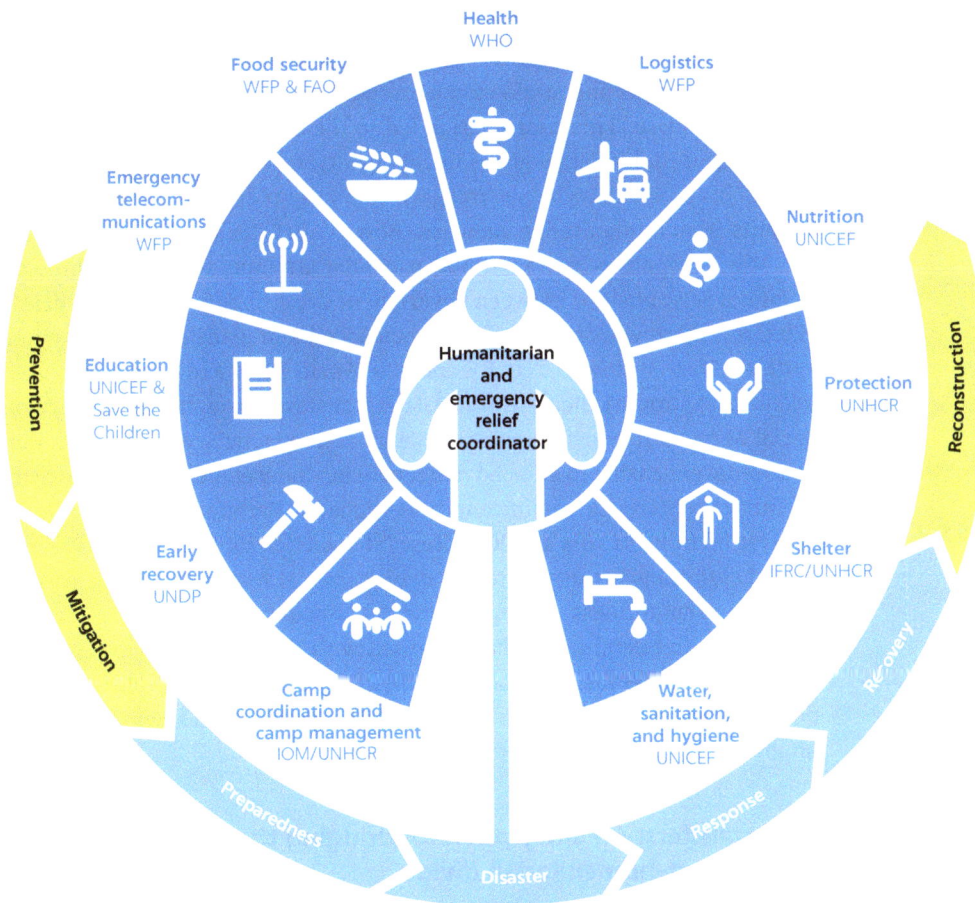

Source: United Nations Office for the Coordination of Humanitarian Affairs Services.
Note: ECHO = European Civil Protection and Humanitarian Aid Operations; FAO = Food and Agriculture Organization of the United Nations; IFRC = International Federation of Red Cross and Red Crescent Societies; IOM = International Organization for Migration; UNDP = United Nations Development Programme; UNHCR = United Nations High Commissioner for Refugees; UNICEF = United Nations Children's Fund; USAID = United States Agency for International Development; WFP = World Food Programme; WHO = World Health Organization.

Where ASP intersects with the humanitarian system, these humanitarian coordination mechanisms will be instrumental in enhancing partnerships. Coordination of international humanitarian interventions at the country level is carried out through Humanitarian Country Teams (comprised of senior leadership from international organizations and sometimes donors) and clusters. The cluster system serves as the mechanism for sector-based planning and implementation discussions with state and nonstate actors. Clusters are tasked with developing strategies for their sectors, which in practice tends to be done by aligning the autonomous programs of different aid agencies (Clarke and Campbell 2018). In the case of disaster response, for example, in some cases, coordination is government-led, with clusters or similar working groups led by government sectoral agencies, as in Mozambique (Kardan et al. 2017). In other cases, coordination is a hybrid of international and government leadership, with clusters being co-led by government departments, as noted earlier in the case of the Philippines (Smith et al. 2017). However, the risk of having parallel systems and lack of coordination remains.

Coordination can lead to and be enhanced by the sharing of data among social protection and humanitarian actors—and can elicit improved knowledge, reduce duplication of efforts, and lead to cost savings. In Turkey, refugees were enrolled into the Emergency Social Safety Net Program through the country's existing information management platform. In the Philippines, the Department of Social Welfare and Development set up a system for coordinating data on typhoon-affected households assisted by aid agencies with its own database. This coordination led to the enrollment of an additional 20,000 households into a government cash transfer program (Smith et al. 2017). This process also helped track which households were receiving which benefits from humanitarian agencies (Bowen 2015). In the Hurricane Irma and Maria responses in the Caribbean, similar attempts were made through bi-lateral relationships between government departments and aid agencies. However, there were trade-offs between speed and using social protection systems. In Dominica, UNICEF and the World Food Programme worked together to support the delivery of cash transfers through the Ministry of Social Services to provide scaled-up support to beneficiary households and horizontal expansion to affected nonbeneficiary households in the aftermath of Hurricane Maria. In Dominica and in Antigua and Barbuda, the International Federation of Red Cross and Red Crescent Societies supported the distribution of cash transfers using prepaid debit cards (already procured as part of regional preparedness measures) and the assistance was timelier. In the British Virgin Islands, two NGOs worked with the Ministry of Health and Social Development to undertake an emergency cash transfer program and to design data collection tools to inform future registration in social protection programs. Even so, implementation faced delays.

Cash transfers: An entry point for bridging the government-humanitarian divide

The humanitarian sector's pivot toward cash transfers over the past decade has helped bridge the "humanitarian–social protection divide." Cash transfers were virtually nonexistent in the humanitarian sector before 2005, whereas cash and vouchers together accounted for $2.8 billion (10 percent) of humanitarian assistance in 2016 (CaLP 2018). The fact that social protection programs often transfer money to populations has led to numerous calls to utilize these systems to a greater extent in times of emergencies and seasonal shocks (see, for example, Bailey and Harvey 2015; Grand Bargain 2016; World Bank 2016). There are cases where humanitarian cash transfers have either paved the way for social protection programs or strengthened the foundations and improved a country's ability to deliver ASP (box 4.4).

Moving beyond dichotomies: Unbundling specific roles and responsibilities to create strategic partnerships

Conceptually, government and humanitarian actors are often viewed simplistically in "either-or" terms. In addition to the entry points for ASP highlighted above, moving beyond a broad commitment to coordination and increased partnerships requires a nuanced approach. It outlines each actor's specific contributions in terms of delivering assistance to the poor and vulnerable to strengthen their preparedness, coping, and adaptation capacities.

BOX 4.4

Cash transfers: A vehicle for ASP development across the government–humanitarian divide

Humanitarian cash transfers can encourage change and reform in the humanitarian system, provide an opening for the development of ASP systems, and result in improved coordination among humanitarian and government actors.

The recent Panel on Humanitarian Cash Transfers and other high-level initiatives, most notably the World Humanitarian Summit, established unequivocally that cash transfers are of strategic importance in improving humanitarian response. As of 2015, approximately 7 percent of international humanitarian assistance is channeled toward either cash transfers or vouchers (ODI 2015). The Summit established a target for the percentage of humanitarian resources to be provided in cash by 2030, ensuring a responsibility among all actors to align and work together. This shift is one of the most fundamental reforms of the humanitarian system over the past decades.

There are multiple cases where humanitarian cash transfers have either paved the way for social protection programs or strengthened the foundations and improved a country's ability to deliver ASP.

- In the Democratic Republic of Congo, the introduction and expansion of cash-based responses has been the biggest evolution in humanitarian assistance in the last decade (ODI 2015). The evidence base built through these initiatives helped establish the case for a national safety net system, which is being financed through the World Bank (Lisungi Safety Nets System Project) and will assist the country in responding to future crises.

- In Nepal, following the earthquake in 2015, the government and the humanitarian actors made great efforts to coordinate humanitarian cash transfers to ensure uniform benefit amounts and coverage of all affected. UNICEF financed a vertical and horizontal expansion of the Social Security Allowance, a cash transfer, in the affected areas (CaLP 2018). Following this, Nepal has engaged in a broad dialogue on ASP and started to establish the building blocks that would promote mobilization of cash transfer programs for disaster response—a robust database of beneficiaries and vulnerable households, electronic payment systems, and institutional coordination across social protection and disaster response agencies. As a result, Nepal is expected to be better equipped to respond to future disasters.

Sources: CaLP 2018; ODI 2015.

Identifying the precise roles and responsibilities of government and humanitarian actors can help establish actionable, operational partnerships for the delivery of ASP. A framework laid out by Seyfert et al. (2019) attempts to facilitate the identification of workable pathways for progress among national and humanitarian actors (figure 4.3). Instead of falling back on the "either–or" choice, the framework lays out four strategic options (parallel systems, alignment, piggybacking, and national-led systems). It also discusses how collaborations may emerge around select programmatic "functions" and the "degrees" of possible connection between national and humanitarian actors within a given function. While a work-in-progress, such a granular analytical approach holds the potential to move beyond strategic dialogue and strategies in support of coordination; that is, coordination toward an operationally relevant delineation of roles and responsibilities based on relative comparative advantages in differing country contexts.

The exact arrangements will differ across countries and contexts, with no predetermined division of labor. Indeed, the creation of actionable, strategic partnerships for ASP requires clear institutional guidelines for delivery. National social protection systems already include a range of service providers to support program implementation along the delivery chain. For example, the data that inform program participation can be generated by government systems or contracted out. The number of organizations may increase as ASP continues to evolve. The additional capacity that is needed to identify, enroll, and pay an increasing number of people can be contracted in or out. This notion of contracting out extends to ASP and humanitarian actors, who may have greater capacity or expertise at key points along the delivery chain in certain contexts (table 4.2).

FIGURE 4.3

Framework: Mix of delivery approaches across government and humanitarian actors

	Parallel systems	Alignment	Piggy-backing	National-led systems
Financing	●			
Legal and policy framework		●		
Setting eligibility criteria and qualifying conditions		●		
Setting transfer type, level, frequency, duration			●	
Governance and coordination				●
Outreach	●			
Registration		●		
Enrollment	●			
Payment			●	
Case management				●
Complaints and appeals				●
Protection			●	
VAM/M&E		●		
Information management	●			

Source: Seyfert et al. 2019.
Note: VAM/M&E = Vulnerability analysis and mapping/monitoring and evaluation.

TABLE 4.2 Kenya and Ethiopia: Features that influence the use of government systems for shock response versus humanitarian actors or NGOs

FEATURE	TYPES	INTERACTION WITH OTHER FEATURES	EXAMPLES
Source of financing	• Development partner humanitarian funds • Development partner development funds • Domestic government financing	**Managing agency:** Higher probability of development funds being channeled through government departments and humanitarian funds through WFP/NGOs. When humanitarian funds are channeled through a government agency these tend to be through a disaster management agency rather than a sectoral ministry. **Coordinating institution:** Humanitarian funds are more likely to be channeled through agencies that are coordinated by a disaster management agency and development funds through a sectoral ministry.	• **Humanitarian funds:** ○ ECHO financing of cash transfers in Ethiopia and Kenya (largely through NGOs/WFP) ○ USAID support for food aid in Ethiopia and Kenya (through NGOs/WFP) ○ European Union financing for the scale-up of HSNP transfers in Kenya • **Development funds:** ○ Development partner contributions to the federal contingency budget of the PSNP in Ethiopia ○ UK Department for International Development financing for the scale-up of HSNP transfers in Kenya • **Domestic government financing:** ○ Ethiopia government budget contributions to food assistance coordinated and implemented by the disaster management agency ○ Kenya government budget for emergency cash transfers managed by department of special programs, targeting coordinated by the National Disaster Management Authority
Needs assessment/ response planning	• National government led system • Ad hoc individual agency led	**Strong coordination by government:** Ethiopia, regarding both geographic resource allocation through needs assessment and management of response **Weak coordination by government:** Kenya, coordination of early warning is fairly strong, but there is little or no ability to influence actions of implementing agencies and therefore avoid duplications and minimize gaps; also, each implementing agency tends to use its own procedures	• **Well-financed government led system:** Ethiopia through the Humanitarian Requirement Document leading to a unified response plan implemented by various actors. • **Individual agency led:** HSNP scale-up in Kenya, which uses a separate system of triggers to the standard needs assessment.
Managing agency or execution	• Government • Outside of government: ○ NGO ○ WFP	In combination with existence or absence of strong coordinating body can affect use of standard procedures (whether needs assessment or implementing procedures) and thus harmonization of response.	• **Government:** Management of cash and food response through the PSNP • **NGO:** Joint Emergency Operations, financed by USAID, in Ethiopia operates within the government framework • **WFP:** Food distribution in Ethiopia operates within the government framework • **WFP-government combination:** Cash transfers in Ethiopia (until recently, has used an ad hoc government funding channel) • **WFP-NGO combination:** Food distributions in Kenya

continued

TABLE 4.2, *continued*

FEATURE	TYPES	INTERACTION WITH OTHER FEATURES	EXAMPLES

Implementing procedures	• Nationally owned, standardized procedures for targeting, benefit levels, etc.
	• Ad hoc, individual agency-defined procedures
			• **Nationally owned and set:** Ethiopia emergency response and PSNP scale-up
			• **Ad hoc, individual agency-defined procedures:**
			  ○ In Kenya, most of the emergency response, although WFP has some standardized procedures
			  ○ In Ethiopia, emergency cash transfers have less standardized procedures than emergency food.

Source: Based on Sandford 2018.
Note: ECHO = European Civil Protection and Humanitarian Aid Operations; HSNP = Hunger Safety Net Program; NGO = nongovernmental organizations; PSNP = Productive Safety Net Programme; USAID = United States Agency for International Development; WFP = World Food Programme.

NOTES

1. Sendai Framework, https://www.unisdr.org/we/coordinate/sendai-framework.
2. National standards (often articulated in the form of guidelines or operational manuals) typically describe the procedures to be followed in implementing program targeting, registration, payments, case management, grievance mechanisms, and exit.
3. The Inter-Agency Standing Committee is a coordination forum of the UN system, bringing together the executive heads of 18 UN and non-UN organizations to ensure coherence of preparedness and response efforts, to formulate policy, and to agree on priorities for strengthened humanitarian action, https://interagencystandingcommittee.org/the-inter-agency-standing-committee.

REFERENCES

Bailey, S. 2018. "Institutions for Adaptive Social Protection: External Linkages and the Humanitarian Sector." Background Paper. Oxford Policy Management, Oxford, UK.

Bailey, S., and P. Harvey. 2015. "State of Evidence on Humanitarian Cash Transfers." Background Note for the High Level Panel on Humanitarian Cash Transfers. Overseas Development Institute, London.

Barca, Valentina, Thea Westphal, and Veronica Wodsak. 2017. "Administration of Non-Contributory Social Protection: Delivery Systems—Manual for a Leadership and Transformation Curriculum on Building and Managing Social Protection Floors in Africa." Transform (Transformation Curriculum on Building and Managing Social Protection Floors in Africa).

Bastagli, F. 2014. "Responding to a Crisis: The Design and Delivery of Social Protection." ODI Working Paper, Overseas Development Institute, London.

Beazley, R. 2017. "Study on Shock-Responsive Social Protection in Latin America and the Caribbean: Ecuador Case Study." Oxford Policy Management, Oxford, UK.

Beegle, K., A. Coudouel, and E. Monsalve. 2018. *Realizing the Full Potential of Social Safety Nets in Africa.* Washington, DC: World Bank. http://documents.worldbank.org/curated/en/657581531930611436/pdf/128594-PUB-PUBLIC.pdf.

Bowen, T. 2015. "Social Protection and Disaster Risk Management in the Philippines: The Case of Typhoon Yolanda (Haiyan)." Policy Research Working Paper 7482, World Bank, Washington, DC. http://documents.worldbank.org/curated/en/681881468181128752/pdf/WPS7482.pdf.

CaLP (Cash Learning Partnership). 2018. *The State of the World's Cash Report: Cash Transfer Programming in Humanitarian Aid.* Oxford, UK. http://www.cashlearning.org/downloads/calp-sowc-report-web.pdf.

Clarke, P. K., and L. Campbell. 2018. "Coordination in Theory, Coordination in Practice: The Case of the Clusters." *Disasters* 42 (4) 655–73.

Development Initiatives. 2018. "Global Humanitarian Assistance Report 2018." Development Initiatives, Bristol, UK.

Devereux, S., and R. Sabates-Wheeler. 2004. "Transformative Social Protection." IDS Working Paper 232, Institute of Development Studies, Brighton, UK.

FAO (Food and Agriculture Organization of the United Nations). 2016. "The World Humanitarian Summit." Position Paper, FAO, Rome.

Grand Bargain. 2016. "The Grand Bargain: A Shared Commitment to Better Serve People in Need." World Humanitarian Summit, Istanbul. https://reliefweb.int/sites/reliefweb.int /files/resources/Grand_Bargain_final_22_May_FINAL-2.pdf.

Harkey, J. 2014. "Experiences of National Governments in Expanding Their Role in Humanitarian Preparedness and Response." Feinstein International Center, Tufts University, Medford, MA.

Harvey, P. 2009. "Towards Good Humanitarian Government: The Role of the Affected State in Disaster Response." Humanitarian Policy Group Brief 37. Overseas Development Institute, London.

Kardan, A. 2018. "Institutions for Adaptive Social Protection Systems." Background Paper, Oxford Policy Management, Oxford, UK.

Kardan, A., S. Bailey, A. Solórzano, and L. Fidalgo. 2017. "Shock-Responsive Social Protection Systems Research Case Study: Mozambique." Oxford Policy Management, Oxford, UK.

Kawasoe, Y. Forthcoming. "Social Protection Disaster Risk Management Case Study for Japan." World Bank, Washington, DC.

Levine, S., and I. Mosel. 2014. "Supporting Resilience in Difficult Places: A Critical Look at Applying the 'Resilience' Concept in Countries Where Crises Are the Norm." Report Commissioned by Humanitarian Policy Group. Overseas Development Institute, London.

O'Brien, C., J. Congrave, K. Sharp, and N. Keïta. 2018. "Shock-Responsive Social Protection Systems Research: Case Study—Social Protection and Humanitarian Responses to Food Insecurity and Poverty in Mali." Oxford Policy Management, Oxford, UK.

ODI (Overseas Development Institute). 2015. "Doing Cash Differently: How Cash Transfers Can Transform Humanitarian Aid." Report of the High Level Panel on Humanitarian Cash. ODI, London.

OPM. 2017. *Shock-Responsive Social Protection Systems Research: Literature Review*, 2nd edition. Oxford, UK: OPM.

Sandford, J. 2018. "Responding to Shocks: Humanitarian Response through National Systems." Unpublished. World Bank, Washington, DC.

Seyfert, K., V. Barca, U. Gentilini, M. Luthria, and S. Abbady. 2019. "Unbundled: A Framework for Connecting Safety Nets and Humanitarian Assistance in Refugee Settings." Social Protection and Labor Discussion Paper 1935, World Bank, Washington, DC. https:// openknowledge.worldbank.org/bitstream/handle/10986/32467/Unbundled-A -Framework-for-Connecting-Safety-Nets-and-Humanitarian-Assistance-in-Refugee -Settings.pdf?sequence=1&isAllowed=y.

Smith, G., Z. Scott, E. Luna, and T. Lone. 2017. "Shock-Responsive Social Protection Systems Research Case Study: Post-Haiyan Cash Transfers in the Philippines." Oxford Policy Management, Oxford, UK.

Stern, N. 2006. *The Economics of Climate Change: The Stern Review*. Cambridge, UK: Cambridge University Press.

World Bank. 2012. "Resilience, Equity, and Opportunity: The World Bank's Social Protection and Labor Strategy 2012–2022." World Bank, Washington, DC. http://documents .worldbank.org/curated/en/443791468157506768/pdf/732350BR0CODE200doc0 version0REVISED.pdf.

World Bank. 2013. *Building Resilience to Disaster and Climate Change through Social Protection: Synthesis Note*. Washington, DC: World Bank. http://documents.worldbank.org/curated /en/187211468349778714/pdf/796210WP0Build0Box0377381B00PUBLIC0.pdf.

World Bank. 2016. "Cash Transfers in Humanitarian Contexts: Strategic Note." World Bank, Washington, DC. http://documents.worldbank.org/curated/en/697681467995447727 /pdf/106449-WP-IASC-Humanitarian-Cash-PUBLIC.pdf.

WWP (World without Poverty). 2019. "Social Assistance." Brazil Learning Initiative for a World without Poverty. https://wwp.org.br/en/social-policy/social-assistance/.

Resilience as It Relates to Adaptive Social Protection

This appendix outlines in greater detail the definition of resilience, the resilience capacities, and their relationship to poverty and vulnerability. Drawing from the expansive literature, resilience is defined in this report as: The ability for households to prepare for, cope with, and adapt to shocks in a manner that protects their well-being, ensuring that they do not fall into poverty or destitution. This definition suggests that a more resilient person will possess three interlinked capacities that help to minimize and resist a shock's negative impacts. The higher the person's capacity to prepare, cope, and adapt, the lesser the implied impact of a shock and the likelihood of a faster "bounce back," recovering to pre-shock levels of well-being. With this definition, the generalized vulnerability of the poor and vulnerable to covariate shocks can be ascribed to a deficit in terms of the capacity to prepare, cope, and adapt.

Poor households tend to be particularly vulnerable to the impacts of covariate shocks. By 2030, an estimated 325 million poor people will live in the 49 countries most prone to hazards, with the majority in South Asia and Sub-Saharan Africa (Shepard et al. 2013) (box A.1). At the same time, by 2030, it is estimated that man-made disasters will lead to half of the world's poorest people residing in very poor countries that are fragile or affected by conflict (OECD 2018). For a poor household that is hit with a shock, factors such as having limited to no savings, access to finance, access to formal insurance, or safety nets can combine and contribute to this excessive vulnerability and a generally limited capacity to cope with the impacts from shocks (see, for example, figure A.1; Dercon 2005; Hallegatte et al. 2016). To protect short-term well-being and consumption after a shock, poorer households may instead turn to negative coping strategies such as removing children from school to work for extra household income, availing high-interest loans, and selling productive assets and forced migration (del Ninno, Pierre, and Coll-Black 2016; Hallegatte et al. 2016; Skoufias 2005). However, such short-term coping strategies often work to the household's longer-term detriment. In this way, at the aggregate level, shocks work to undermine poverty reduction efforts and can cause a country to hemorrhage human capital, also to its long-term disadvantage: international experience overwhelmingly shows that poverty is both a driver and consequence of disasters (UNISDR 2015).

While poor households are especially vulnerable to covariate shocks, the near- and nonpoor similarly struggle to cope with such impacts, in some cases becoming at-risk of impoverishing losses. Globally, an estimated 26 million people fall into poverty every year because of natural disasters—especially frequent floods and drought (Hallegatte et al. 2017). Across Africa, figure A.1 describes the

Unbreakable: The poor suffer disproportionately from natural hazards

A recent study by the World Bank identified five factors that account for the increased vulnerability of the poor to disasters:

- **Overexposure to disasters.** Poor households are overexposed to disasters (floods, droughts, and high temperatures). Informal settlements, for instance, tend to be located in hazard-prone areas (such as on hillsides, close to riverbanks, or near open drains and sewers), making them highly vulnerable to frequent, low-intensity events (such as recurrent floods). The issue of overexposure is expected to worsen, given population trends and climate change.

- **Higher degree of vulnerability.** Poorer populations have a higher degree of vulnerability than nonpoor populations. When the poor are impacted by a disaster, the share of their wealth lost is two to three times that of the nonpoor, mainly due to the nature and vulnerability of their assets and livelihoods. The poor tend to have fewer or no savings to protect against crises and are twice as likely to live in fragile areas.

- **Less able to cope and recover.** Poor households are less able to cope and recover from a disaster. The impact of disasters on well-being and quality of life is larger on poorer households, who receive less support from financial instruments, social protection schemes, and other private financing. The poor have few buffers against the effects of disasters and deploy coping strategies that further-erode well-being. Repeated losses, destruction of assets, or forced displacement degrade economic activity and well-being.

- **Permanent impacts on health and education.** Over the longer term, disasters lead to permanent impacts on the health and education of poorer populations, as households need to make difficult coping decisions, such as withdrawing children from school or cutting health expenditures. In turn, these impacts reinforce the intergenerational cycle of poverty, with children being the most aggrieved victims. In Guatemala, for instance, Hurricane Stan (2005) increased the probability of child labor in affected areas by more than 7 percent.

- **Negative impacts on saving and investment behavior.** From a behavioral standpoint, disasters can impact saving and investment behavior of poorer households, reinforcing poverty. The impact can be present before a disaster hits, such as smallholders planting low-risk crops to protect their yields in case of bad weather.

Source: Hallegatte et al. 2017.

prevalence of "transitory poverty" where two poor households in five are moving into or out of poverty as income fluctuates and they become exposed to shocks (Beegle, Coudouel, and Monsalve 2018). Concretely, between 2006 and 2011, 45 percent of poor households in Senegal escaped poverty, but 40 percent of nonpoor households fell into it, with households affected by a natural disaster having been found to be 25 percent more likely to fall in poverty during the period (Dang, Lanjouw, and Swinkels 2014). Similarly, in Asia, Walsh and Hallegatte (2019) estimate that almost 0.5 million Filipinos per year are vulnerable to poverty due to natural disasters. Indeed, Skoufias et al. (2019) also capture the prevalence of this vulnerability to poverty across the Philippines, relative to chronic poverty, as depicted in map A.1. Turning to a different type of shock, it also has been estimated that globally 20 million people sink into poverty for each percentage point decline in the gross domestic product growth rate that results from an economic downturn (Ötker-Robe and Podpiera 2013). Similarly, Laborde, Lakatos, and Martin (2019) find that the 2010–11 food price spike tipped

Africa: Chronic and transient poverty

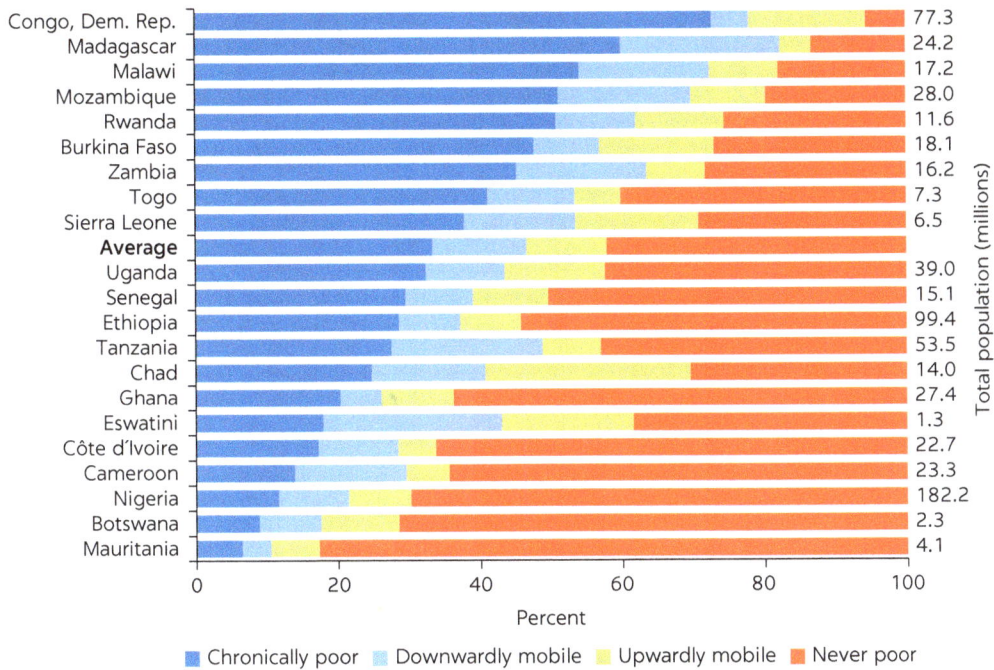

Source: Dang and Dabalen 2017, as cited in Beegle, Coudouel, and Monsalve 2018.
Note: Poverty statistics are from the latest household survey year for each country. "Chronically poor" are households that were poor in both periods of the analysis; "downwardly mobile" are households that fell into poverty in the second period; "upwardly mobile" are those that were poor in the first period but not in the second; and "never poor" are households that were nonpoor in both periods.

The Philippines: Vulnerability to poverty because of typhoons

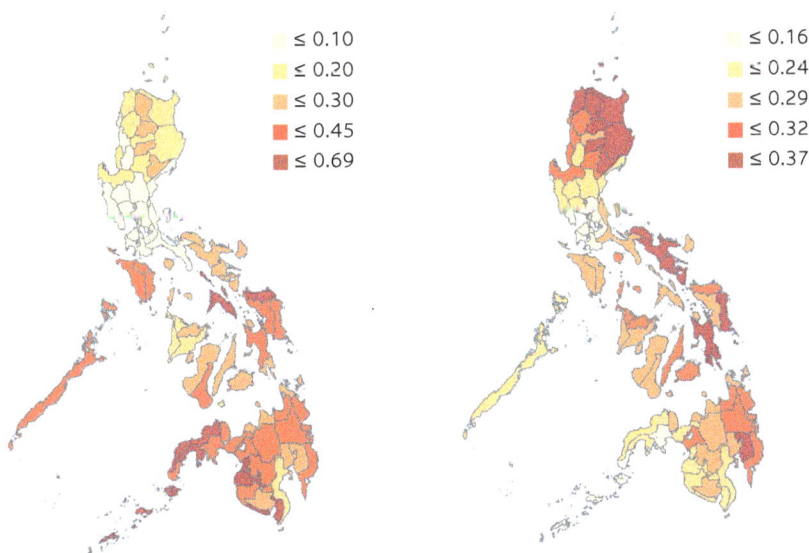

Source: Skoufias et al. 2019.

8.3 million people into poverty, representing nearly 1 percent of the world's poor. The Ebola crisis increased rural poverty 12 percentage points, from 70 percent in the first half of 2014 just before the Ebola crisis to 82 percent in the first half of 2016 following the Ebola crisis (de la Fuente, Jacoby, and Lawin 2019).

These select data points indicate the extent of vulnerability to poverty as a direct outcome of covariate shocks. For this reason, sustainable poverty reduction requires an understanding of both current and future poverty dynamics in the context of vulnerability to poverty among nonpoor households (Diwakar et al. 2019). The notion of future poverty highlights the fact that poverty is a backward-looking concept, where a poor household may have been affected adversely by shocks experienced in the recent or more distant past (Skoufias et al. 2019). However, the conceptual distinction between poverty and vulnerability to poverty rests on the fact that vulnerability to poverty is not about the present but rather about the future (Gallardo 2018). Notably also, women, children, the disabled, and the elderly may not be poor or vulnerable to poverty but belong to vulnerable groups identified as often disproportionately vulnerable to the impacts of shocks (see, for example, Holmes 2019).

The concept of "resilience" to shocks has become widely and ubiquitously applied throughout development and humanitarian institutions in the last decade. This has led to a proliferation of definitions among these actors and across the literature (for a brief sample, see box A.2; for a more detailed synopsis, see Béné, Devereux, and Sabates-Wheeler 2012; IFPRI 2013; De Weijer 2013). In summary, however, resilience can be broadly defined as "the ability of countries, communities and households to manage change, by maintaining or transforming living standards in the face of shocks or stresses without compromising their long-term prospects" (Alfani et al. 2015, 4). The Multi-Agency Resilience Measurement Technical Working Group of the Food Security Information Network (FSIN), led by the World Food Programme and the Food and Agriculture Organization of the United Nations, highlights that the concept of resilience has become compelling in development and humanitarian circles in recent years because it highlights the positive capacity to prepare for and respond to shocks in a way that prevents individuals, households, and communities from suffering long-term adverse consequences (FSIN 2015).

A definition of resilience is offered here as the basis for considering the role of adaptive social protection in building it.[1] Firstly, as noted in the definitions from box A.2, resilience applies to different levels of analysis; for example, the resilience of a society, system, community, household, and individual to shocks. Where the definition used here is concerned, the resilience of the household is the focus specifically. Several definitions of resilience also define resilience as an outcome relative to a benchmark. As the FSIN notes, for conceptual clarity and eventually measurement, it is useful to define resilience as a capacity that prevents households from falling below a "normatively defined level for a given development outcome" including food security, nutrition, well-being, and poverty, for example (FSIN 2014, 7). Accordingly, resilience is defined here as: The ability for a household to prepare for, cope with, and adapt to shocks in a manner that protects their well-being: ensuring that they do not fall into poverty or become trapped in poverty as a result of the impacts.

This definition and the benchmarking of resilience to poverty highlight the previously outlined vulnerability of the poor to shocks as well as the vulnerability of the nonpoor to poverty because of shocks. Accordingly, the definition reflects the necessity of achieving and protecting the long-term development

BOX A.2

Resilience: A brief sample of prominent definitions in the literature and among development and humanitarian institutions

The constituent parts of these multiple definitions of resilience can be grouped in the following ways:

- Resilience as an ability, capacity
- Unit of analysis: system, country, community, society, household, individual
- Mix of specific abilities/capacities of the analysis unit: to resist, absorb, adapt, accommodate, recover, anticipate, prevent, withstand, manage, overcome, maintain, transform, recover from
- Outcomes: without compromising their long-term prospects, do not have long-lasting adverse development consequences; advance the rights of every child; ensuring the preservation, restoration, or improvement of its essential basic structures and functions

United Nations International Strategy for Disaster Reduction: The ability of a system, community, or society exposed to hazards to resist, absorb, accommodate to, and recover from the effects of a hazard in a timely and efficient manner (UNISDR, 24).

Intergovernmental Panel on Climate Change: The ability of a system and its component parts to anticipate, absorb, accommodate, or recover from the effects of a hazardous event in a timely and efficient

manner, including through ensuring the preservation, restoration, or improvement of its essential basic structures and functions (IPCC 2012, 563).

UK Department for International Development: The ability of countries, communities, and households to manage change, by maintaining or transforming living standards in the face of shocks or stresses—such as earthquakes, drought or violent conflict—without compromising their long-term prospects (DFID 2011, 6).

Building Resilience and Adaptation to Climate Extremes and Disasters (BRACED): The ability to anticipate, avoid, plan for, cope with, recover from, and adapt to (climate related) shocks and stresses (Bahadur et al. 2015a, 11).

Resilience Measurement Technical Working Group: The capacity to ensure that shocks and stressors do not have long-lasting adverse development consequences (WFP 2015).

UNICEF: The ability of children, households, communities, and systems to anticipate, prevent, withstand, manage, and overcome cumulative stresses and shocks in ways which advance the rights of every child, with special attention to the most vulnerable and disadvantaged children (UNICEF 2017, 3).

goals of poverty reduction as a driver and a consequence of shocks. In that sense, the definition is directly aligned with the Sustainable Development Goals where social protection (Target 1.3) and building resilience of the poor and vulnerable (Target 1.5) are both contributory targets to the achievement of the goal of ending poverty (Goal 1).

Where this definition of resilience is concerned, resilience and vulnerability to poverty can be simplistically seen as "two sides of the same coin." Jorgensen and Siegel (2019) note an implied[2] symmetry between reducing household vulnerability to poverty and increasing household resilience to poverty, where vulnerability to poverty is related to the exposure and susceptibility of households, and the potential negative impacts and resilience to poverty is related to the ability of households to prevent/resist/recover from their negative impacts over time. The "SRM 2.0 model" for vulnerability and resilience to poverty is outlined briefly in box A.3, wherein all households are separated into four categories based on whether they are expected to be poor in the future.

This concept of vulnerability and resilience to poverty has also been linked explicitly to the mean and variance of the welfare measure used. Skoufias et al. (2019) have developed similar concepts of vulnerability and resilience as being

Social risk management: Vulnerability and resilience to poverty

In social risk management frameworks, a household is defined as vulnerable to poverty if the probability of its future well-being falling below a socially accepted norm (or "benchmark") is high. This definition identifies "at-risk" individuals/households as being "at-risk of falling into poverty."

A household can be vulnerable to poverty because of a specific hazard/risk and/or because of multiple hazards/risks, and vulnerability to poverty can be for one or more period(s) into the future. It is possible to divide all of society into four groups of households that

are either poor/nonpoor or vulnerable/resilient to poverty at a given point in time. If a household's current income is below the poverty line the household is income poor; and if the expected income is less than the poverty line, the household is considered asset poor.

Income poverty is an outcome. Asset poverty is forward-looking and shows lack of opportunity to be nonpoor. Increasing household wealth through asset accumulation (and improved risk management) is critical to moving from vulnerability-to-poverty to resilience-to-poverty.

TABLE BA.3.1 Poor and nonpoor households grouped as vulnerable or resistant to poverty

HOUSEHOLD POOR TODAY		HOUSEHOLD NONPOOR TODAY	
Expected to be poor in future	Not expected to be poor in future, depends on variance in expected income	Expected to be poor in future, depends on variance in expected income	Not expected to be poor in future
Chronic poor	**Transient poor**	**Transient poor**	**Sustainably nonpoor**
Vulnerable to poverty	Exit poverty? Vulnerable/resilient to poverty?	Enter poverty? Vulnerable/resilient to poverty?	Resilient to poverty
	Outcome depends on good/bad luck	Outcome depends on good/bad luck	
Household Group 1	**Household Group 2**	**Household Group 3**	**Household Group 4**
Income poor	Income poor	Income nonpoor	Income nonpoor
Asset poor	Asset nonpoor	Asset poor	Asset nonpoor

Source: Jorgensen and Siegel 2019.

the product of both the mean and variance in welfare, and Hoddinott (2014) has done so using food consumption, asking the questions: is the household poor today, and can it be expected to be poor tomorrow based on its variance in welfare resulting from a shock? In that sense, a household is resilient if the answer to both questions is no, and a household's resilience can be built through interventions that increase mean resilience in excess of the poverty line and/or reduce variance in welfare to ensure it does not fall beneath the poverty line (box A.4).

Broadly speaking, the literature further disaggregates household resilience as being the product of a set of interlinked household capacities. As with the myriad definitions of resilience itself, definitions of these individual capacities, as well as the respective emphases applied to each of them, vary across institutions and within the literature. Nevertheless, taken together they are most often summarized in terms of "absorptive, adaptive, anticipatory, and transformative" capacities (most prominently as found in Bahadur et al. 2015a; Béné et al. 2012; FSIN 2015). To briefly summarize, together, these capacities imply that a household is resilient when it can adequately prepare for a shock (anticipatory), adapt and

BOX A.4

Welfare mean versus welfare variance: Conceptualizing resilience to poverty

The welfare of a household measured by per capita expenditure is assumed to be characterized by two key parameters: the mean value of household per capita expenditure (Is the household poor?) and the variance of household per capita expenditure (Is the household vulnerable to poverty?). Thus, households are assumed to differ with respect to the mean level of their per capita expenditure and the variance of their per capita expenditure around that mean.

Figure BA.4.1 summarizes these two dimensions of welfare, mean and variance, for 10 hypothetical households (households A–J). The mean consumption expenditure of a household (or the average value of consumption expenditures, for example, associated with many different shocks or states of the world over time) is depicted by the blue square. Households differ with respect to the mean level of their expenditure and the variance of their expenditure around that mean, with some households having a low (or high) mean level of consumption and a low (or high) variance of consumption.

- **Poor households.** Households A, D, G, and I are, on average, poor households and their vulnerability is "poverty induced," meaning that it is determined primarily by low endowments of assets and human capital that are the primary determinants of their low mean value of welfare.
- **Nonpoor households.** Households B, C, E, F, H, and J are, on average, nonpoor households as their mean welfare is above the poverty line. However, some of these households are vulnerable to poverty while others are not.
- **Not vulnerable to poverty.** Households B, E, and H, for example, have variability in their consumption but the variance line never crosses the poverty line.
- **Vulnerable to poverty.** Households C, F, and J may end up below the poverty line under some circumstances, as depicted by the fact that the variance of their consumption around the mean crosses the poverty line. For households C, F, and J, vulnerability to poverty is "risk induced."

FIGURE BA.4.1

Vulnerability to poverty characterized by the mean and variance of welfare

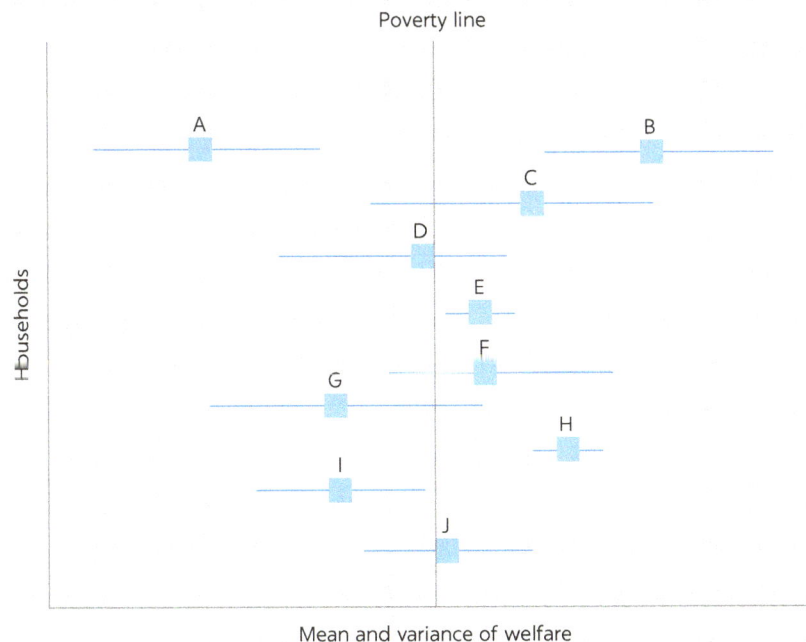

Source: Skoufias et al. 2019.
Note: Hoddinott (2014) applies a similar concept using the food consumption score as the threshold.

reduce its risk to that shock over time (adaptive), cope with its impacts should it materialize (absorptive), and potentially even completely remove its exposure and vulnerability to the shock through a structural transformation in its livelihood, assets, and/or location (transformative). "Transformative" capacity also may be viewed as a constituent part of the household's adaptive capacity (Davies et al. 2009). These definitions, as found in the literature, are expanded upon in greater detail in box A.5.

Drawing from the capacities identified in the literature, a household's resilience to a shock can be seen as the product of its capacity to prepare, cope, and adapt. The higher the household's capacity to prepare, cope, and adapt, the lesser the implied impact and the likelihood of a faster bounce-back (Schipper and Langston 2015), recovering to pre-shock levels of well-being.

For greater precision, taking each interlinked capacity in turn, a more resilient household can do the following:

- **Prepare** for a shock to minimize and mitigate its impact on well-being.[3] Primarily, the degree of preparedness is related to the household's access to information that improves the understanding of the factors that drive its exposure and vulnerability to shocks, as well as the actions taken to minimize these factors (Bahadur et al. 2015a). This preparedness directly enhances the

BOX A.5

Household resilience "capacities" in the literature

Drawing primarily on the absorptive, adaptive, and transformative framework from Béné et al. (2012) and the anticipatory, absorptive, and adaptive framework from Bahadur et al. (2015a), each of which have been widely adopted in the social protection and resilience literature:

- *Anticipatory capacity* is denoted as the ability for the household to be better prepared for the eventuality of a specific shock by proactively acting to avoid or reduce exposure or by minimizing vulnerability to it. The ability to anticipate a shock, to understand the associated risks, and to prepare is instrumental to the other capacities—informing decisions that can assist with short-term coping and long-term adaptation.
- *Absorptive capacities* allow households or systems to absorb and cope with climate-related shocks and stresses during and after their occurrence. It enables households to reduce the immediate negative impact on livelihoods and

basic needs. In other words, they are the various (coping) strategies by which individuals and/or households moderate or buffer the impacts of shocks on their livelihoods and basic needs.
- *Adaptive capacity* is the ability of social systems to adapt to multiple, long-term, and future climate risks and to learn and adjust after a disaster. It capacitates deliberate and planned decisions to achieve a desired state even when conditions have changed or are about to change. Adaptive capacity is realized through "income stability and asset accumulation and retention over time" as a result of proactive and informed choices about alternative livelihood strategies based on an understanding of changing conditions.
- *Transformative capacity* refers to strategies that aim at altering permanently and drastically the household structure or functioning to ensure the long-term "survival" of the individual member/household.

Sources: Based on Bahadur et al. 2015a; Béné et al. 2012; FSIN 2015.

capacity to cope should the shock materialize and better enables adaptation in the longer term.

- **Cope** with a shock's direct impacts to minimize their impact on well-being.[4] That is, a more resilient household will have more assets to draw upon to resist the negative impact on its well-being—to the greatest extent possible—and to bounce back to their pre-shock state in a timely fashion (Bahadur et al. 2015a). To do so, a more resilient household may draw upon a range of skills, resources, and assets to face and manage adverse conditions, emergencies, or disasters, including own savings and private (insurance) and public (social protection) resources.

- **Adapt** in a manner that reduces both the exposure and vulnerability over the longer term and before, during, and after a shock occurs. A more resilient household is capable of acting on information pertaining to its exposure and vulnerability, making longer-term investments and undertaking strategies that reduce both factors. This includes diversifying or adjusting livelihood portfolios away from sources of income that are especially vulnerable to the impacts of a shock; building the household's asset base, including productive, financial, and human capital-related assets to enable it to make these adjustments; and/or, leveraging such assets to relocate away from an area of spatially concentrated risk. Indeed, the ultimate expression of adaptation may be the household's ability to reduce exposure altogether through relocation and planned migration when in situ adjustments to livelihood and assets portfolios fail and where remaining in place would lead to chronic vulnerability and even maladaptation.[5]

This definition of resilience implies that providing a pathway toward achieving a more resilient state is critical for poor and vulnerable households. A key point, as Frankenberger et al. note, is that

> it is important to emphasize that resilience is not synonymous with coping capacity. Whereas coping capacity typically refers to the ability of households to return to their previous state in the wake of disaster, resilience programming must focus on strengthening the adaptive capacity of vulnerable households...this entails taking incremental steps to reduce their exposure...so that they can eventually escape poverty and continually improve their wellbeing. (Frankenberger et al. 2012, 2)

As the FSIN (2015, 7) also notes, it is important to distinguish between resilience capacities that allow households to maintain normative levels of well-being above the threshold (the 'resilient state') and resilience capacities that reflect growth toward and in excess of the normative threshold ('resilient pathway'),

The concept of "bouncing forward" or "bouncing back better" is critical when considering resilience to poverty. Indeed, Tanner, Bahadur, and Moench (2017) and Shelton (2013) note the increasingly popular idea of "bouncing forward" or "bouncing back better." This is in line with the concept of "building back better" after disasters (Priority 4 of the Sendai Framework on Disaster Risk Reduction) wherein the conditions underlying vulnerability to the previous disaster are altered in its aftermath to reduce future risk. Essentially, these concepts emphasize that the household's state prior to the shock may not have been an optimal state, instead being one characterized by vulnerability. This suggests that bouncing back to that state alone will be a less than optimal outcome, underscoring the need for resilience to consider the capacity to adapt in the long term, reducing vulnerability and improving well-being (Schipper and Langston 2015). Without doing so, households may experience recurring cycles of vulnerability.

The concept of resilience can be useful in fostering multisectoral collaboration around a broadly shared, if differently defined, objective. While, as discussed, many definitions of resilience exist, the literature frequently notes that this also has served to create a basis for collaboration and cooperation among institutions and agencies. Broadly speaking, in most cases, differences in definitions of resilience among institutions are slight and semantic rather than significant and substantive. Indeed, Bahadur et al. (2015b) note that the application of the term across disciplines and institutions is helping to break down sectoral silos; while Béné et al. 2012 similarly state that precisely because the term is used loosely in a large number of disciplines and organizations, it can be a powerful integrating concept across different sectors. Indeed, in the original and pioneering concept of adaptive social protection by researchers at the Institute of Development Studies, resilience (and vulnerability) served as the conceptual cornerstone for linking the three traditionally separate sectors of social protection, disaster risk management, and climate change adaptation around a common objective (see box A.5). As noted in chapter 3, resilience also can be seen as a potentially unifying concept and policy instrument that uses humanitarian and development approaches to address the chronic vulnerability of populations exposed to recurrent shocks (FSIN 2015, similarly articulated in FAO 2016).

NOTES

1. While an already poor individual or household cannot "fall" into poverty (although the poor individual or household may fall deeper into poverty), the poor individual or household cannot be considered resilient according to this definition.
2. This symmetry is contested but is defendable. It is contested in the literature where one can be characterized as being both resilient and vulnerable at the same time. This holds in instances where one can return to her/his prior state after a shock, but that prior state may be one characterized by vulnerability. The symmetry is defendable in instances where a benchmark for resilience is set, such as poverty in this case. Here, returning to a previously vulnerable state (that is, remaining poor) cannot be defined as being resilient.
3. This capacity is also referred to as "anticipatory" capacity in the BRACED 3As framework (Bahadur et al. 2015a). The term "preparedness" is used here to more explicitly reflect the meaning of the capacity as used in this report as well as to make a clear linkage to the emphasis on preparedness reflected in the disaster risk reduction and disaster risk management communities.
4. This capacity is also referred to as "absorptive" capacity in the BRACED 3As framework (Bahadur et al. 2015a; similar in Béné et al. 2012). The term "coping" is chosen here because of its widespread use in the social protection community and its interchangeability with the term "absorptive."
5. Defined as a failure to adjust adequately or appropriately to a shock.

REFERENCES

Alfani, Federica, Andrew Dabalen, Peter Fisker, and Vasco Molini. 2015. "Can We Measure Resilience? A Proposed Method and Evidence from Countries in the Sahel." Policy Research Working Paper 7170. World Bank Group, Washington, DC. https://openknowledge.worldbank.org/handle/10986/21387.

Bahadur, A., K. Peters, E. Wilkinson, F. Pichon, K. Gray, and T. Tanner. 2015a. "The 3As: Tracking Resilience across BRACED." Working Paper, Building Resilience and Adaptation to Climate Extremes and Disasters (BRACED), London.

Bahadur, A., E. Wilkinson, E. Lovell, and T. Tanner. 2015b. "Resilience in the SDGs: Developing an Indicator for Target 1.5 That Is Fit for Purpose." ODI Briefing Note. Overseas Development Institute, London.

Beegle, K., A. Coudouel, and E. Monsalve. 2018. *Realizing the Full Potential of Social Safety Nets in Africa*. Washington, DC: World Bank. http://documents.worldbank.org/curated /en/657581531930611436/pdf/128594-PUB-PUBLIC.pdf.

Béné, C., S. Devereux, and R. Sabates-Wheeler. 2012. "Shocks and Social Protection in the Horn of Africa: Analysis from the Productive Safety Net Programme in Ethiopia." IDS Working Paper 395, Institute of Development Studies, Brighton, UK.

Béné, C., R. Wood, A. Newsham, and M. Davies. 2012. "Resilience: New Utopia or New Tyranny? Reflection about the Potentials and Limits of the Concept of Resilience in Relation to Vulnerability Reduction Programmes." IDS Working Paper 405, Institute of Development Studies, Brighton, UK.

Dang, H.-A., and A. Dabalen. 2017. "Is Poverty in Africa Mostly Chronic or Transient? Evidence from Synthetic Panel Data." Policy Research Working Paper 8033, World Bank, Washington, DC. http://documents.worldbank.org/curated/en/172891492703250779/pdf/WPS8033 .pdf.

Dang, H.-A., P. Lanjouw, and R. Swinkels. 2014. "Who Remained in Poverty, Who Moved up, and Who Fell Down? An Investigation of Poverty Dynamics in Senegal in the Late 2000s." Policy Research Working Paper 7141, World Bank, Washington, DC. http://documents.worldbank .org/curated/en/862121468296672365/pdf/WPS7141.pdf.

Davies, M., B. Guenther, J. Leavy, T. Mitchell, and T. Tanner. 2009. "Adaptive Social Protection: Synergies for Poverty Reduction." *IDS Bulletin* 39 (4): 105–12.

De la Fuente, A., H. Jacoby, and K. Lawin. 2019. "Impact of the West African Ebola Epidemic on Agricultural Production and Rural Welfare Evidence from Liberia." Policy Research Working Paper 8880, World Bank, Washington, DC. http://documents.worldbank.org /curated/en/423511560254844269/pdf/Impact-of-the-West-African-Ebola-Epidemic-on -Agricultural-Production-and-Rural-Welfare-Evidence-from-Liberia.pdf.

del Ninno, C., F. Pierre, and S. Coll-Black. 2016. *Social Protection Programs for Africa's Drylands*. Washington, DC: World Bank. *http://documents.worldbank.org/*curated /en/736221471343475745/pdf/107854-PUB-PUBLIC-PUBDATE-8-9-16.pdf.

De Weijer, F. 2013. "Resilience: A Trojan Horse for a New Way of Thinking?" ECDPM Discussion Paper 139, European Centre for Development Policy Management, Maastricht.

Dercon, S. 2005. "Risk, Poverty and Vulnerability in Africa." *Journal of African Economies* 14 (4): 483–88.

DFID (Department for International Development). 2011. "Defining Disaster Resilience: A DFID Approach Paper." DFID, London.

Diwakar, V., J. Albert, J. Vizamos, and A. Shepherd. 2019. "Resilience, Near Poverty and Vulnerability Dynamics, Evidence from Uganda and the Philippines." U.S. Agency for International Development, Washington, DC. https://www.agrilinks.org/sites/default/files /usaid-report-nearpoor_clean_march_508.pdf.

FAO (Food and Agriculture Organization of the United Nations). 2016. *Adapting Agriculture to Climate Change. FAO's Work on Climate Change Adaptation*. Rome: FAO. http://www.fao .org/3/a-i6273e.pdf.

Frankenberger, T., T. Spangler, S. Nelson, M. Langworthy. 2012. "Enhancing Resilience to Food Insecurity amid Protracted Crisis." United Nations High-Level Expert Forum, Rome. http:// www.fao.org/fileadmin/templates/cfs_high_level_forum/documents/Enhancing _Resilience_FoodInsecurity-TANGO.pdf.

FSIN (Food Security Information Network). 2014. "Resilience Measurement Principles: Toward an Agenda for Measurement Design." Technical Series 1. Resilience Measurement Technical Working Group, FSIN Secretariat, World Food Programme. http://www.fsincop.net /fileadmin/user_upload/fsin/docs/resources/FSIN_29jan_WEB_medium%20res.pdf.

FSIN (Food Security Information Network). 2015. "Measuring Shocks and Stressors as Part of Resilience Measurement." Technical Series 5. Resilience Measurement Technical Working Group, FSIN Secretariat, World Food Programme. http://www.fsincop.net/fileadmin/user _upload/fsin/docs/resources/1_FSIN_TechnicalSeries_5.pdf.

Gallardo, M. 2018. "Identifying Vulnerability to Poverty: A Critical Survey." *Journal of Economic Surveys* 32 (4): 1074–105.

Hallegatte, S., M. Bangalore, L. Bonzanigo, M. Fay, T. Kane, U. Narloch, J. Rozenberg, D. Treguer, and A. Vogt-Schlib. 2016. *Shock Waves: Managing the Impacts of Climate Change on Poverty.* Washington, DC: World Bank.

Hallegatte, S., A. Vogt-Schilb, M. Bangalore, and J. Rozenberg. 2017. *Unbreakable: Building the Resilience of the Poor in the Face of Natural Disasters.* Washington, DC: World Bank. https:// www.gfdrr.org/sites/default/files/publication/Unbreakable_FullBook_Web-3.pdf.

Hoddinott, J. 2014. "Understanding Resilience for Food and Nutrition Security." Building Resilience for Food and Nutrition Security 2020 Conference Paper 8. International Food Policy Research Institute, Washington, DC. http://ebrary.ifpri.org/utils/getfile/collection /p15738coll2/id/128165/filename/128376.pdf.

Holmes, R. 2019. "Promoting Gender Equality and Women's Empowerment in Shock Sensitive Social Protection." ODI Working Paper 549, Overseas Development Institute, London.

IFPRI (International Food Policy and Research Institute). 2013. "Definitions of Resilience: 1996–Present." Building Resilience for Food & Nutrition Security. IFPRI, Washington, DC. http://www.2020resilience.ifpri.info/files/2013/08/resiliencedefinitions.pdf.

IPCC (International Panel on Climate Change). 2012. "Glossary of Terms." In *Managing the Risks of Extreme Events and Disasters to Advance Climate Change Adaptation.* A Special Report of Working Groups I and II of the Intergovernmental Panel on Climate Change (IPCC), edited by C. B. Field, V. Barros, T. F. Stocker, D. Qin, D. J. Dokken, K. L. Ebi, M. D. Mastrandrea, K. J. Mach, G.-K. Plattner, S. K. Allen, M. Tignor, and P. M. Midgley, 555–64. Cambridge, UK and New York, NY: Cambridge University Press.

Jorgensen, S., and P. Siegel. 2019. "Social Protection in an Era of Increasing Uncertainty and Disruption: Social Risk Management 2.0." Social Protection and Jobs Discussion Paper 1930, World Bank, Washington, DC. http://documents.worldbank.org/curated /en/263761559643240069/pdf/Social-Protection-in-an-Era-of-Increasing-Uncertainty -and-Disruption-Social-Risk-Management-2-0.pdf.

Laborde, D., C. Lakatos, and W. Martin. 2019. "Poverty Impact of Food Price Shocks and Policies." Policy Research Working Paper 8724, World Bank, Washington, DC. http://documents .worldbank.org/curated/en/863311549375011898/pdf/WPS8724.pdf.

OECD (Organisation for Economic Co-operation and Development). 2018. "States of Fragility 2018, Highlights." OECD, Paris.

Ötker-Robe, I. and A. M. Podpiera. 2013. "The Social Impact of Financial Crises: Evidence from the Global Financial Crisis." Policy Research Working Paper 6703, World Bank, Washington, DC. http://documents.worldbank.org/curated/en/498911468180867209/pdf/WPS6703 .pdf.

Schipper, E., and L. Langston. 2015. "A Comparative Overview of Resilience Measurement Frameworks." ODI Working Paper 422, Overseas Development Institute, London.

Shelton, P. 2013. "Bouncing Back Better: Defining Resilience at the 2013 Global Hunger Index Launch." International Food Policy and Research Institute, Washington, DC.

Shepherd, Andrew, Tom Mitchell, Kirsty Lewis, Amanda Lenhardt, Lindsey Jones, Lucy Scott, and Robert Muir-Wood. 2013. "The Geography of Poverty, Disasters and Climate Extremes in 2030." Research Reports and Studies, October 2013. ODI, London.

Skoufias, E. 2005. "PROGRESA and Its Impacts on the Welfare of Rural Households in Mexico." Research Reports 139. International Food Policy Research Institute, Washington, DC.

Skoufias, E., Y. Kawasoe. E. Strobl, and P. Acosta. 2019. "Identifying the Vulnerable to Poverty from Natural Disasters. The Case of Typhoons in the Philippines." Policy Research Working Paper 8857, World Bank, Washington, DC. http://documents.worldbank.org/curated

/en/326941558453867995/pdf/Identifying-the-Vulnerable-to-Poverty-from-Natural
-Disasters-The-Case-of-Typhoons-in-the-Philippines.pdf.

Tanner, T., A. Bahadur, and M. Moench. 2017. *"Challenges for Resilience Policy and Practice."* Working Paper 519. Overseas Development Institute, London. https://www.odi.org/sites /odi.org.uk/files/resource-documents/11733.pdf.

UNICEF (United Nations Children's Fund). 2017. "Resilience, Humanitarian Assistance and Social Protection for Children in Europe and Central Asia." Social Protection Regional Issue Brief 2, UNICEF Europe and Central Asia Regional Office. https://www.unicef.org/eca /media/2671/file/Social_Protection2.pdf.

UNISDR (United Nations International Strategy for Disaster Reduction). 2009. *2009 UNISDR Terminology on Disaster Risk Reduction.* Geneva: UNISDR.

UNISDR (United Nations International Strategy for Disaster Reduction). 2015. *Making Development Sustainable: The Future of Disaster Risk Management: Global Assessment Report on Disaster Risk Reduction.* Geneva: UNISDR.

Walsh, B., and S. Hallegatte. 2019. "Measuring Natural Risks in the Philippines: Socioeconomic Resilience and Wellbeing Losses." Policy Research Working Paper 8723, World Bank, Washington, DC. http://documents.worldbank.org/curated/en/482401548966120315/pdf /WPS8723.pdf.

WFP (World Food Programme). 2015. "Policy on Building Resilience for Food Security and Nutrition." WFP/EB.A/2015/5-C. WFP, Rome. https://documents.wfp.org/stellent/groups /public/documents/eb/wfpdoc063833.pdf?_ga=2.20959473.817428444.1582152603 -752767465.1554223343.

Considerations for Shock Response along the Social Protection Delivery Chain

The social protection delivery chain can help to think through pertinent questions and challenges that need to be addressed when establishing contingency plans, along with the investment in these core delivery processes that may be needed to support shock response. Despite heterogeneity in program composition and maturity of social protection systems across countries, most rely on common phases of delivery to ensure that programs provide the right amount/composition of benefits and services, to the right persons, at the right time. This delivery chain is centered on four implementation phases, captured in the World Bank *Sourcebook on the Foundations of Social Protection Delivery Systems* (Lindert et al., forthcoming), namely: assess, enroll, provide, and manage. Applying the delivery chain to evaluate whether social protection programs are supporting adaptive social protection (ASP) objectives can help establish whether the essential implementation features required to ensure efficient and effective delivery of ASP interventions are functioning in those programs.

Four common phases apply to the delivery chain for social protection programs and services, with associated business processes for each phase. The assess phase of the delivery chain seeks to determine potential eligibility and includes business processes for outreach, intake and registration, and assessment of needs and conditions among potentially eligible households and individuals. This is followed by an enroll phase which is concerned with making decisions on enrollment and onboarding into programs, and the determination of what benefits and services would be provided to enrolled beneficiaries. The provide phase follows, where implementation begins in earnest with the provision of benefits and services, including payment transactions and services provision etc. Finally, the recurring phase of manage follows, where beneficiary monitoring processes are addressed, including addressing grievances and compliance, exit notifications and case outcomes. The defined operational processes to support program implementation also help to guide program management at all stages of the delivery chain and is a critical tool for supporting the beneficiary monitoring and management processes (figure B.1).

This appendix draws extensively from a background paper by Smith (2018).

Social protection delivery chain

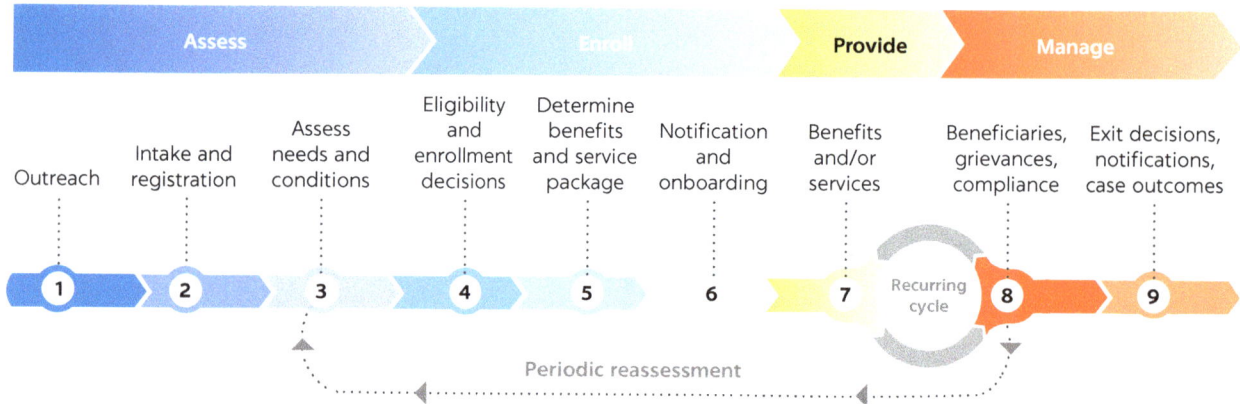

Source: Lindert et al., forthcoming.

ASSESS

Outreach: *How will I let affected households know that they may be eligible for support?*

The objective of the Outreach process is to inform beneficiaries of the social protection program, create awareness, and encourage potential beneficiaries to apply. Outreach activities usually use a variety of communication mechanisms, including public messaging through the media (electronic and print); local information sessions through community structures; word of mouth; visual information campaigns; staff outreach; and digital communications (for example, social media). Outreach activities are necessary to encourage potential beneficiaries to apply, and to inform existing beneficiaries on regular interactions, such as payment dates and times (Smith 2018).

Post-shock considerations. Shocks can disrupt communication channels, undermining outreach activities. Therefore, the communication mechanisms may need to change in a post-shock setting. For instance, where digital communication is interrupted, outreach may need to focus on word-of-mouth or staff outreach campaigns. Also, the type of information to be provided following a shock depends on the type of response to be implemented. In the case of vertical expansions, beneficiaries will already be aware of the program, but may not be aware of the additional payment(s) to be provided. In the case of a horizontal expansion or emergency program/piggybacking, the information provided would need to be more comprehensive, informing potential beneficiaries on the objective of the program, who can apply, how to apply, what kind of assistance they may expect and when, etc. (Smith 2018). In the case of Turkey, the horizontal expansion to include the Syrian refugees undertook innovative outreach processes in order to inform those refugees they may be eligible for support through the Emergency Social Safety Net Program.

Intake and registration: *How should I gather information on the disaster-affected households to assess their needs and potential eligibility for support?*

The objective of the intake and registration process is to collect information on potential beneficiaries (individuals, households, or communities), to be able to assess their eligibility for the social protection program. Intake and registration are completed either on demand, where potential beneficiaries register themselves (typically at social welfare offices), or all together, in which case survey teams visit the population to collect household data. Surveying all households may have been used to establish a social registry containing information on social protection and nonsocial protection beneficiary households. Where a social registry exists, it may not be necessary to complete separate intake and registration processes for each social protection program, but rather the social registry serves as the basis for intake and registration for multiple programs (Smith 2018), as depicted in figure B.2. Some social registries have near universal coverage (Chile, Colombia, the Dominican Republic, Pakistan, and the Philippines). Others cover between one third and one half of the population (Brazil, Georgia, Indonesia, Mexico, Montenegro, and Turkey). Others operate on a much smaller scale, either because they have been implemented in specific geographic areas before expanding to national coverage (such as China, Djibouti, Mali, Senegal, and the Republic of Yemen) or because of strict eligibility verification rules that can discourage applicants (Azerbaijan) (Leite et al. 2017).

Post-shock considerations. In the case of a vertical expansion of an existing program, the registration of beneficiaries is already completed via the existing, regular program. However, depending on program objectives, it may be necessary to leverage additional information, in the event that only some of the existing beneficiaries are to be targeted (for example, only those living in a

FIGURE B.2

Social registry intake and registration

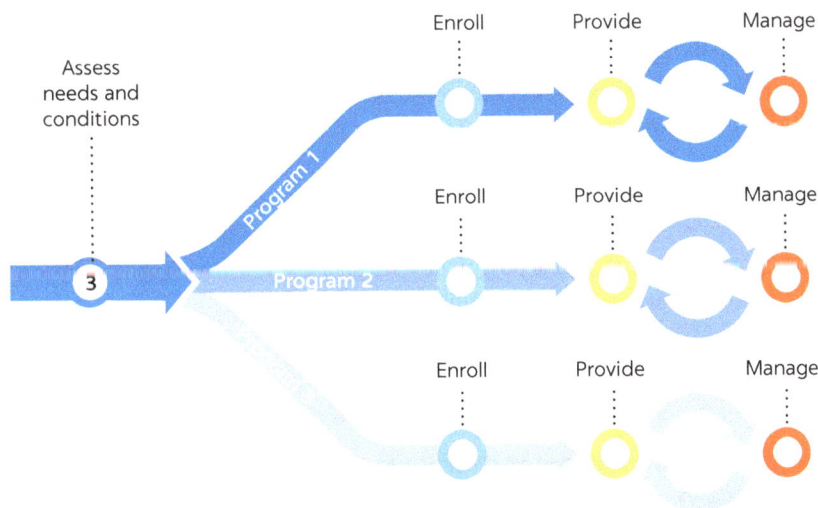

Source: Lindert et al., forthcoming.

shock-affected area), prioritizing categorical vulnerabilities (such as women, children, the disabled, and the elderly). For horizontal expansions or piggybacking, it will depend on the extent of the existing information contained in a social registry, as well as how up to date that information is. Where up to date and complete, the social registry will already contain the information on most of the households in the affected areas. Where otherwise, and even in those cases, additional information will need to be gathered through postdisaster surveys or on-demand registration (see chapter 2 and below related to assessment). Depending on the impacts of the disaster, it may be necessary to change the location and number of registration offices, including through temporary offices to facilitate such on-demand registration.

Assess needs and conditions: *Among the affected, who are most likely to require support?*

The objective of this step is to assess needs of applicants according to eligibility criteria and screening tools, to inform the determination of eligibility for benefits and the composition of the benefits and service package. The assessment of needs and conditions for regular social protection benefits is based on adherence to criteria-based information such as income/consumption, poverty status, age, gender, or geography. These are often relatively static and evolve infrequently. For postdisaster social protection benefits and services, assessment of needs and conditions often requires assessment of postdisaster impacts and needs on affected households to inform eligibility determination for the post-shock benefits and services that may be offered.

Post-shock considerations. As noted, in case of vertical expansions, the eligibility criteria for regular programs are retained in the event of disaster, which can lead to exclusion errors as beneficiaries or households that need assistance may not be among the regular beneficiaries of the program. However, by virtue of already being in the program, and having been selected as eligible in advance, those existing beneficiaries can be reached quickly if financing is available (see chapter 3). By contrast, horizontal expansions or piggybacking can allow for changes in eligibility criteria of the program (using damage to the household as a proxy for eligibility, for example) and most likely the reduction of exclusion errors. Such examples are discussed extensively in chapter 2, including the case of Chile where the Basic Emergency Sheet (Ficha Básica de Emergencia—FIBE) assessment tool is used to assess post-shock household needs, linked to the national social registry (Registro Social de Hogares—RSH). Emergency programs, which are solely deployed after shocks, may combine indicators related to chronic poverty or categorical criteria with shock impacts and needs to assess needs and conditions.

ENROLL

Eligibility and enrollment decisions: *Based on intake, registration, and assessment, who should be enrolled into the program?*

As part of the eligibility and enrollment decision process, program implementers decide which of the potential beneficiaries who completed intake and registration are included in the program as beneficiaries.

Both applicants who are included in the program as beneficiaries, and applicants who are not included in the program, are informed of the decision. For beneficiaries, the enrollment process then includes the collection of additional documents (if applicable), as well as registration for the programs in which they are being enrolled, and preparation of the delivery of benefits and services packages, for instance, through establishing a payment mechanism and/or setting up a bank account. Beneficiaries are then provided with a beneficiary identification (ID), or other means, to verify their status as a beneficiary.

Post-shock considerations. In cases where shocks such as fast-onset disasters are disruptive, beneficiaries may lose their means of ID and documentation. Similarly, the forcibly displaced will most often lack ID. Depending on the type of ID required, processes may need to be adapted. For instance, where ID is based on beneficiary IDs, these may need to be reissued following a disaster by program staff. Where ID is based on national IDs, the process to replace these documents is outside the jurisdiction of the social protection program institution, such that assistance from the issuing authority would be required. In post-disaster contexts, biometric data are typically most easily verifiable. For the case of horizontal expansion, processes need to be adapted to enable enrollment of new beneficiaries, ensuring accessible and convenient locations and times for enrollment; mechanisms to relax or waive documentation requirements or facilitate referrals to have document processes expedited for beneficiaries who do not possess them.

Determine benefits and service package: *Once enrolled, what kind of benefits will they receive?*

As part of the Determination of the Benefits and Service Package, the beneficiary list is finalized prior to each payment, the amount of the transfer is set, and provision points are determined. The determination of benefits and services packages will seek to ensure that the benefits and services provided are appropriate in light of need and will depend on resource availability and political feasibility. For regular social protection programs, benefits and service packages are often determined so as to smooth consumption, to reduce chronic poverty, to provide assistance in the event of unemployment, or to ensure an adequate pension.

Post-shock considerations. Post-shock benefits can have a range of objectives from smoothing income and consumption to addressing lost livelihoods and replacing lost assets. Typically, benefits and service packages are designed to address chronic, rather than transitory, multifaceted post-shock needs. Therefore, benefits and service packages may need to be modified to address the needs generated in postdisaster situations. For instance, where benefits are provided in cash, it is important to ensure that the amount provided is enough to purchase an appropriate amount of food for the household, and where benefits are provided in-kind, the amount should suffice to meet nutritional requirements. Moreover, coordination with other actors that are providing post-shock benefits is critical to ensure alignment of benefit packages. If transfer values and durations provided by different actors vary widely, this may lead to perceptions of inequity and have further implications for beneficiaries' expectations of transfers provided by regular programs once emergency support ends.

Notification and onboarding: *What is the best way to let the selected beneficiaries know they will receive support?*

As part of the Notification and Onboarding step, beneficiaries receive notification that they have been selected as a beneficiary. Beneficiaries are informed of the benefits and service package they will receive, the timing and duration of payments and services, and the steps required to avail themselves of benefits and services.

Post-shock considerations. As a result of a destructive or disruptive shock, such as a fast-onset disaster that has generated significant displacement, it may be difficult to notify beneficiaries of their selection as into a program. As with the outreach stage, alternative mechanisms will need to be created to inform beneficiaries of the decision. Ideally notification (and in some cases even payment or initiation of public works activities, for example) could be delivered when the beneficiary applies for entry into the program, where possible. This was successfully undertaken through the utilization of one stop shops in Pakistan as part of the Citizen's Damage Compensation Program, where applicants passed from the assessment to payment phase in as little as 13 minutes in one location.

PROVIDE

Benefits and/or services: *How will I physically deliver this assistance to the selected beneficiaries in the post-shock setting?*

The benefits and/or services process focuses on the provision of payments to beneficiaries. This requires providing the correct payment amount to the right people with the right frequency and at the right time (Grosh et al. 2008). Payment modalities include physical cash, transfers to bank accounts, and mobile money. For electronic transfers, such as bank transfers or mobile money, this involves two steps: the provision of funds to the bank account/mobile money account, and the collection of funds by the beneficiary.

Post-shock considerations. In the event of destructive disasters, payment and other benefit delivery processes can be disrupted. For instance, pay points and offices of banks or payment service providers can be destroyed or rendered inaccessible, and a lack of connectivity can affect mobile money and automated teller machine (ATM) networks. Therefore, in the event of disasters, it is important to understand what the payment and benefit delivery infrastructure is; what markets exist; what is convenient and accessible for beneficiaries; and what is quick, timely, transparent, less subject to fraud and error, and can be reconciled with confidence. For instance, it can be useful to temporarily switch to manual cash payments where electronic payment delivery is not feasible. Moreover, temporary pay points can be set up to ensure accessibility, as was the case in the Philippines. In the cases of vertical and horizontal expansion after a shock, additional transactions will increase the workload of staff and the payment service provider; and additional financial resources at the local level will be required for distribution. Frequency of payments may also need to be revisited in situations of crisis to ensure that they reach beneficiaries quickly and to reduce the administrative burden in these complex payment environments.

MANAGE

Beneficiary monitoring, grievance redress, and compliance monitoring: *Is the program functioning effectively, responding to needs, and do I need to make any adjustments?*

The objective of this step is to conduct beneficiary monitoring and ensure that grievances made by beneficiaries and nonbeneficiaries are addressed. This includes, for instance, monitoring payment receipt, ensuring that beneficiaries meet conditionalities, such as health and education conditions, recording grievances and complaints,[1] addressing administrative issues related to delivery, and facilitating case management processes. To ensure that these processes are implemented effectively, it is important that the processes are supported by adequate human resources, and that systems are in place to record these processes.

Post-shock considerations. Following a destructive disaster, damaged offices, a breakdown of communication channels, and limited staff (who themselves may be among the affected) can create challenges in maintaining program operations. Further, postdisaster contexts may be associated with additional demands on the system. Additional complexities include changed program conditionalities, the inclusion of new beneficiaries, and introduction of temporary modifications. These challenges can be addressed by temporarily deploying staff from other regions, ensuring the availability of alternative data management options, and backing up systems (for example, using the cloud). Where program conditionalities are in place, these can be waived temporarily; however, in such cases, this must be communicated clearly to program staff, beneficiaries, and partners. As noted previously in the discussion around timeliness versus accuracy, functioning grievance redress mechanisms will be critical to addressing exclusion errors, a priority during shock response.

Exit decisions, notifications, and closing cases: *When should the program be wound down and how is it best to inform beneficiaries?*

As part of the exit decisions, notifications, and case outcomes process, it is assessed whether beneficiaries have met the conditions to graduate from the program and are notified that they will exit. Where there are changes in regulations and exit conditions, these would need to be communicated to beneficiaries. After beneficiaries exit the program, cases are closed.

Post-shock considerations. Programs that undergo vertical and horizontal expansion need to be scaled down after the emergency. Scaling programs down following an emergency can be difficult. Different approaches include scaling down the program after a certain amount of time or number of transactions or following a change in household vulnerability indicators after the assistance was provided, for example. While scaling down following a vertical expansion requires a termination of additional payments, scaling down following a horizontal expansion can be more challenging as it involves reducing the caseload. In some cases, however, beneficiaries who have been newly included in an existing social protection program as part of the horizontal expansion may qualify for continued assistance; where this is the case, these decisions need to be communicated carefully to ensure there is clarity on which beneficiaries will continue to receive benefits and which will exit the program. In each case, social protection case workers should connect beneficiaries to additional, longer-term (non–shock specific) social protection programs for which they may be eligible. Similarly, stand-alone emergency programs should have a defined temporality that is well communicated to beneficiaries so they know for how long they will receive the temporary assistance.

NOTE

1. Examples of grievances include: Beneficiaries did not receive information about the program, were misinformed, did not receive the information they needed, were not notified, were treated poorly, were incorrectly classified in a certain category, did not receive payments, and received an incorrect amount.

REFERENCES

Grosh, M., C. del Ninno, E. Tesliuc, and A. Ouerghi. 2008. *For Protection and Promotion: The Design and Implementation of Effective Safety Nets*. Washington, DC: World Bank. https://siteresources.worldbank.org/SPLP/Resources/461653-1207162275268/For _Protection_and_Promotion908.pdf.

Leite, P., T. George, C. Sun, T. Jones, and K. Lindert. 2017. "Social Registries for Social Assistance and Beyond: A Guidance Note and Assessment Tool." Social Protection and Labor Working Paper 1704, World Bank, Washington, DC. http://documents.worldbank.org/curated /en/698441502095248081/pdf/117971-REVISED-PUBLIC-Discussion-paper-1704.pdf.

Lindert, K., T. George, I. Rodriguez-Caillava, and Kenichi Nishikawa. Forthcoming. *A Sourcebook on the Foundations of Social Protection Delivery Systems*. Washington, DC: World Bank.

Smith, G. 2018. "Responding to Shocks: Considerations along the Delivery Chain." Oxford Policy Management, Oxford, UK.

www.ingramcontent.com/pod-product-compliance
Lightning Source LLC
Chambersburg PA
CBHW080425270326
41929CB00018B/3164